NUMBER 134

Yale French Studies

The Construction of a National Vernacular Literature in the Renaissance: Essays in Honor of Edwin M. Duval

SPECIAL EDITORS: JESSICA DEVOS AND BRUCE HAYES

Yale French Studies

Jessica DeVos and Bruce Hayes,
  Special editors for this issue
Alyson Waters, *Managing editor*
Editorial board: Maurice Samuels (Chair), R. Howard
  Bloch, Morgane Cadieu, Tom Connolly, Sophia
  Helverson, Jill Jarvis, Alice Kaplan, Christopher L.
  Miller, Richard Riddick, Pierre Saint-Amand
Assistant editor: Robyn Gail Pront
Editorial office: 82-90 Wall Street, Room 308
  Mailing address: P.O. Box 208251, New Haven,
  Connecticut 06520-8251
Sales and subscription office:
Yale University Press, P.O. Box 209040
New Haven, Connecticut 06520-9040

Designed by James J. Johnson and set in Trump
  Medieval Roman by Newgen North America.
  Printed in the United States of America.

ISSN 044-0078
ISBN for this issue 978-0-300-23599-9

JESSICA DeVOS AND BRUCE HAYES

Editors' Preface: French Renaissance Literary and Scholarly Legacies

In presenting a volume on the construction of a national vernacular literature during the Renaissance, we feel the need to offer a few caveats. First, we recognize that poets and authors did not spontaneously decide to start writing in French during the sixteenth century. From the *Chanson de Roland* to the *Roman de la Rose*, from Marie de France's *Lais* to Chrétien de Troye's Arthurian *romans*, not to mention the poetic tradition created in the south by Occitan troubadours and soon imitated by their northern counterparts, the *trouvères*, there was a vast and well-established tradition of composing poems and prose in the vernacular long before the sixteenth century. Moreover, while many sixteenth-century writers, artists, and thinkers advocated for an innovative "rebirth" within their respective fields, using the term "The Renaissance" to designate a specific historical period is, of course, anachronistic. Before we discuss this period with such terminology, we should also first acknowledge similar historical moments of artistic and intellectual flourishing such as the Carolingian Renaissance of the late eighth and ninth centuries or the Renaissance of the twelfth century.

However, writers and poets during the sixteenth century viewed the medieval poetic and scholastic traditions of their forebears unfavorably and were consciously engaged in an effort to replace them. The very conception of a French vernacular evolved as the notion of French nationhood became more explicit in the sixteenth century, in part because previously independent territories such as Brittany and Navarre were brought under the direct control of the French monarchy. As they consolidated and centralized their power, the French kings, beginning with François I, increasingly turned to artists and

YFS 134, *The Construction of a National Vernacular Literature in the Renaissance: Essays in Honor of Edwin M. Duval*, ed. DeVos and Hayes, © 2018 by Yale University.

1

poets to praise the crown. By the end of the sixteenth century, the French nation was understood very differently from the way it had been only one hundred years earlier.

Moreover, sixteenth-century France was marked by dramatic historical developments that distinguish this period from previous epochs. Indeed, beyond France's domestic borders, all of Europe experienced profound, irreversible cultural changes. The discovery of the so-called "New World" brought into question previous certainties, and European principalities accrued wealth through the cruel exploitation of these lands and their peoples. The advent of the printing press provided a new method for the rapid exchange of ideas. Its impact on European society was as radical and profound as that of the internet on our own world today. Exchanges with Italy and northern Europe, aided by the printing press, permanently transformed the intellectual landscape in France, and no change had a larger or more destabilizing impact than what would come to be known as the Protestant Reformation.

Of the many new ideas brought about by this multifarious movement, the insistence on accessing sacred texts in the vernacular was among its most radical propositions. In France, nine years after Jacques Lefèvre d'Étaples completed his translation of the Bible into French, François I signed into law the Ordinance of Villers-Cotterêts (1539), which established French as the language of all legal documents in the kingdom. Two years later, Jean Calvin published in French his foundational *Institution de la religion chrestienne*, first published in Latin five years before. French Protestantism would be a movement propagated almost entirely in French. Joachim du Bellay's *Deffence et illustration de la langue françoyse*, published in 1549, is now often seen as the symbolic dividing line between France's two Renaissances; the first half dominated by Erasmian, evangelical humanists such as François Rabelais, Marguerite de Navarre, and Clément Marot, and the second half dominated by Pléiade poetics and deeply entrenched religious and political divides that would send the kingdom spiraling into almost four decades of civil war.

In the midst of these transformations, du Bellay and his entourage called upon poets, authors, and dramatists to establish a new national literary tradition, with the grand ambition of replacing Latin with French as the *lingua franca* both in France and beyond. Individual writers drew upon other linguistic traditions to innovate and create (or rediscover) new forms of expression in French. *Innutritio* and *imi-*

tatio provided the key framework for literary and poetic production. Through the agricultural and even cannibalistic metaphors employed in the *Deffence* and elsewhere, French writers actively sought to raise the stature of French by borrowing and stealing from the literary traditions of Antiquity and Italy.

A closer examination of this *translatio studii* reveals, however, that despite the optimism and energy often associated with the Renaissance, the literature and artistic production contained a corollary shadow of doubt from the very beginning. For example, while the literature of ancient Rome might be extolled as a model, sixteenth-century writers were also acutely aware that this empire no longer existed. Perhaps Joachim du Bellay's *Les antiquitez de Rome* best captures this tense ambivalence. The attempt to resurrect the language of an empire now buried under the rubble of ruins, in conjunction with the *Deffence*'s imperative to imitate it, causes the reader to wonder what the future of French might be.

The civil wars that racked France in the latter half of the century added a concrete analogue to the more ethereal musings that marked the first half of the sixteenth century. The first four books of Pierre de Ronsard's epic poem, the *Franciade*, appeared in print just days after the St. Bartholomew's Day Massacre. Is it any wonder that in such a climate the national epic that would extol a unified French identity never came to fruition and that the ultimate realization of such a project would be d'Aubigné's *Les tragiques*, a poem filled with an inexorable sense of belatedness and failure? There is something particularly modern in these attempts at control. They reveal not simply aesthetic preferences, but the authors' attempt to provide structure and attribute meaning to the chaotic events that surround them.

In addition to its stated theme on the construction of a vernacular literature, this volume also serves as a *liber amicorum* dedicated to Edwin (Ned) M. Duval. The contributions come from Duval's former students and long-time colleagues. Due to the space limitations of *Yale French Studies*, we are unable to be comprehensive either in our examination of the birth of a new literary tradition in Renaissance France or in our inclusion of the many scholars who would have loved to take part in this tribute to Ned Duval. The authors included here acknowledge Duval's many and diverse contributions to our field. David Quint once referred to Duval as a "code cracker," in an allusion to his colleague's scholarship, with its particular focus on teasing out hidden structures and symmetries in Renaissance poetry and prose. In honor of Duval's literary "sleuthing," the contributors we have assembled for this issue explore the symmetries—as well as the dissymmetries, the fragility, ambiguities, and contradictions—of French Renaissance literary production. This volume addresses evolving literary practices, innovations in genre, and intellectual developments in sixteenth-century France.

The first author studied here, Rabelais, produced books that show the author's deep interest in hidden meanings and hermeneutics, and call into question traditional modes of interpretation. Over the course of his illustrious career, Duval has published on a vast array of writers and poets, but unquestionably his greatest contribution to the field is to be found in his groundbreaking work on Rabelais. It should come as no surprise, then, that the first and largest section of this volume centers on Rabelais's writings. François Rigolot begins by asking a question that others have probably pondered as well—while Duval published a book on each of the Pantagrueline Chronicles, he did not publish a book on Rabelais's *Gargantua*. One of Duval's most important articles, however, which instigated a vigorous debate between Duval and Gérard Defaux on one side and Terrence Cave, Michel Jeanneret, and François Rigolot on the other, centered on the much-debated meaning of the prologue of *Gargantua*. While other critics have argued that the polysemous nature of Rabelais's works contributes ultimately to an indeterminacy of meaning, Duval has labored diligently to argue for a clear and forceful structural, epistemological, and above all else, hermeneutical "design" in Rabelais's oeuvre. Rigolot pays homage to Duval's approach and focuses on one particular structural aspect of *Gargantua*, the possible "higher meaning" at its center. In a play on words, chapter 29 (vingt-neuf) becomes the locus of "vin neuf" ("new wine") offered to the diligent reader who is able to make sense of the structure and meaning of this complex work.

Rigolot's article is followed by François Cornilliat's intertextual study of a panegyric written by Rabelais's contemporary, Jean Bouchet. Cornilliat skillfully shows how, as with other established genres, Rabelais calls into question, if not subverts and undermines, the moral and ethical dimensions of the panegyric tradition. In examining Panurge's excessive craftiness and deceit in battle, the Renaissance ideal of *mediocritas* is problematized and challenged. While these traits have been extolled by others, including Rabelais's friend Bouchet, Panurge's actions highlight the ethical and moral aporia at the heart of such formulations. Examining further conflicts in the *Chroniques*,

Edward Tilson offers a reading of the *Tiers livre* prologue that high-lights the competing tensions between its cynical, Diogenic subtexts on the one side and its Christian, Erasmian message on the other. This hybridity underscores the heterogeneous and unexpected nature of Ra-belais's project, an issue that dominates the prologue. Rabelais's work explicitly violates accepted norms, drawing on two distinct traditions to do so. The author does not simply seek to temper Diogenic excess with Christian restraint; his aim is to create a hybrid, or as Tilson de-scribes it, a "meta-hybrid" whose very eccentricity is an essential key to the proposed liberation that the author offers to his readers.

This section on Rabelais ends with Mireille Huchon examination of the "final word" in Rabelais's work. She addresses the modalities of encryption in Rabelais by turning to a set of terms, polysemous and suggestive, that appear in the *Brief Declaration* that the author included at the end of the *Quart livre*. Huchon focuses on one set of terminology that groups together priests, prophets, and interpret-ers, connecting this to the overall challenge of interpreting Rabelais's work. She moves from the *Brief Declaration* to the books themselves to reveal various patterns and hidden clusters that expand possible meanings in the text, steganographic encryptions that reveal previ-ously hidden meanings.

In the second section, two contributors, Richard Cooper and Rich-ard Keatley, leave the borders of France and travel to Italy in order to consider new aspects of Italian influence in Renaissance France, and explore questions surrounding authorial identity in Montaigne's *Journal de voyage*. While the poets of the Pléiade would ultimately select the Petrarchan sonnet as their model for lyric verse, Richard Cooper reminds us of Dante's significant, yet often overlooked, role in sixteenth-century cultural exchange and his influence on both the French and Italian Renaissance. By documenting the transmission and commission of texts as well as the exchange of ideas, Cooper highlights both the concrete and abstract ways in which Dante serves as an important source of *translatio imperii* and *translatio studii*. Turning to Montaigne's *Journal de voyage*, Richard Keatley examines how authorship and authority are blurred and problematized through the collaborative nature of the journal. It is difficult at times, if not impossible, to distinguish between Montaigne's writing and that of his secretary. The secretary's unique position both renders him ser-vile and allows him to assume an authoritative voice on behalf of his lord. A constant interplay between Montaigne's "il," the secretary's "je," and the "nous" of the troop accompanying Montaigne on his travels further complicates the authorial voice. The closeness of the secretary and his master plays out in a text that is both collaborative and intimate.

This volume's third section centers on the roles played by women in the fashioning of poetic legacies by male poets. Brooke Di Lauro's reading of Maurice Scève's adoration and idolatry of his beloved, Délie, deciphers the poet's complex and composite poetics. As the author of the first French *canzoniere*, Scève "domesticated" foreign poetic models, renewing and inverting them in order to distinguish himself from his poetic predecessors. Jessica DeVos examines Pierre de Ronsard's personal and poetic relationship with Madeleine de l'Aubespine, focusing in particular on how the two collaborated to designate her as Ronsard's literary heir. Building upon Duval's scholarship on collaborative self-crowning, DeVos argues that Ronsard not only accepted the woman poet as a member of his literary community, but also considered her to be an equal participant in the ambitious project of forging a new national literature in the vernacular. Finally, Cathy Yandell brings together two poems by Ronsard dedicated to Mary Stuart and Catherine de Medici, both titled *Discours*, a term connected to the new polemics of religious and political conflict in sixteenth-century France. She examines how both the poetics and politics of Ronsard evolved as he was thrust into an increasingly uncertain court and kingdom and tried to establish a space for himself in this perilous terrain.

Studies of the Wars of Religion-era propaganda comprises the penultimate section of this collection of essays. First, Dora Polachek takes the very different accounts of the assassination of the Guise brothers on the orders of Henri III to highlight the fraught nature of discursive practices that constantly challenge the boundaries between fact and fiction. She uses another example of the skewed portrayals of Catherine-Marie de Lorraine, the Duchesse de Montpensier and the sister of the assassinated brothers, to illustrate how the works of two writers, Pierre de Brantôme and Pierre de L'Estoile, reveal divergent embedded biases that are inextricably linked to their respective narrations. She concludes by emphasizing the pertinence of these examples to our own time, filled with "fake news" and vastly different ways of interpreting and understanding events. Shira Weidenbaum explores an important Renaissance genre, the dialogue, which was extremely popular in the sixteenth century. Dialogue represented a significant change from the rigidity of medieval dialectic due to its greater openness and thus contributed to a gradual fragmentation of authority. The dialogue format became ubiquitous in the religious polemical works widely produced in much of sixteenth-century France. Using as a case study the anonymous *Le pacifique* (1590), a pamphlet that appeared a year after the assassination of Henri III when the controversy over Henri IV's succession intensified, Weidenbaum shows how this pamphlet simultaneously emphasizes concord between Catholics and Huguenots, while also advocating for a clear ideological position. In this pamphlet, polemics are masked in calls for religious harmony, a decidedly modern method for approaching religious difference. French unity is associated with religious tolerance, a concept tested and challenged repeatedly well beyond the sixteenth century.

This volume concludes with an important contribution from David Quint on Montaigne, who, along with Rabelais, is traditionally viewed as the other literary and intellectual bookend of French Renaissance prose. Quint addresses a particular instance of Montaigne's radical effort in the *Essais* to replace classical moral philosophy with a modern, vernacular ethics, one that proposes a code of conduct for noblemen during the Wars of Religion. In "De la cruauté," Montaigne challenges classical thought, addressing human weakness through an examination of the mistreatment of other humans (slaves in Antiquity) and animals. Treatment of animals becomes a metaphor for humans' capacity for good and evil. Domesticating our own potential to do harm, more than reading the inimitable experiences such as Cato the Younger's graphic suicide, keeps us from the savage brutality that manifests itself even in the writings of the Ancients who are the putative exemplars of morality. Montaigne's ethics are both more modest and more radical than his classical predecessors' moral reasoning, centered as they are on our shared embodiedness.

As a scholar and a teacher, Ned Duval moved away from the *idée reçue* of a spontaneous artistic flourishing during the Renaissance, helping us to better understand the methodical crafting of a new national literature in the vernacular. Throughout his lifetime, du Bellay cast himself as the tortured poet, in opposition to the divinely inspired Ronsard. Like du Bellay, in much of his scholarship Ned Duval has striven to reveal the Ronsardian dissimulation of spontaneous artistic creation. Indeed, a passage of the *Deffence*, often cited by Ned, could easily refer to his own labors as a scholar:

> He who wishes to fly through the hands and lips of men must long dwell in his study. And he who desires to live in the memory of posterity must, as though dead unto himself, often sweat and tremble and, just as our courtier poets drink, eat, and sleep at their ease, endure hunger, thirst, and long vigils.[1]

In a variety of ways, all of the contributions in this volume pay tribute to a scholar whose "long vigils" have produced some of the most thoughtful and erudite scholarship on Renaissance France. Whether one agrees or disagrees with him, one is always aware that Ned Duval's scholarship is the product of a careful examination not just of the texts themselves, but also, and more importantly, of the myriad intertextual echoes contained within them. In the *Deffence*, du Bellay calls on his fellow poets to engage in a poetics based on *innutrio* and *imitatio*. Classical texts must first be ingested and digested to the point that they become a part of the poet. Before producing poetry, poets must first be careful, rigorous readers of their literary forebears. Among scholars today, Ned Duval stands out as someone who has taken du Bellay's call to heart, who has labored intently and diligently to reveal to his students and colleagues new and unexpected worlds contained within the poetry and prose of Renaissance France.

1. Joachim du Bellay, *The Defense and Enrichment of the French Language. A Bilingual Edition*, ed. and trans. Richard Helgerson. (Philadelphia: University of Pennsylvania Press, 2006), Book 2, Chapter 3, 370–72.

I. Rabelais's Innovations

FRANÇOIS RIGOLOT

The "Design" of Rabelais's *Gargantua*: A Note on Structure and Meaning at Midpoint

> My purpose here has been to discover the coherence of both form and meaning in a work usually assumed to be fragmentary, disjointed, open-ended, and thus inconsistent, ambiguous and perhaps uninterpretable.[1]

With these words Edwin M. Duval presented his goal and explained his method in prefacing his third and final volume of an important series of scholarly books devoted to the design of Rabelais's Pantagrueline epics. His remarkable project began twenty-five years ago with the first book of *Pantagruel* (1532), and continued sequentially over the years with the *Tiers livre* (1546) and *Quart livre* (1548-52), thus constituting an in-depth study of the three epics of which Pantagruel is the hero.[2]

Today no serious scholar of sixteenth-century French literature can ignore Duval's impressive series of critical studies. Gérard Defaux, another bright and indefatigable Rabelais scholar, acclaimed the publication of Duval's last volume on the Pantagrueline epics in these words: "Like Duval's two earlier books [on Rabelais], this one is a pure delight. We already had M. A. Screech's monumental *Rabelais*; we now have Duval's doubly monumental one."[3]

---

1. Edwin M. Duval, *The Design of Rabelais's* Quart livre de Pantagruel (Geneva: Droz, 1998), 11.

2. Duval, *The Design of Rabelais's* Pantagruel (New Haven: Yale University Press, 1991); *The Design of Rabelais's* Tiers livre de Pantagruel (Geneva: Droz, 1997); *The Design of Rabelais's* Quart livre de Pantagruel, ibid.

3. Gérard Defaux's review in *Bibliothèque d'Humanisme et Renaissance* 61/3 (1999), 845. In her own later review of Duval's last two design-themed books, Hope Glidden also eulogized them: "No critic can work seriously on Rabelais without taking

YFS 134, *The Construction of a National Vernacular Literature in the Renaissance: Essays in Honor of Edwin M. Duval*, ed. DeVos and Hayes, © 2018 by Yale University.

Even those "Rabelaisants" who may disagree with some aspects of Duval's approach are deeply indebted to him for illuminating the French writer's three arguably most difficult works. Three times, in the 1990s, Duval proposed a rigorous approach that concentrates on structural features and reveals a hidden comprehensive meaning. Turning away from radical hermeneutic indeterminacy rooted in polysemous textual criticism, he consistently argued for the legitimate presence of specific meaning, beyond ambiguous signs that denote the structure of profoundly "literary" books. His coherent investigative method uncovered the presence of a "Christlike epic" masterfully hidden in the fabric of the "*Pantagruelian* mythologies."

We cannot help but wonder, therefore, why the scholar passed over Rabelais's other famous masterpiece, *Gargantua* (1534–35), published chronologically as the second book although fictionally set at the beginning of the narrative cycle. *Gargantua* tells the story of Pantagruel's father and develops characters originally borrowed from the anonymous *Chroniques gargantuines*, a series of popular tales published, with or without Rabelais's help, shortly before *Pantagruel* (1532).[4] Given the impact of Duval's demonstrations, developed within the context of the period's evangelical debates, one may ask why he did not extend his productive approach to the reading of *Gargantua*, arguably the best-known book of Rabelais's oeuvre.

One possible answer is that the three Pantagruel-themed books on which Duval focused are thematically and stylistically different from *Gargantua*: they have a common hero, Pantagruel, and a coherent fictional narrative. They move from Pantagruel's birth, education, and heroic deeds to ideological considerations based on peace, harmony, and moderation—virtues that are continually threatened by monsters of all sorts. By contrast, the design of a Christian epic can hardly be found in *Gargantua*, despite its obvious thematic filiation. As far as we know, Duval has never related why he did not devote a book-length analysis to the story of Pantagruel's father. In the Preface to his study of the *Quart livre*, he announced that this would be "the third and final volume of a series of books devoted to the design of

---

these exquisitely documented readings into account." *Renaissance Quarterly* 56/2 (Summer 2003), 501.

4. See Mireille Huchon, *Rabelais grammairien. De l'histoire du texte aux problèmes d'authenticité* (Geneva: Droz, 1981); and more recently *Rabelais* (Paris: Gallimard, 2011).

Rabelais's books."[5] Of course, he may someday change his mind and surprise us with an unexpected fourth volume to complete his earlier trilogy. That would be wonderful news for the international community of "Rabelaisants."

In the meantime, although it is tempting to take up that challenge here, it would be foolish *hubris* to do so. Instead, my goal is simply to select a few key elements in the complex Duvalian methodology and try to apply them to the relationship between structure and meaning in *Gargantua*, focusing on the midpoint and the bipartite format of a book that has attracted so much interest over the centuries both among specialists and the wider community of cultivated readers.

Before addressing the question of structure and meaning in *Gargantua*, it is useful to recall the medieval literary tradition in which a major poetic event occurs at the midpoint of an epic or a romance. This often involves uncovering a hero's identity to give a deeper sense to the whole work. Half way through the *Chevalier de la Charrette*, for instance, Guenievre reveals the name of Lancelot; in the middle of the *Chevalier au Lion*, Yvain meets the Lion that explains his name and fame; similarly, the central part of *Cligès* illuminates the meaning of the romance. In his *Roman de la Rose*, Guillaume de Lorris awaits the middle of his poem to reveal its allegorical meaning as the "Miroër aus Amoreus."[6]

The deliberate placement of significant meaning at the midpoint of an epic is, of course, exemplified by Dante's *Divine Comedy*. From the first line of the *Inferno* ("Midway in the journey of our life" ["NEL MEZZO del cammin di nostra vita"]),[7] we are prepared to expect the crucial illumination that strikes the protagonist in the middle of his life, and precisely in the middle of the *Divine Comedy*. The midpoint of the *Purgatorio* is itself the middle of the "cantica centrale" in the *Commedia*. There Dante's Virgil announces the Christian theme on which the moral order of the whole poem rests: "He [Virgil] began: 'Neither Creator nor creature, my son, was ever without *love*, either

5. Preface to *The Design of Rabelais's* Quart livre de Pantagruel, 11.

6. More specific details on this issue can be found in François Rigolot, "Structure du texte et mémoire intertextuelle," *Le texte de la Renaissance: des Rhétoriqueurs à Montaigne* (Geneva: Droz, 1982), 155–70.

7. Dante Alighieri, *The Divine Comedy*, translated with a commentary by Charles S. Singleton (Princeton: Princeton University Press, 1970). *Inferno*, Canto I, 1.1, 2–3. All quotations from Dante's *Divine Comedy* will refer to this edition.

natural or of the mind, and this you know.'"[8] Here *love* appears as the universal force that animates and binds together the Creator and his creatures, God's universe as manifested in the Poet's own creation.[9]

Given this long tradition, Rabelais's readers may not be surprised to find a similar structural pattern in the *Pantagruel:* it seems to follow a numerological order. Just as the *Purgatorio* consists of thirty-three cantos, the final version of *Pantagruel* is composed of thirty-three chapters framed by a Prologue and a Conclusion. Comparing the midpoints of the two texts (canto 17 in one, chapter 17 in the other), we can discern a reversal of moral values in the French comic parody. Panurge, Rabelais's anti-hero, excels in multiplying mischief, and rejects the "higher virtue" of Love, taught by Dante's *Commedia*. He even invites the narrator, Alcofribas, Rabelais's fictional persona, to join him in doing his devilry: "My friend . . . you have no pastime in this world. I have some, more than the king; if you wanted to join forces with me, we'd do the devil's own trick."[10]

This comic temptation scene offers a counter-rendition of the *Purgatorio*'s central scene with its Neo-Platonic exaltation of Love as the motor of the universe. In chapter 17 of *Pantagruel*, Panurge enacts what Dante calls the "mal diletto" ("sinful pleasure"; Canto 17, l. 99), the rebellious human drive to refuse God's love for a perverted selfish satisfaction: "Hence you can comprehend that love must needs be the seed in you of every virtue and of every action deserving punishment."[11] Panurge, whose name (*panurgos* in Greek) means "omnium gnarus" in Latin ("capable of everything"), thus promotes himself as the creator of a new purgatory based on an inverted theology in which Love is excluded.[12]

8. *Purgatorio*, Canto XVII, ll.91–3, ibid., 184–85. Emphasis mine.

9. See Charles S. Singleton, "The Poet's Number at the Center," *MLN* 80 (1965): 1. For a critique of Singleton's thesis by R. J. Regis ["Numerology and Probability in Dante," *Medieval Studies* 29 (1967): 370–73] see John Logan's response in "The Poet's Central Numbers," *MLN* 86 (1971), 95–98. On the central positioning of numbers in Boccaccio, see Cesare Segre, "Strutture e registri nella *Fiametta*," *Strumenti critici* VI (1972): 141–43, and Robert Hollander, "The Validity of Boccaccio's Self-Exegesis in His *Teseida*," *Medievalia et Humanistica* 8 (1977): 169 ff.

10. *Pantagruel*, chapter 17, in *Œuvres complètes*, ed. Mireille Huchon (Paris: Gallimard, 1994), 280. *The Complete Works of François Rabelais*, trans. Donald M. Frame (Berkeley: University of California Press, 1991), 193. All quotations of Rabelais's text will be taken from *Oeuvres* for the original French, and *Works* for English translations.

11. *Purgatorio*, Canto XVII, ll.103–05, *ed. cit.*, 184–85.

12. Rabelais probably found the meaning of "panourgos" in Suidas's *Lexicon graece et latine*, of which he owned the 1499 Milanese edition. See Rigolot, "La

As Duval has clearly shown, this structural device, consisting in placing a "higher sense" (*altior sensus*) at the center of the book will be used again by Rabelais, fourteen years later, in the next installment of his Pantagruelian epics, the *Tiers livre*, in which an older Panurge is foolishly driven by his own *philautia* as opposed to Pantagruel's Christian generosity and philosophy based on *caritas*. In his compelling interpretative reading of the *Tiers livre*, Duval carefully uses the midpoint strategy to show that the imbricated episodes are constructed around a unique center occupied by the Socratic injunction "CONGNOIS TOY" ("know thyself"):

> The entire *Tiers livre* pivots on these two words and frames them at the very center of its multiple concentric frames, highlighting them as the unique focal point of the quest and the book. The two words are even printed in upper case letters, lest having come this far the reader mistake the precise point around which the entire book turns.[13]

Given the powerful significance of this strategy, largely recognized by scholars of Medieval and Renaissance literature and exemplified by Rabelais both in his *Pantagruel* (1532) and *Tiers livre* (1546), the well-informed and curious reader may therefore expect to find another version of that same compositional device in the design of *Gargantua* (1534–35), a book composed and published between the first two segments of these "Pantagrueline epics."

La vie treshorrificque du grand Gargantua, pere de Pantagruel (1534–35) begins with a complex prologue that challenges readers' assumptions about the interpretative act of reading a comic story patterned after folkloric tales. Through a series of appealing metaphors (the "bone marrow" being the most famous), we are made to understand that a deep, serious meaning might be hidden behind the narrator's apparent "mockeries, tomfooleries, and merry falsehoods" ("mocqueries, folateries et menteries joyeuses"),[14] and we should follow the example of well-trained biblical scholars who do not remain

---

conjointure du *Pantagruel*: Rabelais et la tradition médiévale," *Littérature* 41 (February 1981): 93–103.

13. *The Design of Rabelais's* Tiers livre de Pantagruel, 126. Those crucial "two words" are found in chapter 25 of the *Tiers livre*, in which Panurge takes counsel of Her Trippa "who claims to predict all things to come." *Tiers livre*, in *Œuvres*, 428, and *Works*, 329. In a footnote, Duval specifies that "this [capitalization] is true of both the first edition of the book, published in 1546 by Wechel and the definitive edition published in 1552 by Fezandat." *The Design*, 126, note 17.

14. *Gargantua*, "Prologue de l'auteur" in *Œuvres*, 6 and *Works*, 3.

at the literal level of the sacred text but seek higher, deeper meanings in the stories they read. Here is the crucial paragraph of the Prologue:

> And, even in case in the literal sense you find these matters rather jolly and corresponding to the name, you should not stop there, as the Sirens' song, but interpret in a higher sense what peradventure you thought was said casually.[15]

Much has been said about the narrator's controversial invitation to go beyond literalness and search for "lofty matters and profound knowledge" ("haultes matieres et sciences profundes").[16] It is not my purpose to revive that late 1980s polarizing debate about the Prologue.[17] Suffice it to say that the two interpretations, comic versus serious, remain a key issue for readers to ponder.

Gargantua is largely patterned like *Pantagruel*: it starts with the hero's birth, then his education and his remarkable deeds, comically reactivating the common notion of filial imitation summed up in the motto, "tel père, tel fils" (like father, like son). But the familiar schema is framed by two enigmatic texts: the "Fanfreluches antidotées" at the beginning (chapter 2) and the "Enigme en prophetie" at the end (chapter 58). If, as we might expect, Rabelais was once again using the midpoint strategy to convey a "higher meaning," it behooves us to pay special attention to the center of the definitive edition. The 56 chapters in the original *Gargantua* (Lyon: François Juste, 1535) increase to 58 in the final edition (Lyon: François Juste, 1542), but the change appears to be merely cosmetic, reflecting an editor's wish to turn two long chapters into four more manageable ones.[18]

---

15. *Works*, 4.

16. *Œuvres*, 7; *Works*, 5.

17. See Terence Cave, Michel Jeanneret, François Rigolot, "Sur la prétendue transparence de Rabelais. Réponse à Gérard Defaux," *Revue d'histoire littéraire de la France*, 86/4 (1986): 709–16. This vigorous debate, initiated by three English, Swiss, and French Renaissance scholars, was originally triggered by an earlier article by Duval on the Prologue to *Gargantua*.

18. Chapter 4 of the original *Gargantua* (1534–35) stops after "it was heavenly fun to watch them sport" ["c'estoit passetemps celeste les veoir ainsi soy rigouller"]: *Œuvres*, 17; *Works*, 14]. A new chapter 5 opens with the title "The palaver of the potted" ["Les propos des bienyvres"]: *Œuvres*, 17; *Works*, 15. Also the original long chapter 20 is divided. The new chapter 21 stops after "The cork in his slippers swelled upward a half a foot" ["le liege de ses pantoufles enfloit [en hault] d'un demy pied"]: *Oeuvres*, 58; *Works*, 50]. A new chapter 22 opens with the title "Gargantua's Games" ["Les jeux de Gargantua"]: *Œuvres*, 58; *Works*, 50. One should also note two errors in the numbering of the definitive edition: chapter 6 is wrongly numbered 7, and chapter 33 becomes 28.

The modification does not undermine a numerological hypothesis based on the significance of chapters 29 and 30 at the midpoint of the definitive edition.

Chapter 29 is clearly set up as a father's sermonizing letter to his son.[19] Grandgousier's rhetorical purpose is to question the power of a humanist education if it is not harnessed to actual political practice. He writes: "Vain is the endeavor and counsel which at the opportune time is not carried out and put into effect."[20] This typical Erasmian lesson to the Christian prince is followed by a dissertation on divine grace that must be read in the context of the contemporary quarrel between Erasmus and Luther concerning the existence of free will: "Eternal God has abandoned him [Picrochole] to the rudder of his own free will and sense, which cannot but be wicked if it is not continually guided by divine Grace."[21]

As the Prologue warned us, there is much substantial "marrow" contained in this paternal letter, which amply justifies its position at the very center of the book. However, far from remaining pure theoretical verbiage, in the next chapter the pronouncement is followed by Grandgousier's "Realpolitik" decision to send his ambassador and start negotiations with the enemy:

> This letter dictated and signed, Grandgousier ordered Ulrich Gallet, his Master of Requests, a wise and discreet man whose valor and good counsel he had tested in varied and contentious affairs, to go to Picrochole and remonstrate to him what had been decreed by them.[22]

The paternal letter is dated "The twentieth of September" ("Du vingtiesme de Septembre") (*Œuvres*, 85; *Works*, 72). Why such a precise date? We know, of course, that the month of September refers in Rabelais's works to the beloved period of grape harvesting ("les vendanges"). That's why wine is often called "Septembral potion" ("purée Septembrale") (*Œuvres*, 219; *Works*, 138); dating the letter in September is certainly meant to remind us that Picrochole's aggression takes place at a "sacred" time for all honest wine drinkers. When the tyrant's soldiers invade the Abbey of Seuilly, Frère Jean urges the other monks to save the one essential thing in their lives:

19. For another famous example of this oratory device, see *Pantagruel*, chapter 8, *Œuvres*, 241–46; *Works*, 158-62.

20. *Œuvres*, 84; *Works*, 71.

21. Ibid.

22. *Gargantua*, ch. 30 in *Oeuvres*, 85; *Works*, 72.

the vineyard. And, when the prior rebukes him for disturbing the church service ("le service divin"), the monk retorts with a significant pun: "But the wine service, let's see to it that it is not disturbed" ("Mais le *service du vin*, faisons tant qu'il ne soit troublé.").[23] In the face of destructive vandals, prayer is no longer appropriate: "These responses you're singing, by God, are not in season";[24] concrete action is necessary. For Frère Jean it is best to turn the ceremonial cross into a weapon, and push back the invaders to save the harvest: "So saying, he [Frère Jean] took off his great monk's habit and seized a staff of the cross [. . .] and fell so lustily upon his enemies, who were gathering grapes without order, or ensign, or trumpet, or drum, amid the close."[25]

Although the harvesting scene offers one explanation for choosing September, it does not clarify the specific day of the letter: 20. But if we consult the meteorological calendar, which often informs early modern practices, September 20 corresponds to the Autumn Equinox, characterized by the equal length of day and night. Whether or not Grandgousier attributes importance to this equal division of diurnal and nocturnal time, it may provide a valuable clue to the bipartite structure of the book since it comes at the very moment when the first set of twenty-nine chapters ends and the second begins. In other words, by dating Grandgousier's crucial letter on the equinoctial day, Rabelais may indicate an allegorical similarity between natural phenomena and the fictional composition of his work. Grandgousier's signature would then serve as a reminder of a Neo-Platonic universe in which macrocosm and microcosm mirror each other.

Could arithmosophy play a role in having 29 chapters in each half of the book? Perhaps, if we remember Rabelais's passion for homonyms. In chapter 9 ("neuf"), the narrator, grand "Abstracteur de Quinte Essence," starts by making fun of rebus-based riddles, which he ridicules as "homonyms so stale, so uncouth and barbaric" ("homonymies tant ineptes, tant fades, tant rusticques et barbares"); in their place, he eulogizes the ancients' sacred writings which, he claims, contain deeper meaning:

> Very differently did the Egyptian sages act once upon a time, when
> they wrote with letters they called hieroglyphics, which no one

23. *Gargantua*, ch. 27 in *Œuvres*, 78; *Works*, 66.
24. *Works*, 66.
25. *Œuvres*, 79; *Works*, 67.

understood who did not understand, and everyone understood who understood, the virtue, property, and nature of the things represented by these.[26]

Obviously, number 29 (in French: "vingt-neuf") can be read as a homonym of "vin neuf," a possibility that makes sense in the harvest season when a "new wine"—"how much more appetizing, laughing, inviting, heavenly, and delicious it is" ("combien plus friant, riant, priant, plus celeste et delicieux")[27]—will become available if the vineyards are not plundered by robbers. If this is the case, then the date of the paternal letter would be another signal that, metaphorically, a "new wine" (meaning a new "purée septembrale") is about to be drawn, which will give a "higher meaning" ("plus hault sens") to the whole epic.

When, at the end of the book, Gargantua and Frère Jean read the "Enigme en prophetie," they offer different, yet complementary interpretations. The monk's comic verve is no less admissible than the king's serious message. Each protagonist has his own version of what this "new wine" should be, in conformity with the ambiguous invitation given by the narrator in the Prologue. True, the monk will remain at the level of the literal sense, but the Giant may favor too sophisticated an interpretation. This reading does not exclude the idea of a Christ-like narrative that, as Edwin Duval has amply demonstrated, is at the core of the three books of the Pantagrueline epics. The design of La vie treshorrificque du grand Gargantua, in short, is not radically different from the rest of Rabelais's fiction: the book hides an ambiguous message, and beckons the diligent reader to make sense of its structure and appreciate the meaning of this new "September broth" ("purée de Septembre").[28]

26. Œuvres, 29; Works, 26.

27. Œuvres, 7; Works, 5.

28. Œuvres, 336; Works, 244. On the dichotomy of this dual search for meaning, see Rigolot, "A plus bas sens interpreter: Frère Jean et la matière de bréviaire," in Rabelais pour le XXIe siècle. Actes du Colloque du Centre d'Études Supérieures de la Renaissance (Chinon-Tours, 1994), ed. Michel Simonin (Geneva: Droz, 1998), 41–53.

FRANÇOIS CORNILLIAT

Panurge and the Blameless Knight: From Bouchet's *Panegyric* to Rabelais's *Pantagruel*

The great Rabelais scholar Mireille Huchon was the first to point out that a few words from the portrait of Panurge in Rabelais's *Pantagruel* (1532) were borrowed from the *Panegyric du chevallier sans reproche*, published a few years earlier (1527) by Rabelais's friend, the "rhétori-queur" Jean Bouchet.[1] The *Panegyric*[2] is an epideictic biography of its author's employer, the military commander Louis de la Trémoille,[3] who had been killed at Pavia (1525) along with many of his peers. Here is Bouchet, at the narrative's beginning, describing his young protagonist:

> He was as beautiful as a half-god: his body was of medium height, neither too tall nor too small, well-proportioned in all its limbs, with a noble head, a high, handsome forehead, green eyes, a medium-sized, slightly aquiline nose, a small mouth, a cleft chin, a dark but radiant complexion, verging on white and red rather than on black, and curly hair shining like fine gold. (*Panegyric*, 5 r°)[4]

---

1. See Mireille Huchon, "Rabelais, Bouchet et la *Nef des Folz*," in *Les grands jours de Rabelais en Poitou*, ed. Marie-Luce Demonet and Stéphan Geonget (Geneva: Droz, 2006), 83-103 (103 in particular); and *Rabelais* (Paris: Gallimard, 2011), 94–99 and 103–107. See also Romain Menini, *Rabelais altérateur. «Græciser en François»* (Paris: Garnier, 2014), 219–20.

2. (Poitiers: Jacques Bouchet, 1527). A critical edition of the *Panegyric* is being prepared by Laurent Vissière and François Cornilliat (forthcoming from Éditions Classiques Garnier). On its author's career and œuvre, see Jennifer Britnell's masterful study, *Jean Bouchet* (Edinburgh: Edinburgh University Press, 1986).

3. On La Trémoille, see Vissière's definitive account, *Sans poinct sortir hors de l'orniere. Louis II de La Trémoille (1460–1525)* (Paris: Champion, 2008).

4. My translation, from the 1527 edition (henceforth *Pn*), as in all references below. The portrait mixes poetic tropes with La Trémoille's actual features (see Vissière, "Les signes et le visage. Étude sur les représentations de Louis II de la Trémoille," *Jour-

YFS 134, *The Construction of a National Vernacular Literature in the Renaissance: Essays in Honor of Edwin M. Duval,* ed. DeVos and Hayes, © 2018 by Yale University.

And here is Rabelais describing the more mature Panurge:

> [He] was of medium height, neither too tall nor too small, and he had
> a rather aquiline nose, shaped like a razor handle; and at that time he
> was of the age of thirty-five or thereabouts, fit for gilding like a lead
> dagger, in his person a very likely fellow, except that he was some-
> what of a lecher [. . .] (*Pantagruel*, ch. 16)[5]

While Panurge is no longer a pretty boy, his body could still pass for harmonious, were it not for details that underline his dishonesty, lechery,
and greed; with derisive images, Rabelais appears to subvert not just
beauty, but the new canon of physical "mediocrity" (neither tall nor
short) touted by authors like Castiglione, and recommended for soldiers
in particular.[6] This intertextual nod can certainly be read as an exercise in parody; but we know that questions about parody's intent and
effect are not so easily answered. Are we dealing with a friendly joke
about what La Trémoille represents, and/or about the manner in which
Bouchet represents him—or is this a satirical jab, and, if so, is Rabelais
targeting the protagonist, or the text, or the author, or perhaps all three?[7]

---

nal des savants 2/1 (2009): 211–82. As Adeline Desbois-Ientile has shown (*L'histoire
écoutée aux portes de la mythologie: l'écriture du mythe troyen autour des* Illustrations de Lemaire de Belges, II, 4, 2 [Université Paris–Sorbonne Doctorate, 2015. Pub
lication forthcoming]), the portrait of young Louis is itself a remake of that of Pâris in
Jean Lemaire's *Illustrations de Gaule et Singularitez de Troye* (book I, chapter 21). The
Panegyric as a whole borrows a number of poetic devices from Lemaire, who had made
seductive use of mythological beauty (most famously in his tableaux of clothed and na-
ked goddesses) only to show this kind of seduction compromised by Pâris's judgment, as
though the narrative's meaning disavowed its very form. Bouchet thought that Lemaire
had taken this equivocal art too far; he made no use of it in his own major history work,
the *Annales d'Aquitaine*, yet still allowed himself to combine history with the charms
of fable in the *Panegyric*, albeit within strict limits designed to moralize Lemaire's art.
See François Cornilliat, "La persuasion dans le *Panegyric*," in *Jean Bouchet, Traver-
seur des voies périlleuses*, ed. Jennifer Britnell and Nathalie Dauvois (Paris: Champion,
2003), 149–74; and "Imaginer Minerve? Horizons de la 'fantasie' dans le *Panegyric*."
Camenae 8 [online journal] (Paris: Université Paris-Sorbonne, 2010). Thus La Trémoille
is cast as an anti-Pâris, guided by a personal "Minerve," capable of resisting Venus's
temptation, and schooled in the art of government by a Juno-like figure.

5. Chapter 12 in the original edition, published in 1532; the text quoted was not
modified in subsequent editions. *The Complete Works of François Rabelais*, trans.
Donald M. Frame (Berkeley: U. of California Press, 1991), 86 (henceforth *Pt*).

6. As a complement to Vegetius's criteria (*De Re Militari*, I, vi), see Baldassare
Castiglione, *The Book of the Courtier*, I, xx; and Marie Madeleine Fontaine, "L'athlète
et l'homme moyen: le nouveau regard de la Renaissance," in *Sport and Culture in Early
Modern Europe*, ed. John McClellan and Brian Merilees (Toronto: CRRS, 2009), 127–45.

7. Either way, Lemaire may have served as implicit foil. Both Rabelais and
Bouchet admired the *Illustrations* yet objected to their blend of truth and fiction;

I will not attempt to assess the full extent of *Pantagruel*'s debt to a work whose very title seems to be echoed in the sound of Panurge's name: because the *Panegyric* is a collage of borrowings from sources with which Rabelais was also familiar, the required sorting-out would exceed the limits of this essay.[8] What I will do is compare La Trémoille and Panurge through the age-old question of the morality of deceit. One problem with this type of comparison is that it cannot possibly proceed as though the characters involved belonged in the same genre: it has to consider the chasm that separates a biographical eulogy written in earnest from a work of (wild) fiction written in sardonic jest. Indeed, good method would seem to require that we measure this chasm before asking what, if anything, our characters might have in common. Taking the opposite tack, I will start from the fact that our heroes are both cunning, and use the question of cunning's moral worth as a touchstone of generic difference—revealing (and perhaps helping to determine) what separates Rabelais's take on fiction from Bouchet's take on history. This is a tale of two narratives, one of which ends up lampooning not just the other, but the other's very premise.

Again Huchon paves the way for this analysis by noting that Bouchet's La Trémoille, like Panurge, is an image of what the Greeks called *metis*—a two-faced intelligence, at once wise and sneaky.[9] How does this ambiguity play out in our texts? On Rabelais's side, the relevant notion is *panourgia* (cunning as a readiness to "do any-

---

Rabelais made the criticism more biting. See, in particular, Walter Stephens, *Giants in Those Days: Folklore, Ancient History, and Nationalism* (Lincoln: University of Nebraska Press, 1989); Mawy Bouchard, *Avant le roman. L'allégorie et l'émergence de la narration française au XVIe siècle* (Amsterdam: Rodopi, 2000), 129–89; and Menini, *Rabelais altérateur*, 217–36. On the relevance of Lucian's *True Story* and *How to Write History*, see Mireille Huchon's comments in Rabelais, *Œuvres complètes*, ed. Mireille Huchon and François Moreau (Paris: Gallimard, Bibliothèque de la Pléiade, 1994), 1214–17, as well as Menini, ibid. Yet Rabelais may *also* have thought that Bouchet's way with history was not immune from the same problem. See Guy Demerson, "Géant de *Chroniques* et Géants de chronique. Rabelais entre Jean Bouchet et Érasme," *Réforme, Humanisme, Renaissance* 37/1 (1993): 25–50; Emmanuelle Lacore-Martin, *Figures de l'histoire et du temps dans l'œuvre de Rabelais* (Geneva: Droz, 2011), 122–26; if so, the *Panegyric* would have struck him as a bad case of *mélange des genres*. Menini (*Rabelais altérateur*, 221, 225–26, 244) argues that criticism is softened in this case, with Rabelais's friendly pastiche playing Lucian to Bouchet's Herodotus.

8. Only one of which will be used here: Francesco Patrizi's *De Institutione Reipublicae* (quoted below from Galliot du Pré's 1518 edition).

9. See Huchon's analysis (inspired by Marcel Detienne and Jean-Pierre Vernant) in Rabelais, *Œuvres complètes*, 1221–24.

thing"), which gave Panurge his name. Aristotle defines *panourgia* as cleverness (*deinotes*) applied to unworthy goals.[10] But this evil twin of *phronesis* (prudence, *deinotes* applied to noble goals) has also been understood as prudence itself;[11] and the Christian terms in which Rabelais casts the concept further deepen its ambivalence since in the eyes of God, human wisdom *is panourgia*, as Edwin Duval has memorably demonstrated.[12] The *Panegyric*'s attention to what it calls "cautelle," "subtilité," "astuce" (*astutia*), or "versucie" (*versutia*) is more narrowly framed in terms of military merit. La Trémoille embodies a commander's ability, theorized by a long tradition,[13] to come up with "ploys, tricks and ruses" ("finesses, cautelles et ruzes"), under the rationale that "more battles [are] won by cunning and trickery [. . .] than by force" (*Pn* 60 v°[14]). Bouchet, however, feels compelled to add that "astuce et cautelle" must come from the right place ("procedans de bon esprit"). This restriction is a symptom of the author's own double mind on this double-edged subject: in the *Panegyric*, "bon esprit" signals a sound moral disposition rather than just keen intelligence. Dubious means cannot be justified by their good outcome or intent, let alone by their own cleverness: the means themselves, deceptive as they are, have to remain worthy of the virtuous mind that conceived them.

While Panurge is indeed capable of anything, military ruse, as Duval has also demonstrated,[15] is one of *panourgia*'s most important applications; Rabelais's treatment, however, problematizes the "bon esprit" caveat. In *Pantagruel*'s "walls of Paris" chapter (to which I will return), Duval points out that Panurge alludes to Lysander, the Spartan general who held that fraud is fair game in war, and that "if

10. *Nicomachean Ethics*, VI, 12, 9.

11. See for example Everett L. Wheeler, *Stratagem and the Vocabulary of Military Trickery* (Leiden: Brill, 1988), 33–35.

12. See Edwin M. Duval, *The Design of Rabelais's* Pantagruel (New Haven and London: Yale University Press, 1991), 63-64 (and notes on 171–72); also Huchon, ibid.,1273. *Panourgia* is positive in the Old Testament's sapiential books (Septuagint version) and negative in the New Testament (see Eph 4.14, I Cor 3.19, II Cor 4.2 and 11.3).

13. On which the *Panegyric*'s take comes from Patrizi (*De Inst.*, IX, 2), itself inspired by Vegetius's *De Re Militari* (III, 9; compare *Pn* 60 v°).

14. See, for example, Giles of Rome, *De Regimine Principum*, III, 3, 5: "Nam sagacitas et versucia aliquando plus faciunt ad obtinendam uictoriam quam corporis fortitudo."

15. *Design of Rabelais's* Pantagruel, ch. 5.

the lion's skin is not enough, a fox's must be added."[16] La Trémoille's Minerve, likewise, explains to her pupil that a commander must be "astucieux et cauteleux," and cites a number of examples—but Lysander, perhaps the most canonical one, is not mentioned. Her best case is Philip of Macedon, who

> achieved all his conquests and earned his victories by art and *versucie*, that is to say cunning, and rejoiced when he had deceived his enemies, which got him to be deemed wise and prudent, beloved by his entire military, and feared by his opponents. (*Pn* 60 v°)[17]

This is as far as Bouchet is willing to go theoretically. Yet his La Trémoille did not assume that fooling enemies is enough to earn the love of friends. As a boy already, he outclassed his peers in both force and guile, but won their affection thanks to a third quality, "humility" (*Pn* 5 r°): Bouchet weaves a "good" form of cunning into his hero's original disposition.[18] Rabelais, by contrast, adds craftiness to *mediocritas* only to heighten their tension, since Panurge's endless schemes (which neither cause nor harm Pantagruel's extraordinary love for him) typically prove as nasty as they are excessive.

The trickster's greatest military exploit occurs during the Dipsode war, when he persuades his master to let him take on 660 attacking horsemen: with two ropes, a barrel of gunpowder, and his companions' help, he designs a trap in which all but one of the aggressors become ensnared and they are "burned like damned souls" (*Pt* ch. 25, 215). The moral, delivered moments later by Pantagruel's celebratory trophy, is that "wit conquers might" ["engin mieulx vault que force"] (*Pt* ch. 27, 219). The real La Trémoille's own "subtil engin" (*Pn* 125 v°) would agree; so would Bouchet; and both might even laugh at the mock-fearsome manner in which this lesson is taught. Yet it does not follow that they share Rabelais's provocative sense of what "engin" can do. Simply put, La Trémoille is not a scoundrel, playing a part as such in a tall tale's redemptive "design" (to use Duval's term). In fact, working from a long-established tradition that understands deceit as accessory to military action and facing the related ethical

---

16. Erasmus, *Adages*, III, v, 81, trans. Denis L. Drysdall, *Collected Works of Erasmus*, vol. 35 (Toronto: University of Toronto Press, 2005), 114. Cf. Plutarch, *Life of Lysander*, 7. See Duval, *Design*, 97–98, for the demonstration.

17. Paraphrased from Patrizi (*De Inst.*, IX, 2, 131 r°).

18. Lemaire's young Pâris is also a brilliant yet humble athlete, but not a wily one: it is the "cautelle" of Fortune (*Illustrations*, I, 22, 146) that will turn him into a cheat.

conundrum of whether deception ever be justified,[19] our two authors take opposite routes.

Like Rabelais's Epistemon (Pt ch. 24, 213), La Trémoille is familiar with all the *stratagemata* worth trying on the battlefield. However, he uses cunning moderately, as an instrument of prudence. Prudence remains the over-arching virtue that both manages his "force" (in the moral sense of courage, preventing it from falling into temerity) and mitigates the use of "force" (in the physical and material sense) in war operations. It is by being prudent that the hero proves himself to be not just a great combatant but a great commander. This virtue also makes him a good political leader in his roles as an advisor to his king and, from 1506 on, governor of a crucial province, Burgundy. Further, prudence and courage call for justice and temperance, because cardinal virtues form a chain, a *catena* made even tighter by La Trémoille's unswerving loyalty to king and kingdom. As a prudent warrior, the king's servant does not hesitate to recommend and apply force when appropriate,[20] but we also see him using his wiles to avoid battle, a result that legitimizes deceit as a tool to *limit* the cost of war (as in Thomas More's *Utopia*).[21] This is what happens, for example, when La Trémoille's clever eloquence[22] persuades the Swiss to abandon the cause of Lodovico Sforza (Pn 76 v°), or convinces them, a few years later, to lift the siege of Dijon (Pn 143 r°–145 v°). In fact, compared to other examples of its genre[23] (to say nothing of *romans de chevalerie*), the *Panegyric* pays little attention to prowess for its own sake. Bouchet is often cursory, if not silent, on his hero's exploits in battle.[24] While La Trémoille's bravery is a given, his craftiness is best demonstrated when combat is eschewed. Even major campaigns are treated spottily (in contrast to the character's love life, which the

---

19. Thus Bouchet's model, Patrizi (De Inst., ibid.), reaffirms that fraud is not tolerable in a republic before conceding that it has its uses in certain war situations (though it remains better to fight cleanly) and that large armies can be routed by ambushes. Machiavelli is less cagey (see The Prince, 18).

20. In part because the French lack perseverance; so a commander is wise to unleash their "furie" promptly. Prudence is not caution: it knows when it is imprudent to wait. Too much waiting is presented as the direct cause of the disaster at Pavia.

21. More, Utopia, book II; see Duval, Design, 101–02.

22. A commander must also be eloquent. Bouchet tends to associate speech and cunning in La Trémoille, not to underline the former's trickery, but the latter's dignity.

23. Such as the Life of Bayard published by Symphorien Champier in 1525.

24. While La Trémoille's victory at Saint-Aubin is described in some detail (Pn 62 v°–63 r°), the "great honor" he earns at Agnadello (132 v°) is left unexplained.

panegyrist chronicles in great detail),[25] and typically reduced to a few symbolic episodes.[26]

One example of this pattern is the brilliant Picardie campaign of 1523. Dispatched with threadbare forces to face a massive English invasion while King Francis prepares to send the bulk of his army into yet another Italian adventure, La Trémoille (himself only half-recovered from a horse-riding accident) would not be able to field "more than sixty horsemen and a thousand foot soldiers" (*Pn* 176 v°) at any given moment. So he avoids battle, sacrifices undefendable castles and towns, and moves his troops around at night to hold the remaining ones, keeping one step ahead of enemy movement and appearing to have many more men than he actually does.[27] The invaders soon withdraw, losing "a vast number of their people" along the way: "a great service rendered to king and kingdom" (*Pn* 176 v°). This is "astuce" at its least glamorous and most effective—the reverse image of the doomed Italian campaign in which the king is about to lose everything but his honor.

Even more telling is the panegyrist's choice to linger on events that might appear dishonorable, such as the 1513 siege of Dijon. The governor persuaded the Helvetic invaders to lift the siege through sweet-talking and a hefty pay-off (*Pn* 142 r° and 145 v°). Far from downplaying the episode, which he says earned La Trémoille some enmity at court and the temporary displeasure of Louis XII, Bouchet makes it a showpiece. The matter of fortifications—a permanent concern for La Trémoille—comes up with particular urgency. In his welcoming words to the new governor, the "chief of citizens" brings up King Agesilaus's famous boast (asked why his city did not have walls, the king pointed to his men: "These are Sparta's ramparts"),[28] with a twist: the renown of La Trémoille's victories alone will protect Dijon. The hero demurs, and reverses the image: actually fortified cities are critical to a kingdom's security (*Pn* 126 r°–v°).[29] By the time

25. It is worth noting that La Trémoille uses deceit to meet Gabrielle de Bourbon, whom he is supposed to marry: the ruse justifies itself by allowing the future spouses to know each other truthfully.

26. For instance, the *Panegyric* skips the latter part of Charles VIII's "voyage" from Rome to Naples and the king's short-lived victory there—focusing instead on the storied return.

27. See Vissière, *Louis II*, 287–89.

28. Plutarch, *Apophthegmata laconica: Agesilaus* 29–30; Erasmus, *Apophthegmata*, 1, 30; quoted by Duval about *Pt* ch. 15 (*Design*, 93 and 98).

29. Argument borrowed from Claude de Seyssel's *Monarchie de France*, III.

the Swiss arrive, he has begun to improve Dijon's weak defenses, but not enough to repel the enemy; the citizens panic. La Trémoille tries to shore up their resolve in a speech that uses (correctly this time) the same *topos* he was served before: a city's greatest defenses *are* its citizens' courage. But the Dijonnais do not feel encouraged, and the governor, seeing that he will not be able to hold the city for long and that Paris may well be next, decides to buy the invaders' retreat.

One cannot read this without thinking of the debate between Panurge and Pantagruel (*Pt* ch. 15, 182–86) on the subject of Paris's dilapidated ramparts, as interpreted definitively by Duval.[30] The giant quotes Agesilaus's heroic metaphor. Panurge objects that "some semblance of stone" remains necessary, then farcically recommends a much cheaper material (the genitals of Parisian women and monks), and then recounts the pornographic tale of the lion and the fox that alludes to Lysander, Agesilaus's cynical counterpart. Dijon's woes as narrated in the *Panegyric* may have inspired this *morceau de bravoure*. Bouchet's account toggles, as it were, between the literal (stone defenses) and the metaphorical (moral defenses), in a situation where both are necessary—and found equally lacking. A city needs strong ramparts *and* strong citizens, but in the absence of the former, the latter might be found wanting too: the Agesilaus *topos*, designed to remedy this very situation, fails to do so. This leaves a savvy commander with his own "astuce" as the only option: in this case playing on the invaders' greed[31] to purchase peace, at a price that the king will deem exorbitant.[32] Rabelais radicalizes this dialectic by making "astuce" as cynical as it could be, mocking even itself: if citizens can neither play the role of ramparts nor afford to build actual ones, then ramparts might as well be replaced with prostitution.

Such instances show how Bouchet softens the ethical tension between deceit and courage, while Rabelais (in *Pantagruel* at least) ratchets it up.[33] Like La Trémoille, the giant is the epitome of prudence and bravery. No one should be surprised if his wisdom also

---

30. *Design*, 92–102.

31. Swiss avarice is also a *topos*. Still, Bouchet, taking pains to emphasize La Trémoille's own perfect integrity, highlights the speech more than the money.

32. On the siege, the deal, and the controversy, see Vissière, *Louis II*, 224–30; also his contribution to *1513. L'année terrible*, ed. Vissière, Alain Marchandisse, and Jonathan Dumont (Dijon: Faton, 2013), 92–115.

33. *Gargantua* will take a different course (see Grandgousier's efforts to "buy peace").

includes a measure of deceit in war (though it appears that he learned this skill from his friend).[34] Yet the mere presence of Panurge *adds* something that *remains* tacked on, as suggested by Lysander's image of the two skins. Thus it is not enough, in *Pt* ch. 28, for Pantagruel to trick the enemy by administering a drug that makes them drink uncontrollably (and fall asleep). Panurge tricks Pantagruel by feeding him a drug of his own, which makes him piss uncontrollably (and drown the enemy). Like every commander worth his salt, the giant should have something of both lion and fox; however, true prudence, which controls cunning and bravery, would make the image moot by assuming seamlessness: Bouchet would argue that a prince's "cautelle" is not a separate quality and would prove immoral should it become one.[35] But Panurge's cunning, which requires neither courage nor prudence and procures gratuitous, cruel fun, keeps standing out. By contrast, La Trémoille cannot possibly turn (nor even appear to turn) into one of the "foxes" whose maliciousness Bouchet denounced in his first work.[36] The Picardie episode shows that "engin mieulx vault que force" because a much stronger aggressor suffers disproportionate losses. Yet it does not belabor this point, depicting instead the triumph of wit as an exercise in restraint, which may even prevent (as happens at Dijon) loss of life on both sides. Rabelais's horsemen massacre is driven by an opposite logic, with emphasis on the savagery of the winning trick. The point of Panurge's cunning is to beat force at its own game, but the meaning of this point remains ambiguous. The episode can be taken to mean, in hyperbolic jest, that "cautelle" is an alternative to the brute force symbolized by the horsemen (whose horrible fate must not be taken literally), or that "cautelle" *is* force pursued by other means, only made even more violent and ruthless instead of less so.[37] In the first case, Panurge's actions can be assimi-

34. See Duval, *Design*, 100, about *Pt* ch. 28, where the giant practices the art of bluffing recommended by military manuals.

35. Thus Bouchet's *Temple de Bonne Renommée* (1517), an allegorical work written in memory of Charles de La Trémoille (Louis's son, killed at Marignano), lists examples of cunning, whether military (Fabius Maximus, Bertrand Du Guesclin) or political (King Louis XI), alongside other forms of prudence in the "tabernacle" dedicated to that virtue.

36. *Les regnars traversant les perilleuses voyes des folles fiances du monde* (1502).

37. Cicero wrote that of two manners of injustice unworthy of man, fox-like fraud is even worse than lion-like violence (*De officiis*, I, 13). Here fraud *is* the worst kind of violence. See also Machiavelli (*Prince*, 18), who notes that both the lion and the fox are beasts—which a warrior should combine as needed with his own humanity.

lated into the prudence model; the fireworks are but a colorful way of showing that both qualities are required to achieve victory. In the second, Panurge remains a dissident figure, whose excess could suggest (for example) that a wise leader might benefit from ignoble actions. This is the ambiguity (however we choose to resolve it) that Rabelais's art thrives on—and from which Bouchet's recoils.

A good symptom of this divergence is our authors' treatment of guns and gunpowder, which are called a "diabolical invention" in both texts.[38] Without condemning guns in his own name (if only because their use by La Trémoille can hardly be denied), the panegyrist underplays their importance.[39] Nevertheless, after the hero's death from an arquebus shot, grieving servants deploy the anti-artillery *topos* in all its pathos: "artificial fire," they howl, cuts down the deserving without allowing them any possibility of self-defense, thus bringing chivalry to an end. On the other hand, Panurge's victims, "chevaliers" wiped out without a fight by the trickster's inferno, illustrate this point for laughs. Yet Bouchet's mourners insist that the devil's technology causes both the "bastardization of true force" *and* the "annihilation of military cunning" ("astuce militaire," *Pn* 189 r°), whereas Rabelais makes gunpowder an emblem of "engin" at its wiliest. Bouchet's earnest representation of virtues avoids dwelling on those weapons, which preserves his hero's moderate form of "astuce" from their unholy fire. Alcofrybas's comedy welcomes them and not only unleashes, but aggrandizes the fire, leaving us to ask how (in what world) a form of cunning that is now lethal to the point of barbarity should be praised by the most humane of princes—and even chalked up to the will of a loving God.

Rabelais deepens the problem of gunfire by forcing us to think about it within a moral framework that is no longer merely "cardinal," but also involves the "theologal" (God-inspired) domain of "faith and hope," brought to the fore by the same Pantagruelian trophy that celebrates the triumph of wit over force (*Pt* ch. 27, p. 219–20). If victory does in fact belong to divine providence,[40] does it follow

38. See *Pn* 189 r° (lament on the Pavia dead) and *Pt* ch. 8 (Gargantua's letter).

39. For instance, the *Panegyric* elides one of the chevalier's most brutal feats, the artillery-led assault and massacre at Monte San Giovanni, but heralds his hauling of Charles VIII's artillery through the Apennines, an exploit that does not consist of *firing* the guns.

40. Bouchet would of course agree, but in the *Panegyric* his treatment of this idea does not go beyond rote acknowledgment.

that God allowed the clever to incinerate the strong—just like He will assist the strong who have the strength to humble themselves, as Pantagruel will show in the prayer he offers before his own old-fashioned, bona fide combat against Werewolf (Loupgarou) (*Pt* ch. 29, 226–27)? Whatever the answer, Rabelais makes us look at the question (of good and evil) in its highest *and* lowest instances, stretched all the way from human perversion to divine salvation; he does not reduce it to a manageable format somewhere in between, for the sake of a great man worth praising. Bouchet's historical account keeps a problematic aspect of current reality at arm's length, to prove itself (and its protagonist) ethically coherent at the literal level. Rabelais's fictional account not only welcomes the challenge but exaggerates it *beyond* moral acceptability while *also* endowing it with spiritual significance, thereby making the literal level even more grossly incoherent. The resulting clash of tones and values makes us laugh and puzzles us, requiring not just interpretation, but a form of it that will have to juggle this jumble of objects, for we cannot hope to hold all of them at the same time.

The starkest contrast between our two figures of *metis* is drawn by virtue's ultimate test: the willingness to give one's own life. The subtext of the *Panegyric* is a veiled criticism of King Francis, who is courage incarnate and blessed with a number of other qualities, but (royal propaganda notwithstanding) seems to lack prudence.[41] He exhibits this flaw to disastrous effect in his 1525 Italian campaign, most notably when he rejects the advice of his most experienced captains.[42] This decision ends up costing them their lives, as they are left with no choice but to die by his side. With not a little *hubris* of his own, Bouchet presumed that the king, freshly released from captivity, was ready to learn from his errors by reading the *Panegyric*.[43] This assumption helps explain why prudence and (good) cunning are given such pride of place in the work, while deeds of courage are downplayed in comparison. What makes the lesson complete, however, is the ending. The crafty La Trémoille dies for king and country, demonstrating

---

41. Royal propaganda presents Francis as a most prudent king. See Anne-Marie Lecoq, *François Ier imaginaire* (Paris: Macula, 1987), 115–17, 244, 415.

42. See *Pn* 177 r°; and, even more clearly, Bouchet's *Annales d'Aquitaine* (Poitiers, 1532, IV, 174 r°), where the king is shown ignoring La Trémoille's prescient advice.

43. He (predictably?) failed in this ambition, and the work was never reprinted.

his bravery one last time in a desperate situation that he blames, at least partly, on his master's ill-considered decisions. Charging alongside Francis and already wounded in the face, the 64-year old warrior helps kill "two or three hundred" enemy horsemen before his own horse is mortally hit. He finds another one, and immediately returns "to the place where the king was. And there surrounded by enemies he was shot dead by an arquebus" (*Pn* 188 r°). Unlike Epistemon, La Trémoille will not be resurrected.

Panurge's behavior is, of course, the opposite. Before Pantagruel's fight against Loupgarou, the trickster expresses total confidence in the outcome; he dismisses the giant's doubts by praising his force, promises that he and his companions will not fail him, and asserts that "a man is as good as he thinks he is" (*Pt* ch. 29, 226). Wiliness has turned (back) into recklessness. The strong Pantagruel, by contrast, offers a humble prayer to God (227), in whom all hope and faith reside. And when, in a moment of distress, he calls for his friend ("Panurge, where are you?"), it is Carpalim who wants to leap to his aid while Panurge merely babbles. The weapon-deprived hero is left to move and think fast before finding the opening that will ensure his victory. Thus, having established the need to complement force (in either sense of the term) by a troubling form of cunning, Rabelais upends the lesson by showing not only the latter's inability to help the former, but *panourgia*'s tendency to encourage force at the risk of making it fall into temerity—a risk that force ultimately eschews not by earning cunning's help, but by doubting itself and turning to God. Where Bouchet shows prudent "astuce" sacrificed by the reckless courage it tried to guide, then sanctified in death by its own inner bravery, Rabelais portrays *panourgia* first as imprudence (i.e., the kind of trust in force to which it was supposed to offer an alternative), and then as cowardice, which renders it unable to help at all. Force is left to draw on its own inner agility, while its only (and sufficient) outside assistance is grace.

Again Bouchet seeks to close the ethical circle by showing how prudence (ethical deceit included) *and* courage lead La Trémoille to an unfair but (as far as the hero's own values are concerned) lucid and coherent death, whereas Rabelais breaks the circle by preventing values from "adding up" in a world defined by unfair events. In Rabelais's work a wildly unethical form of deceit complements ethical force, but ultimately fails to do so: the hinges break down, the chain of cardinal virtues becomes dysfunctional. Reckless fiction is being invented to make this scandalous point,[44] which prudent history—let alone when it is written in order to praise and to teach by praising—would rather not make. While Pantagruel's victory still attests to the desirable, laudable conjunction of force and prudence in a prince, the real key, as Duval has shown, is elsewhere—in the humility that reaches beyond both virtues to uphold the Gospel. As for Panurge's wiliness, then recklessness, then haplessness, they are paradoxically needed to establish the superior necessity of such a key—one that does not lock the *catena* of virtues but unshackles us from our faith in its solidity.

Metis, in our two authors, proves an ambiguous, unstable substance indeed. In the case of Bouchet, "astuce" must be reabsorbed, over and over, into prudence, so as to maintain the coherence of the narrative's ethical outlook—and, more generally, of military and political history as the *Panegyric* understands it. In the case of Rabelais, *panourgia* must be embraced as a subversive factor, then dismissed by another blow of the same subversion, so that an outrageously fictional narrative may find the only coherence it claims: one that proves impossible, "unless in point of laughter," at the literal level of either writing or reality. Whether or not Rabelais intended to make fun of his friend's earnest praise of a wily commander in an age of violence, greed, and arbitrary death, he did show, by virtue of his own contrarian "engin," what vertiginous moral aporia lurked at the heart of such an endeavor.

44. *Gargantua* will walk some of the distance back by creating a sidekick (Frère Jean) who is recklessly brave and also learns prudence over time. *Gargantua*'s relation to the *Panegyric* deserves its own study, which I have sketched out, since the completion of the present article, in "'Cautelles et ruzes' chez Bouchet et Rabelais: *Panegyric, Pantagruel, Gargantua*," to appear in a volume of *Mélanges* honoring Mireille Huchon (Paris: Presses Universitaires de la Sorbonne, forthcoming).

EDWARD TILSON

Cynic Charity and Christian Satire: Blending Genres and Programming Readings in the "Prologue of the Author" to Rabelais's *Tiers livre*

The Lucianic background to the prologue of the *Tiers livre des faicts et dicts heroïques du bon Pantagruel* has received a good deal of critical attention of late, especially in connection with the parable of the black camel and the motley slave.[1] The Erasmian background to the Pantagruelism that the prologue requires of the reader is also well known. The way the prologue entwines these two intertexts to create an overture that models both the novel and its intended reception, however, merits further attention.

Compared to the Silenus model of the previous prologues, with its opposition of a frivolous exterior and a precious interior, each of these constellations of sources (the Lucianic dialogues that emblematize the message and the Erasmian texts that encode its reception) functions more like a Russian doll, with each intertextual group containing multiple other sources in a pattern of recession. The relations of these nested texts are more complex than the diminishing iterations of a matryoshka doll, however, in that each cluster elaborates an ambiguous, somewhat antagonistic rapport with a normative tradition—Aristotelian philosophy in the case of the literary, Lucianic intertext, and the Old Testament in the case of the theological, Erasmian intertext—which each claims to supersede. At the core of each textual cluster is a body of rules that it transgresses and transcends through the creation of new, hybrid forms that reconcile

---

1. See Edwin M. Duval, "En quoi les œuvres de Rabelais sont-elles hybrides?" and François Rigolot, "Le griffon, l'hippocentaure et l'esclave bigarré. Hybridité et métalangage dans le prologue du *Tiers Livre*" in *Rabelais et l'hybridité des récits rabelaisiens*, ed. Diane Desrosiers, Claude La Charité, Christian Veilleux, and Tristan Vigilano, *Études rabelaisiennes* 56 (Geneva: Droz, 2016), 25–43 and 345–61, respectively.

YFS 134, *The Construction of a National Vernacular Literature in the Renaissance: Essays in Honor of Edwin M. Duval*, ed. DeVos and Hayes, © 2018 by Yale University.

the antinomies—between art and Nature, between freedom and the Law—bequeathed by the old rules. For each of the textual filiations evoked and employed by the prologue's author, the key theme is freedom: the freedom of the poet in the face of the grammarians' rules and their anchorage in the categories of Aristotelian philosophy, and the freedom of the Christian in the face of veterotestamentary and "Judaizing" laws and observances.[2] At the same time, the attitude toward the rules of peripatetic grammarians and "Mosaic" institutions is nuanced by the need to maintain safeguards against the insufferable poetaster and the prideful libertine. It is this balance between the freedom granted to poetic genius and to the follower of Christ on the one hand, and the need to maintain the codes of communication and to avoid giving offense on the other that the prologue attempts to negotiate, and that will be developed throughout the exchanges that make up the body of the *Tiers livre*.

The various parts that make up the "Prologue of the Author" are quite distinct: the larger part is devoted to the narrator/author Rabelais's reworking of Lucian's account in the dialogue *How to Write History* of the reasons that prompted him to take up his pen. This first development is followed by a concessive one, built around a second Lucianic borrowing, this time from the dialogue *You're a Prometheus in Words*, which sets forth the author's fears that his works may be ill received because of their innovation in blending genres that were previously considered incompatible. The author then allays his own fears by surveying his readers and discerning in all of them a "specific form and individual property"[3] of Pantagruelism that will ensure that his latest installment is taken in good part. The author then emphasizes his role as the host of the banquet that is to follow, insists on the exclusion of certain types of readers from the "table" of the *Tiers livre*, enacts their expulsion, and concludes by cursing them.

2. In Rabelais as in Erasmus, "Judaism" signifies a superstitious submission to rituals, a belief that salvation comes from the sedulous observance of ceremonies rather than from a love of one's neighbor in Christ. For Christian humanism, mention of "Judaic" or "Mosaic" rules refers to Catholic institutions such as lent or monasticism rather than to any historical Jewish beliefs or practices. See Duval's exposition of the sense of the term, in *The Design of Rabelais's* Tiers livre de Pantagruel, *Études rabelaisiennes* 34 (Geneva: Droz, 1997), 155–62.

3. "Prologue of the Author" in *The Complete Works of François Rabelais*, trans. Donald Frame (Berkeley: University of California Press, 1991), 258.

The first Lucianic borrowing from the dialogue to *How to Write History* serves both to introduce Diogenes as a personification of the cynic character of the work to follow and to bring up the question of composition. The anecdote about Diogenes rolling his barrel up and down the Cranion hill is presented as a parallel with Lucian's animadversions on the subject of historiography—just as the citizens of Corinth were caught up in their collective frenzy of preparations to repel the Macedonians, so it seems, says Lucian, that in his day the fad for writing history is such that there is no one who does not fancy himself a historian. The real point of Diogenes's spectacle is to ridicule the citizens of Corinth, both for the futility of their preparations for an assault that would never come and that could never be withstood were it to happen and, more essentially, for the idea that these outward preparations might somehow safeguard a freedom of which the only true guarantee is a virtue built on self-knowledge rather than on conformity. In the same way, Lucian's dialogue purports to be concerned with correcting histories (and the *Tiers livre* does present itself as a historical account of "the heroic deeds and sayings of the good Pantagruel") that fail to observe the rules of proper historiography, but is really more concerned with mocking the poor taste of his contemporaries and their predilections for foolish fashions.

Among other foibles Lucian is at pains to ridicule are proœmia that do not correspond to the body of the text and, more generally, any lack of harmony in the composition of a work:

> [T]he whole should be homogeneous and uniform, and the body in proportion to the head—not a helmet of gold, a ridiculous breastplate patched up out of rags or rotten leather, shield of wicker, and pig-skin greaves. You will find plenty of historians prepared to set the Rhodian Colossus's head on the body of a dwarf; others on the contrary show us headless bodies, and plunge into the facts without exordium.[4]

Lucian recommends that a prologue should summarize the causes and outcome of the matter so as to prepare the ground for the ensuing account, which should itself "be adorned with the virtues proper to narrative, progressing smoothly, evenly and consistently, free from

---

4. *How to Write History*, § 23, in *Lucian in Eight Volumes*, Loeb Classical Library 6, trans. K. Kilburn (Cambridge, MA: Harvard University Press, 1939), 35.

humps and hollows" and be marked by its "limpid" clarity.[5] As Edwin M. Duval remarks in his discussion of this passage,[6] however, the *Tiers livre* is far from fulfilling these criteria:

> Yet in the *Tiers livre*, Rabelais apparently remains one of those impenitent, raving historiographers for whom Lucian played his Diogenes in vain. Uncured by the tub-rolling of *How to Write History*, he rolls his own tub by putting down whatever comes to mind with no respect for the art of composition—that essential art by which, Lucian promises, the writer may never "stray from the straight path that leads directly onward" and that consists in knowing precisely "what kind of beginning to begin with, what kind of order to impose on the parts, what proportion to give to each part, what to leave out, what to dwell on, what to mention only in passing, and how to express and arrange everything harmoniously." (*How to Write History*, 6)[7]

Duval's discussion of this apparent paradox extends to Rabelais's return to this matter in the Raminagrobis chapters of the *Tiers livre*, an examination of which would take us beyond the scope of these remarks, as would any attempt to detail the variety of genres—from the incongruous association of philosophical dialogue and comedy to the perplexing incorporation of (burlesque) epic, (mock) encomia, declamations, diatribes, farce and *facéties*, among others—that combine to form the body of the *Tiers livre*, but it will be sufficient to consider the prologue itself to see the same dynamic in action.

Lucian's treatment of the aims of prefatory materials—to "appeal for a favourable hearing and give his audience what will interest and instruct them"—first excludes the cultivation of goodwill from the tasks that are appropriate for the historian and then advises that the audience's interest be secured through a demonstration of the greatness of the events to be related or else of their importance to the reader, while the open mind required for instruction is to be encouraged by a succinct exposition of the "causes and outlines of the main events."[8] Needless to say, Rabelais's "Prologue of the Author," with its rambling version of the Diogenes anecdote, its kyrielles of verbs and literary associations, its embroidering of the story of the camel

---

5. Ibid., § 55, 67.
6. Duval, *The Design of Rabelais's* Tiers livre de Pantagruel, ch. 1, "Rabelais's *Art et manière d'escrire histoires*": 15–28.
7. Ibid., 21. The translation of § 6 of *How to Write History* is Duval's own.
8. *How to Write History*, § 53, ed. cit., 65–67.

and the slave, and its omission of any mention of the events to be related or of their relevance to the reader, makes no attempt to fulfill the Samosatan's recommendations for historical prooemia. Nor does the narrator appear to succeed any better if we consider the prologue as an attempt to follow the rules of composition as they apply to the cultivation of goodwill customary for literary works. On the contrary, the only way the prologue seems to announce the work to come is by its similar disregard for the established rules of composition and its apparent lack of structure. As for goodwill, while the prologue starts with a cheerful, if idiosyncratic, salutation to the good folk, illustrious drinkers, and precious gouty gents who had enjoyed the previous installments of Pantagruel's feats, it winds up in a litany of imprecations against various types of potential readers before finally degenerating into animal language and curses.

The second borrowing from Lucian is the much-discussed parable of the camel and the slave drawn from the dialogue *You're a Prometheus in Words*. Summing up his determination, in the face of the frenetic activity of his countrymen, to do his part by offering his readers another draft of Pantagrueline exploits, the narrator underlines the new flavor of this latest barrel, explicitly enrolling the work to follow under the banner of the cynic, Diogenes:

> For the combatants I'm again going to pierce my barrel, and [. . .] draw them, from the vintage of our afterdinner pastimes, a gallant third draft and consecutively a merry fourth, of Pantagruelic sayings; by me it will be licit to call them Diogenic. And since comrade I may not be, they shall have me as loyal steward of the feast.[9]

But the narrator has no sooner resolved to offer up this cynical draft than he is seized with doubts about whether it will be to the taste of readers. The misfortunes of Ptolemy are thus adduced as the prologue passes from the work's message to its reception:

> However, I remember reading that when Ptolemy, son of Lagus one day, among other spoils and booties of his conquests, offered the Egyptians, in the midst of the theater an all-black Bactrian camel and a slave motley, colored in such a way that half of his body was black, the other white [. . .], he hoped by these novelties to augment the people's love for him. What comes of it? At the presentation of the camel all were frightened and indignant; at the sight of the motley-colored

9. "Prologue of the Author," 258.

man some sneered, others abominated him as an infamous monster, created by an error of nature. In sum, the hope he had of pleasing the Egyptians, and by this means extending the affection they naturally bore him, slipped out of his hands. And he understood that they took more pleasure and delight in things beautiful, elegant, and perfect, than ridiculous and monstrous.[10]

For Rabelais, as for Lucian, the oddly colored camel and the pied slave are metaphors for the hybrid nature of the literary form they are offering to their public. The implications of these metaphors warrant close consideration. Regarding the question of Rabelaisian hybridity, Duval, in his *The Design of Rabelais's* Tiers livre de Pantagruel, has suggested that there is an important distinction to be drawn between natural hybrids and the composite constructions of art. Artificial productions such as the goat-stag, or *tragelaphos*, that symbolize poetic fancy, or the goat-man satyr that is the emblem of satire are ridiculous because they juxtapose elements from the same category (body parts) but drawn from different wholes without integrating or blending them, such that the resulting form loses its coherence, whereas natural hybrids such as mules combine different traits of each whole (the horse and the ass) into a completely fused form.[11]

These remarks on the prologue's treatment of hybridity support the reading developed in Duval's *Design* which elucidates the symmetry placing the *Tiers livre*'s Delphic and Evangelical injunctions to self-knowledge at the center of the book in such a way as to provide a highly ordered structure and a clear, univocal message. For this reading, the references to Lucian's dialogues are understood as grounding serious rules of composition. *You're a Prometheus in Words* is seen as condemning artificial hybrids in favor of a seamless blending of comedy and dialogue that more closely resembles the successful genetic mixes of Nature, while *How to Write History* is read as a manual for would-be historians. Moreover, Duval's readings are buttressed by the identification of the Horatian intertext of Lucian's dialogues, as also of the *Tiers livre*.[12] The famous opening lines of the *Epistle to the Pisones* (re-branded as the *Ars Poetica* by the rhetorician Quintilian) are:

10. Ibid., translation modified.
11. For examples of the goat-stag emblem of poetic fancy, see Aristophanes, *Ra*, 931, 937; Plato, *Republic*, 488 a; Aristotle, *Poetics* 927 b 7; *Physics* 208 a 30; on the link between the satyr and satire, see below, note 32.
12. In addition to the indirect echoes of Horace conveyed in the Prologue's references to Lucian's dialogues, there is an explicit evocation of the *Epistle to the Pisones*

If a painter chose to join a human head to the neck of a horse, and to spread feathers of many a hue over limbs picked up now here now there, so that what at the top is a lovely woman ends below in a black and ugly fish, could you, my friends, if favoured with a private view, refrain from laughing?[13]

This opening is seen as a rejection of the type of composite works symbolized by chimeras, a stern warning against poetastic fancy that is further developed in the rest of the epistle and that will serve as a sort of commandment to both Lucian and Rabelais. In light of the *Tiers livre*'s further treatment of the rules of composition in chapter twenty-four,[14] and of the coherent and significant design of the work as a whole that is conveyed through the concentric chapter structure elucidated by Duval, the prologue should thus be understood as announcing a work that:

[w]hile appearing and even claiming to violate all the norms of good narrative structure, [. . .] respects with almost comic literalness the Lucianic and Horatian requirement that histories and epics have a beginning, a middle, and an end, and that the middle be congruent with the beginning and the end with the middle: "primo ne medium, medio ne discrepet imum."[15]

However, like the idea that the Samosatan's historiographical animadversions authorize a normative rhetoric, the idea that there is a sharp distinction to be drawn between natural and artificial hybrids, and that Rabelais's prologue only appears to align the *Tiers livre* with the ridiculous creations of fancy while actually following Lucianic and Horatian statutes in presenting the reader with a work that is more like the harmonious hybrids found in nature calls for further qualification if one looks closely at the passages in question, at their function in the texts from which they are drawn, and at the overall aspect of these texts.

---

in the exchange between Epistemon and Panurge in chapter 24, 325–27. This exchange adduces both Lucian and Horace through the nexus of Erasmus's *Proverbs* (1.9.14), which effectively joins the *Tiers livre*'s meta-textual considerations about its classical, Diogenic message with those intended to shape its Erasmian, Evangelical reception.

13. Horace, *Satires, Epistles, Ars Poetica* V. 1-5, trans. Henry Rushton Fairclough, Loeb Classical Library (Cambridge, MA: Harvard University Press, 1970), 450.

14. See the discussion of ch. 24's references to Lucian and Horace in Duval, ibid., 21–28.

15. *Epistle to the Pisones*, v. 152; Duval, ibid., 115.

It should not be forgotten that Lucian's dialogues are written in the genre most associated with the cynics, satire,[16] and that Horace's *Epistles* are themselves identical in tone and form with his earlier satires, the chief difference being simply their greater length.[17] In looking at *How to Write History*, it is not altogether clear whether the Samosatan's observations are intended to profit the historians of his day as much as they are to provide amusement at their expense. Certainly, if we look at Lucian's own practice as a "historian" in the *True History*, he seems to care very little for the precepts he laid down in his ostensibly didactic dialogue.[18] The examples of the camel and the slave from the prologue's second borrowing are particularly interesting for their treatment of the distinction between a spatial and mechanical form of composition that juxtaposes motley, heterogeneous elements and that belongs to the sphere of art, and a true type of hybridization that fuses normally disparate but potentially complementary elements, sometimes with the advantage of heterosis, and that belongs to the sphere of nature.

If Lucian were condemning artificial composites and claiming that his own poetic inventions more closely resemble the hybrids found in nature, one would expect to see an example of an unusual but successful hybrid, one distinguished by its grace and coherence. On the contrary, the examples the anecdote draws from nature seem to be chosen to resemble the fruits of unrestrained artistic imagination. The pied slave is in this sense an example of nature producing a mix that appears more composite than successfully blended, the implication being that if nature can produce motley hybrids, then art might produce—in the form of Lucian's comic dialogues (or Rabelais's "gal-

16. The connections between Diogenes's tub-rolling as a mockery of the pointlessness of the Corinthians' martial preparations, the apparent formlessness of Lucian's style of Menippean satire, and the apparently shapeless and aimless narrative of the *Tiers livre* are underlined by Duval, ibid., 16–21.

17. As Fairclough observes in his introduction to the Loeb Library edition of Horace's *Satires, Epistles and Ars Poetica* (Cambridge, MA: Heinemann, 1945): xx, "The Epistles belong essentially to the same literary class as the Satires."

18. A capital source for Rabelais's Pantagrueline chronicles, Lucian's *True History* parodies both Herodotus and Thucydides in relating the author's travels to the moon and Venus, with particular attention to the strange creatures he encounters. Of course, the *True History* is in one sense a further satire of the credulity of historians, but the fact remains that Lucian has no investment in objective historiography and shows instead a marked predilection for imagining fantastic creatures.

lant third draft of Pantagruelic sayings")—a blend of disparate parts that will yet appear harmoniously fused rather than simply juxtaposed.[19] This understanding of the sense of the anecdote for both Lucian and Rabelais as a "meta-hybridization"[20] of the categories underpinning the distinction between nature and art is confirmed at the close of *You're a Prometheus in Words* when Lucian rejects accusations that he might have, Prometheus-like, stolen his invention by declaring that if anyone else before him had invented "such seahorses and goat-stags," it was quite without his knowledge.[21] Here again, the distinctions between art and nature are deliberately blurred, this time through the pairing of a natural creature that appears to join a horse's head to a fish's tail with the rather more plausible seeming goat-stag emblem of poetic invention.

Rather than supposing that the hybrids of Rabelais's prologue and, behind them, the various chimeras of Lucian's dialogues and Horace's epistle are intended as admonitions to follow received precepts of composition, it may be more useful to ask whether their purport is not more satirical than serious. Taking a step back to look at the source of the precepts adduced in the texts of Lucian and Horace, we find the canonical statements of Plato—"every discourse must be organized, like a living being, with a body of its own, as it were, so as not to be headless or footless, but to have a middle and members, composed in fitting relation to each other and to the whole"[22]—and of his yet more categorical student, Aristotle:

> A whole is what has a beginning and middle and end. [. . .] Well constructed plots must not therefore begin and end at random, but must embody the formulae we have stated. Moreover, in everything that is beautiful, whether it be a living creature or any organism composed

19. As Michel Jeanneret has pointed out, the Renaissance follows Roman and Hellenistic aesthetics in attributing composites to nature (more specifically to the unbridled fecundity of *natura naturans*) just as it attributes hybrids to art. In general, mannerism plays on the distinctions between the mechanical and the organic in such a way as to blur the distinctions between nature and art. See the chapter, "Grotesques and Monstrosities" in Jeanneret, *Perpetual Motion*, trans. Nidra Poller (Baltimore: Johns Hopkins University Press, 2001), 104–143.

20. On meta-hybridization, see Duval, "En quoi les œuvres," 38 and Rigolot, "Le griffon," 360.

21. *You're a Prometheus in Words*, § 7 in *Lucian in Eight Volumes* 6: 427, translation modified (ἱπποκάμπους and τραγελάφους in the Greek).

22. Plato, *Phaedrus* 264 c, *Plato in Twelve Volumes*, Loeb Classical Library 9, trans. Harold North Fowler (Cambridge, MA: Harvard University Press, 1925), 529.

of parts, these parts must not only be orderly arranged but must also have a certain magnitude of their own.[23]

If we then ask what the relation of our satirists might be to philosophy's rules about how to write poetry, it begins to appear that the echoes of received wisdom opposing chimeras to the regular compositions of Nature actually convey a double-edged irony, both self-deprecating and aggressively anti-dogmatic. Viewed from this angle, the horse-necked fish-tailed bird-woman of Horace's epistle is an emblem of the poet's famously incoherent epistle, just as the goat-stag *tragelaphos* is embraced as an image of the comic dialogue invented by the Samosatan.

It is not that Lucian does not aspire to a gracefully fused invented form or that Horace does not condemn artless composition; they certainly do. The target of their satires, however, is philosophy's claim to dominion over poetry. The satirical tradition dismisses the pretention of dogmatic philosophy to regiment the poet's creations according to the categories and forms of Nature, mocking the latter as products of the philosophers' imaginations, the only distinction between the Ideas or forms of philosophy and the chimerical constructions of poetry being that the poets, at least, understand their works to be fictions.[24] Alongside the attack on simplistic and old-fashioned laws of poetry, what is defended in Rabelais as in Lucian and in Horace is the poet's right to transgress and transcend any particular rule, to build forms that are risible in their disparate originality and yet possess a unique, intrinsic coherence. What is being championed, in other words, is the freedom of genius from the rules of pedantic philosophers, rhetoricians, and grammarians—or, transposing the aesthetics of satire into the ethics of cynicism, the freedom of the introspective philosopher from the dictates of custom and the doxa of popular belief.

Following on the heels of Diogenes's fustigation of the futility of the Corinthians' labors (a metaphor in Lucian for the fashion that made every man fancy himself a historian and in Rabelais for the

23. Aristotile, *Poetics*, 1450 b, *Aristotle in Twenty-Three Volumes*, Loeb Classical Library 23, trans. William Hamilton Fyfe (Cambridge, MA: Harvard University Press, 1932), 31.

24. For the Renaissance, this defense of art goes hand in hand with the critique, typically in the Augustinian tradition, of philosophy's pretention to set the bounds of Nature, to limit what She can or cannot do, and to decide which productions follow Her laws and which are aberrations.

spate of publications setting up every man as a theological authority),
the parable of the black camel and the motley slave is an emblem
for the satirical work to follow. As such, it serves as much to defend
the digressive eccentricity of both the prologue and the narrative it
announces as it does to intimate the existence of an inner coherence
beneath the appearance of aimlessness. It is this tension between outward eccentricity and inner meaning—between individual freedom
and collective understanding—that is addressed in the prologue's turn
from metatextual parables about the *Tiers livre*'s message to optative
and hortative considerations on its reception.

The parable from the second Lucianic intertext leads into confi-
dences about the author's trepidation, which is illustrated by a further series of anecdotes, references, and puns involving positive and
negative alternatives, before being summarily dismissed by the invocation of the reader's Pantagruelism:

> This example makes me oscillate between hope and fear, afraid that in
> place of anticipated contentment I encounter what I abhor, my trea-
> sure proves to be lumps of coal, instead of Venus, I come up with
> Whiskers the shaggy dog, instead of serving them, I offend them, in-
> stead of pleasing them I displease, and my outcome be such as that of
> Euclion's Rooster, made so famous by Plautus in his *Pot* and by Au-
> sonius in his *Gryphon* and elsewhere, who, for having discovered the
> treasure in his scratching, had his coat thrust (eut la couppe guorgée).
> Should that come to pass, would it not be enough to make me turn
> into a nanny goat? It has happened in the past; happen it still could.
> No it won't by Hercules! I recognize in them all a specific form and
> individual property that our ancestors called Pantagruelism, on condi-
> tion of which they never take in bad part things they know issue from
> a good, free, and honest heart. I have seen them ordinarily take good
> will in payment and be content with that, even when weakness in
> power has been associated with it.[25]

The series of contrasting outcomes begins with the fear that instead
of the reward he anticipates for his work ("my treasure," that is, the
appreciation of his readers), he may receive nothing but ingratitude
and incomprehension ("lumps of coal"). Again, the idea is that the
Tiers livre's motley appearance may be misunderstood. The proverb
about treasure and coal was used by Lucian to describe the disap-
pointment he felt when he realized that, just as the proportion and

25. "Prologue of the Author," 258, translation modified.

symmetry of Zeuxis's painting of a family of centaurs was overlooked
by spectators who only had eyes for the strangeness of its subject, the
praise his work had elicited was based only on the freshness of his
paradoxes and the novelty of his style, and not on the power of his
insights or the Attic grace and good construction of his writing.[26] Nor
is Lucian the only source for the proverb, which finds its way more
directly into the prologue via Erasmus's *Adagia*,[27] thus doubling the
echo of the Samosatan's satire of his contemporaries' bad taste with
the moral inflection of the Sage of Rotterdam's explanations. These
intertexts do not just create a thematic *mise en abyme* of the author's
discourse on blending genres; the mash-up of Lucian and Erasmus illustrates in miniature the fusion of different hybrid discourses that
will define the work to follow.

A dicing metaphor then opposes the highest throw to the lowest,
the goddess of love to a shaggy dog, clearly encoding the alternative
between the transformative message of good cheer and charity the
author hopes will be conveyed by his hybrid text, and the possibility that it might be seen as nothing more than a mildly amusing but
poorly constructed amalgam of digressions that never lead anywhere.
The latter outcome is developed in the doubly authorized anecdote
about Euclion's rooster, which again relays a dense network of hybridizing allusions. The pot of Plautus's work (*aularia* in Latin, *mar-
mite* in French) is a receptacle for a stew made up of all sorts of ingre-
dients, a mix such as the *salmigondis* that gives its name to the land
administered by Panurge, while the poem of Ausonius is presented
as having been discovered in the dust of a library, an ironically self-
deprecating image for a work composed of various borrowings. Interestingly, as François Rigolot has recently pointed out, the title of the
poem is altered in Rabelais's French from *Gryphus* to *Gryphon*,[28] the
lion-eagle griffon, yet another fantastic creature in the emblematic
series that runs through Lucian from Horace to Rabelais. The relation

26. Lucian, *Zeuxis or Antiochus*, § 2, in *Lucian in Eight Volumes*, Loeb Classical
Library 6, trans. K. Kilburn (Cambridge, MA: Harvard University Press, 1939), 157.
The dialogue develops a parallel between the reception of Lucian's works and those of
the painter Zeuxis. Lucian expresses his intense admiration for the artistry of Zeuxis's
painting of a family of centaurs, describing the tableau in detail and singling out for
praise the subtle fusion of the two bodies in the depiction of the female centaur before
deploring the attitude of the painting's viewers.

27. Erasmus, *Adagia*, I, ix, 30, *Thesaurus carbones erunt*.

28. "Le griffon," 357–59.

of the anecdote itself, about the unfortunate fate of the rooster that gave away the location of a treasure by scratching in the dust that covered it, provides the occasion for further word play in the spoonerism transposing of the first letters of *throat* and *cut*.

The series of oppositions and the anxiety it expresses culminates with the evocation of what would happen to the author should the negative scenario come to pass, that is, were the reader fail to properly understand the import of the work's hybrid form: "would it not be enough to make me turn into a nanny goat?" ("Ne seroit ce pour chevreter?"). This would be so very vexing, the author tells us, that it might have an effect of retroversion: instead of animating the work and transforming its disparate parts into a marvelous whole, the hybridizing force he has attempted to conjure might bounce back on him, changing both his species and his sex, metamorphosing him into a human nanny goat. The French, *chevreter*, from *chèvre*, or nanny goat (as opposed to the *bouc*, or male goat), means to get hopping mad, like goats that jump about and quiver with rage when angered.[29] The context, however, brings the reader back once again to Lucian's discussion of hybridity. The idea of a mistake leading to a transformation of sex is brought up by Lucian in *You're a Prometheus in Words*,[30] where he supposes that his detractors may have associated him with Prometheus because of an ineptitude in assembling parts similar to that of the God—his mixing of the masculine genre of dialogue with the female comedy would in that regard recall Prometheus's inebriated botching of his models for humans.[31] And of course, the goat-human satyr is the emblem of satire, its model according to the etymology that derives the genre's name from the satyr's habit of jumping from subject to subject and dishing out insults.[32] All of which amounts to saying, somewhat circuitously, that if the author's satire were to miss its mark, it would transform him into a satirist!

29. On the French expression, see Rigolot, "Le griffon," 358–59.
30. Ibid., 427.
31. Phaedrus writes (*Liber fabularum*, 4, 16) that Prometheus was working on making men and women and had got to the genitals when he was perturbed by Bacchus, who dragged him off to a drunken revel, and that when he returned, much the worse for wear, he stuck the wrong parts on the wrong bodies. See *Aesop's Fables*, trans. Laura Gibbs (Oxford: Oxford University Press, 2002), number 517.
32. On the Renaissance's reception and diffusion of the link between satyrs and satire, see Pascal Debailly, "La poétique de la satire classique en vers au xvie siècle et au début du xvie," *L'Information littéraire* 5 (1993): 20–25.

But, with an oath to Hercules, the author suddenly gets a grip on his fears and declares that nothing of the sort will happen thanks to the "specific form and individual property" he discerns in all of his readers. With the heavy irony of its scholastic language, the idea that all of his readers will find the blend of his new, Diogenic draft graceful and harmonious is no more to be taken seriously than the fears it allays. What is of central importance, on the other hand, is the nature of the felicitous condition that is to ensure the successful reception of the *Tiers livre*. Already extensively elaborated in the earlier installments of the Pantagrueline gesta, Pantagruelism as a quality that leads its possessors to interpret the words or deeds of others in the best possible way is based on the ideal of Christian charity as developed in the Gospels and in the epistles of the apostle Paul, and explicated in a wide array of Erasmian commentaries.[33] The context of these Biblical remarks on interpretation is vital for understanding the strategy and import of the prologue, as is the context of their reception in Rabelais's day.

Paul's discussion of the matter in Romans starts from the freedom conferred on the Christian by the New Law of the Gospel, which replaces the myriad observances of the Old Law with the sole duty of love, or charity.[34] The Christian is thus free from the burden of religious institutions and customs, which, from having been thought essential for salvation, henceforth appear indifferent. The question addressed by the apostle is how the Christian should realize his freedom under the New Law without scandalizing those whose weakness or superstition keeps them in the thrall of the Old Law and without thus impeding the progress of his brethren toward an understanding of the redemptive and emancipatory message of Christ. Romans teaches that whether people follow a given observance or not, charity requires that their conduct be imputed to good motives, and that Christian freedom must not lead to contempt or license. It is in this

33. Among the most important Biblical texts on charity in interpretation are the epistles to the Galatians and, above all, to the Romans. Related commentaries of Erasmus include the *Paraphrases'* commentaries on Romans 13-15 and on Luke's (6.37) and Matthew's (7.1) injunctions against judging one's neighbor, the *Apologetic Letters*, and the Proverbs' expositions of the meanings of the Delphic sentence "know thyself," and of Luke's parable of the mote and the beam. For the *Paraphrases* discussion of Luke, see Duval, *The Design of Rabelais's Tiers livre*, 188–89; on the Proverbs' exposition of "Nosce teipsum" (Proverb 1.6.95) and "Festucam ex alterius oculo ejicere" (1.6.91), 205–07.

34. Romans 13–15.

spirit that Erasmus's letter "On the Prohibition on Eating Meat" insists on the need for harmony among the different parts that compose the metaphorical body of Christ:

> In addition to this there is the important matter of order, without which there is no lasting harmony among mortals. Harmony is maintained either by equality or by each having his given place, each his given office. In the body hands, eyes, feet, and ears are equal; but between the eyes, the stomach, and the feet it is not equality that maintains harmony but order. If harmony is taken away, what, I ask, remains of value among Christians, that is, as the apostle Paul teaches, among those who are members of the same body?[35]

Erasmus's letter invokes Christian charity to justify respect for established institutions, whether or not they have anything to recommend them from a spiritual point of view, in the name of harmony between Catholics and Evangelicals or Reformers. The Sage's tolerance cloaks his impatience with the supporters of rigid alimentary restrictions rather thinly, but it is this letter's formulation of the rule of charitable interpretation that most closely parallels the golden rule of Pantagruelism: "It is the duty of Christian charity to interpret in a kindly manner whatever may be done with a good intention."[36]

The prologue's treatment of its Pantagruelic (Christian) reception thus revolves around the same themes as its presentation of its Diogenic (cynical) message. In both cases, a call to introspection and freedom risks encountering incomprehension if not scandal because of the novelty of the message and its lack of regard for received opinion. But in both cases, this novelty—whether we consider the provocations of Democritus's paradoxes or the scandal of Christ's teachings—is inseparable from the message itself. The casting aside of convention—whether in customs, in religion, or in letters—is not just a prelude to liberation, it is part of the enactment of philosophical metanoia (a changing of one's thinking) or religious conversion that provides the

35. "A Letter by Erasmus of Rotterdam Defending his Views Concerning the Prohibition on Eating Meat and Similar Human Regulations" in *Collected Works of Erasmus* 73, ed. and trans. Denis L. Drysdall (Toronto: University of Toronto Press, 2015), 66–67.

36. Ibid., 100. The similarity is remarked (122, n. 328) by Anne-Pascale Pouey-Mounou in her study of the theological context of the *Tiers livre*. See *Panurge comme lard en pois: paradoxe, scandale et propriété dans le* Tiers livre, *Études Rabelaisiennes* 53 (Geneva: Droz, 2013): ch. 2, "Scandale dans les moissons," 65–154.

telos of the traditions invoked by the prologue's author as well as programming the ideal reception of the work to follow.

Moreover, the hybridity of the cynic message (and of its literary transposition into the generically blended form of satire) has a clear parallel with that of the Gospels. Just as Democritus combines a rude exterior with an unparalleled nobility of mind, and just as his affronts to the dogma and doxa of his fellow citizens are actually intended to succor them by shocking them into a philosophical metanoia triggered by the realization that the customs and beliefs they consider important are really *adiaphora*, or indifferent matters, the message of Christ in the Gospels is one of emancipation from the chains of false doctrine and superstitious observances. Indeed, as François Rigolot has recently underlined, the Incarnation is the example *par excellence* of hybridity.[37] Not only does the fusion of man and God in Christ violate all received beliefs about the separation of the human and the divine, the scandal of the cross seems designed to smash all accepted social norms in celebrating the ignominy of crucifixion as the apotheosis of the Messiah. This, indeed, is the message underlined by Christ himself when he reminds his followers that he has not come to bring peace on earth, but rather a sword.[38] And this caustic but liberating side of Christian charity is precisely what was underlined in Erasmus's early work, the *Enchiridion Militis Christiani* (1503), whose pun on *enchiridion* as both handbook and sword (dagger, hanger, *bracquemard*, etc.) reverberates in rather freer echoes throughout the Pantagrueline gesta.[39]

The problem with this type of radical hybridity faced by the prologue's author is the same one addressed in Paul's letter to the Romans and in Erasmus's letter "On the Prohibition on Eating Meat." Like Diogenes's contempt for the customs of his fellow citizens, the reduction of the practices of the Judaic Law (or its Renaissance avatar, the observances of the Catholic Church and the newly instituted dogmas of the Reformers) to the status of indifferent matters risks alienating the very audience the message is intended to liberate, just as the affront to literary canons inherent in the satirical hybridiza-

37. "Le griffon" 355–61.
38. Matthew 10.34.
39. Already in the prologue's embroidering of the parable of the Corinthians' martial preparations, we are told that "Everyone was exercising his poniard; everyone was scouring the rust off his hanger" (255). See also, among other such *double entendres*, the exchange between Friar John and Panurge, ch. 23, 324.

tions of Rabelais's models, Horace and Lucian, entails the risk of their either being dismissed as risible or, worse yet, taken seriously as the works of new grammarians. In all of these cases, the question is how to maximize freedom without it degenerating into incoherence or vulgar license on the one hand, or hardening into a hypocritical new dogmatism on the other. The solution devised by Rabelais is encoded in the genetic double helix of the *Tiers livre* as mapped out by the "Prologue of the Author."

Returning to the series of alternatives that voiced the author's trepidation, we may now see that the solution is actually encrypted in the expression of the fear. Culminating in the spoonerism that transposes the first letters of *throat* and *cut*, the allusions to and examples of mixes and hybrids that saturate the passage, from Zeuxis's centaurs to the griffon and the transgendered nanny goat satyr image of the author himself, all illustrate the transfer of elements or characteristics from one genus or genre to another. The semiotic heterosis achieved by this pattern of cross-grafting, the plurality of comic and serious meanings it engenders, is the means by which the author can deliver a message of good cheer along with a scathing critique of his contemporaries' follies, and can edify his reader while avoiding the collapse of his own text into pedantic or Pharisaical pontificating.

After the anecdote about Euclion's rooster first transfers the property of the hoped-for treasure away from the author himself (it is no longer "*my* treasure"), the layering of these different types of transference rehearses the passage's culminating shift of responsibility for the work's reception from the author to his reader and, ultimately, to the Grace of Christ. The "weakness" of Rabelais's composition is to be redeemed by the reader's Pantagrueline charity just as the weakness of the reader himself is to be redeemed by the power of the Cross, at once the greatest and most scandalous image of hybridity. Whereas the humanist works of Horace and Lucian revel in transgressing the grammarians' rules and make a show, once one reads through their ironies, of uniting disparate parts and genres into a graceful whole by virtue of their authors' genius, the author of the *Tiers livre*'s prologue avoids such presumption by devolving responsibility for the apprehension of the depth of the work's insights and the inner harmony of its outwardly shambolic form to the reader.

In parallel, the emancipatory charge and the explosive potential for conflict carried by Christian militancy is shifted to the satirical, cynic aspect of the text, allowing the Pantagruelic message to focus

on self-knowledge and fraternity, and avoiding the distinctly un-
charitable problem of excoriating the Christianity of the narrator's
contemporaries in the name of his own. Rather than being smitten
with the sword of faith, the "hood-brained pettifoggers," "nitpicking
sticklers for details" and, above all, "pious hypocrites, coffin haunt-
ing spooks and Cerberian curs" of the prologue are thus to be "clob-
bered" with the staff of Diogenes,[40] just as the text will develop its
savage satire of Catholic superstition and hypocrisy under the cloak
of Panurge's cynic prosopopœia.

The model developed by the "Prologue of the Author" does not
simply temper Diogenic license with Christian charity. It takes the
mixed nature of each of these traditions and forges a "meta-hybrid";
it splices cynic philosophy's *spoudogeloion* (its fusing of the serious
and the laughable) with the Evangelical material of Pantagruelism
to develop a heterotic version of Erasmus's "serious play";[41] and it
puts forward the freedom of the hilarious, even shocking form invented through this process as the expression of a natural truth. As
the prologue winds up, just before it tails off into imprecations, the
narrator-steward of the feast offers his reader a mug of wine. Drawn
from a barrel that is at once the font of a new miracle of Cana, the
emblem of cynic intransigence, and "a real cornucopia of joyfulness
and jesting,"[42] this first swig serves to prepare the reader for a satirical narrative whose liberating humor depends on the eccentricity of
its form.

40. "Prologue of the Author," 259–60.
41. The Erasmian idea of serious play (*serio ludere*) is best illustrated in *The Praise
of Folly*.
42. "Prologue of the Author," 259.

MIREILLE HUCHON

Rabelaisian Encryptions

Rabelais supplements his *Quart livre* of 1552—the last work published during his lifetime—with a *Brief Declaration of Some of the
More Obscure Terms in the Fourth Book of the Heroic Deeds and Sayings of Pantagruel*.[1] This *Brief Declaration* provides an explanation of
lexical difficulties, and a key to coded words that reveal modalities
of encryption in the text. Certain terms used in Rabelais's work and
highlighted in the *Brief Declaration* serve as privileged markers of
steganography, the practice found in both painting and writing that
consists of hiding, behind one image, an additional image, which can
only be seen from a secret spot designated by the artist, as in the
paintings of Archimboldo.[2] Rabelais uses rare, mysterious, polysemic

---

1. The *Brief Declaration of Some of the More Obscure Terms Contained in the
Fourth Book of the Heroic Deeds and Sayings of Pantagruel*, which explains, in nine
pages, 178 terms or expressions, was added to certain copies of the edition of the *Quart
livre des faicts et dicts Heroiques du bon Pantagruel, Composé par M. François Rabelais docteur en Médecine* (Paris: Michel Fezandat, 1552). All English translations of
Rabelais's work are taken from *The Complete Works of François Rabelais*, trans. Donald M. Frame (Berkeley: University of California Press, 1991).
  2. See Beroalde de Verville, *Le voyage des princes fortunez, œuvre steganogra-
phique* (Paris, C. de La Tour, 1610), a4v°:
  "Advice offered to those of fine discernment concerning the voyage of the fortu-
nate Princes, which is a steganographic work containing, under the pleasant disguise
of Love's discourses, all that is most exquisite about the secrets sought after by those
curious and of good understanding.
  [. . .] And to those who do not yet know what this craft is through which we hide, it
is our pleasure to reveal, I say that Steganography is the ART of representing naturally
a pleasant conceit, and which nevertheless, under concealed attributes of its appearance, hides entirely different subjects than those that seem to be intended: It is what is
practiced in painting when one presents some landscape, or port, or other portrait that
nevertheless hides under it some other figure that one discerns when one looks from
a certain position that the master has designated. And this is also practiced in writing,

YFS 134, *The Construction of a National Vernacular Literature in the Renaissance:
Essays in Honor of Edwin M. Duval,* ed. DeVos and Hayes, © 2018 by Yale University.

terms charged with the weighty power of allusion and suggestion in this way. The *Brief Declaration* offers an exceptional repertoire of such terms. For instance, the glossary's first entry, *"Mythologies*: fabulous narratives," is the notable characterization that Rabelais assigns to his French oeuvre. The terms he glosses are from a variety of domains, such as medicine, architecture, mathematics, philosophy; and they often find their first attestation in French here, or take on new connotations: *symbole* and *sympathie*, for example.

One series, unique in its genre for a multiplicity of occurrences, stands out: it groups together priests, interpreters of scripture, and prophets, all of ambiguous status in Rabelais's books, in contrast with other imprints of Rabelais's related to evangelism that he always endorsed. From one passage to another, from one book to another, steganographic figurations play off one another or are scrambled together, offering a nonlinear reading in which subtle correspondences are established among elements of each of Rabelais's "designs" that have been of central interest to Edwin Duval's scholarship.[3]

PROPHETS, INTERPRETERS, AND PONTIFFS

Prophets, priests, and interpreters of various religions occupy a select place in the glossary of the *Quart livre*. Pantagruel and his companions are on a quest to find the Divine Bottle, in search of an answer to the question of the marriage of Panurge; they are also in search of knowledge, a journey that in its very essence can have no end.

On the last two islands where they stop, the heroes encounter Papimaniacs, Engastrimyths, and Gastrolaters, "names made up at will,"[4] as Rabelais would say; behind these characters, he castigates interpreters, priests, and false prophets. In the episode about the Papimaniacs—worshipers of the pope—their bishop Homenaz evokes "one of their hypophetes, a degreaser and glossator of their holy

---

when one discusses at length plausible subjects that enclose other matters of exceeding worth that are only understood when one reads by a secret way that uncovers occult and magnificent matters beneath common appearance; but they are clear and seen by the eye and the understanding of the one who has received the light that allows him to penetrate into these perfectly impenetrable and otherwise unintelligible discourses."

3. See Edwin M. Duval, *The Design of Rabelais's* Quart livre de Pantagruel (Geneva: Droz, 1998).

4. *Brief Declaration*, Edwin M. Duval, 598.

Decretals" (QL 49:542)[5] who had written that, just as the messiah would come for the Jews, the pope would one day come to the island. The *Brief Declaration* gives the definition of this hapax in Rabelais's work: "*Hypophetes*: who speak of things past as prophets speak of future things."[6] Homenaz, referring again to the Decretals, mentions the commentary by one of our "ancient Decretaline scholiasts" (QL 49:543) and in the *Brief Declaration* Rabelais translates this other hapax, "scholiasts," as "expositors."[7] On the island of Gaster, the world's "first master of arts," Pantagruel encounters Engastrimyths and the Gastrolaters, two groups whom he detests (QL 57-58). Three consecutive glosses are concerned with them:

> *Engastrimythes*: speaking from the belly.
> *Gastrolatres*: worshipers of the belly.
> *Sternomantes*: divining through the chest.[8]

In the very text of the *Quart livre*, after giving ancient and biblical references for Engastrimyths (the synonym of which is *sternomantes*, used by Sophocles), the narrator denounces them as "diviners, magicians, and deceivers of the simple people" (QL 58:562). He illustrates his comment with the example of the Italian Jacobe Rodogine. Around 1513 in Ferrara, people including Rabelais himself had heard the evil spirited voice of Rodogine who went by the name of Crespelu or Cincinnatus and who, when questioned about the present or the past, answered quite pertinently, but when asked about the future would always lie: he often delivered his answer as a huge fart or a mumbling of unintelligible words with barbarous endings. As for the Gastrolaters, they worship, serve, and honor Gaster as their God, and make sacrifices to him. Staged in their processions and rites, they are nothing but "scurvy rabble of sacrificers" (QL 60:569). Rabelais offers in this passage, as Duval has shown, both a parody of the Mass and a critique of "formalistic, idolatrous Judaism."[9]

---

5. *Quart Livre* 49:542. From this point forward, all references to Rabelais's works will follow the following format: P for *Pantagruel*, G for *Gargantua*, TL for the *Tiers livre*, QL for the *Quart livre*, and CL for the *Cinquiesme livre*. These will be followed by chapter and page number from the English translation with a colon separating the two.

6. [Chapter 48]: 602.

7. Ibid., 603.

8. *Brief Declaration* [Chapter 58]: 604.

9. Duval, "La messe, la cène et le voyage sans fin du *Quart livre*," in *Rabelais en son demi-millénaire, Études rabelaisiennes* 21 (Geneva: Droz, 1988): 132–34.

Along with these fictional characters, representatives of the Roman Catholic Church and objects of a virulent satire, is a group of technical and seemingly neutral terms designating the clergy from the Hebrews to the Gauls:

Pastophores: pontiffs among the Egyptians.[10]
Musaphiz: in Turkish and Slavonic language, doctors and prophets.[11]
Massorethz: interpreters and glossators among the Hebrews.[12]
Druydes: the pontiffs and learned men of the ancient French, of whom Caesar writes, *De Bello Gallico*, Book 6; Cicero Book 1, *De Divinatione*; Pliny, Book 16, etc.[13]

It is worth considering these rare names in Rabelais's work, but it is also worth noticing the terms used in the definitions, like "pontiff," "prophet," "interpreter," or "glossator." Throughout all five books (including the posthumously published *Cinquiesme livre* bringing together Rabelais's drafts), Rabelais refers to "our ancient druids" (*QL* 57:560) and describes their specific customs and beliefs. These include numeration: "more than forty times forty nights back, to reckon as the ancient Druids did" (*P* 1:137); funerary rites: "in the time of our ancient druids, who had the dead bodies of their relatives and lords burned" (*TL* 52:410) or "When once upon a time in Gaul, by the ordinance of the druids, serfs, servants, and attendants were all burned alive at the funerals and obsequies of their masters and lords" (*TL* 45:393); and mythology: "erroneous belief of our ancient druids who thought that Mercury was the first inventor of the arts" (*QL* Prol:427).

Other terms are used in their proper sense or are applied pejoratively to the clergy of the Catholic Church. *Pastophores*, a word that designates Egyptian priests responsible for carrying statues of the gods into temple chapels, keeps its original meaning when Rabelais evokes their clothing along with that of the priests of Isis (*TL* 51:408). But in the *Quart livre*, Rabelais denounces the guilty actions of members of the present-day clergy, referring to them as "mole-catching image-bearers ("pastophores taulpetiers")," priests who officiate at marriages without the consent of the parents (*TL* 48:398); or he al-

10. *Brief Declaration* [In the Prologue]: 595.
11. Ibid., 594.
12. Ibid., 595.
13. Ibid., [Chapter 57]: 604.

ludes negatively to the politics of Pope Julius III and "the tragedies that are being aroused by certain pastophores" (QL Prol: 430).

The word *musaphiz* (corresponding to *mushafi*, "commentator on the Koran") appears starting in *Pantagruel*—the first of Rabelais's five books to be published—as a term of civilization, connected with Turkish pashas (P 14:180). In the *Tiers livre*, in regard to Triboulet the fool, in whose gestures and words Pantagruel has observed notable mysteries, he is no longer as stunned as before that fools are revered by the Turks as musafis and prophets (TL 45:393). Then later Rabelais playfully transposes the term to contemporary France when he mentions the musafis of Saint-Ayl near Orléans, who boast of having the body and relics of little Zaccheus, whom they call Saint Sylvanus (QL Prol:427).

Massorethz, in the first two books, retains its proper meaning of "Jewish doctor who compiled and established the Masorah (Hebrew text of the Bible)," but Rabelais makes amusing use of it. In *Pantagruel* (where the term appears for the first time in French), with regard to Hurtaly sitting astride Noah's ark, the narrator cites the authority of the Masoretes, "good ballocky types and fine Hebraic bagpipers" (P 1:140); and to justify his theivery, Panurge does not hesitate to refer to the biblical commentaries of all the Masoretes (P 17:191); these commentaries are also invoked in the amusing antidoted Frigglehaggles of *Gargantua* (G 2:10). In the prologue to the *Quart livre*, the most learned Masoretes claims that Chinon is the oldest town in the world. In the two occurrences in the *Tiers livre*, the word, accompanied by *cabalistes*, is used for theological discussions about angels and devils: Pantagruel says he remembers that the cabalists (the first attestation of the word in French) and Masoretes, "interpreters of Holy Scripture," determined how to recognize angelic apparitions: Satan's angel seduces first and then leaves man perplexed, whereas the good angel frightens and then consoles man (TL 14:300). Panurge, in response to the question of why devils never enter the terrestrial paradise, says that the Masoretes and cabalists give as the sole reason the presence of a cherubin at the gate (TL 23:324) Just as, for *musaphiz*, there is a joke about the cabalists of Saint Louand who ordered that Gargantua's gloves be made from goblin skin and werewolf skin. (G 8:24)

On the basis of these scholarly terms cross-referencing other religions, Rabelais suggests an image of the present-day Church. But they are not the only terms that prompt another reading. The same is true for more current and more intelligible words used in definitions. Such is the case of glossators, used with the term interpreters in the gloss on Masoretes and to which the uses of "gloss" can be connected. Rabelais frequently condemns these glossators, for example: the twelfth-century jurist Accursius, for his gloss on the *Pandectes* (the compendium of Roman law) considered by Pantagruel to be a fringe of excrement on the beautiful golden gown that the law books comprise (*P* 5:159); or the mirific gloss hidden in a little corner of the holy Decretals according to which the contributions made to the collection must be allotted to food and drink for Homenaz (*QL* 51:546); or the glossators of an entry in the Decretals invoked by Panurge (*TL* 14:300). In the *Cinquiesme livre*, the gloss is curiously incorporated into action. After eliciting the word of the Bottle, "Trinch," the pontiff Bacbuc makes Panurge swallow the chapter and gloss where the word of the Divine Bottle was interpreted (*CL* 44-45:709-10); she also delivers the message of the Divine Bottle: "you yourselves be the interpreters of your own undertaking." (*CL* 45:710) Panurge thus becomes the equivalent of the aforementioned cabalists and Masoretes—making the *Cinquiesme livre* as apt as the *Tiers livre* to be read as the book of interpretation.[14]

The word "Pontife" appears in the definitions of two words in the *Brief Declaration*, for pastaphors and for druids. It is a term used for any person invested with a holy ministry, no matter what the religion, and more specifically for the pope, who is the sovereign pontiff. This polyvalence is manifest, as much in the *Tiers livre*, where one finds mention of the pontiffs of Cybele in Phrygia (*TL* 48:398) and the noble pontiff, the bishop of Auxerre (*TL* 33:358), as in the *Quart livre*, with the pontiffs of Mosaic Law (*QL* 28:498) and the pontiff of Jupiter (*QL* 61:575). In the *Cinquiesme livre*, where the Egyptian pontiffs in Hieropolis are mentioned (*CL* 19:652), the reader cannot help but be surprised by the feminization of Jupiter's pontiff (*CL* 33: 686–87) and, especially, by the invented character Bacbuc, the noble pontiff, pontiff of all mysteries (*CL* 34:688). Rabelais describes Bacbuc at length in the exercise of her ministry as she outfits Panurge for the word of the Bottle, has him perform a series of gestures, with a few conjurations

14. See Duval, "Interpreting Rabelais" in *The Design of Rabelais's* Tiers livre de Pantagruel (Geneva: Droz, 1997), 187–221.

in the Etruscan language, referring to a "ritual book" brought to her by one of her mystagogues (this being the first attestation in French of the adjective *rituel*). The narrator points out that neither Numa Pompilius (second king of Rome who established religious legislation), nor the Caerites of Tuscia (from which the term *cérémonie* would come), nor the "holy Jewish captain" (Moses) instituted as many ceremonies, and that neither for Apis in Egypt nor for Jupiter Ammon did the Ancients make use of such religious observances (*CL* 43:705).

In the following chapter of the *Cinquiesme livre*, in order to present Panurge before the Bottle set in the center of the chapel fountain, Bacbuc again has him perform various actions before laying open her ritual book and whispering into his ear a song of invocation to the mystery-filled Bottle. After something unknown is thrown into the fountain, the word *trinch* issues forth from of the Bottle in the most distinct manner ever heard by Bacbuc since she has been "ministering here to her most sacred oracle" (*CL* 44:709). The book swallowed by Panurge is revealed to be a true breviary (a term designating at the time a book, but also a small bottle) full of Falernian wine. Bacbuc maintains that drinking is a distinctly human behavior and that truth is hidden in wine, before she mentions the necessity of being the interpreter of one's own undertaking. "Panurge himself becomes the passive medium of a truth stronger than himself and which speaks through the intermediary of his voice, just like the Cumean Sibyl described by Virgil, or like the Pythia of Delphi."[15] To be the interpreter of one's undertaking is to be compared with the key expression at the center of the *Tiers livre*, "CONGNOIS TOY,"—know thyself—recognized as such by Edwin Duval.[16] Moreover, Duval has shown just how many vestiges of the primitive *telos* from the episode of the Divine Bottle, "an entirely authentic conclusion to an unpublished and lost *Tiers livre*,"[17] abandoned at the end of the *Tiers livre*, are incorporated in the very body of the *Tiers livre* in the episodes of Raminagrobis, Her Trippa, and Triboulet.

15. Duval, "De la dive Bouteille à la quête du *Tiers livre*," in *Rabelais pour le XXIe siècle*, *Études rabelaisiennes* 32 (Geneva: Droz, 1998): 274.

16. Duval, "Panurge, perplexity and the ironic design of Rabelais's *Tiers livre*," *Renaissance Quarterly* 35 (1982): 381–400; "The Word at the Center," *The Design of Rabelais's* Tiers livre de Pantagruel, 107–32.

17. Duval, "De la dive Bouteille à la quête du *Tiers livre*," 266.

The pontiff Bacbuc, through whose character Rabelais satirizes the clergy and ceremonies, is part and parcel of a particularly subversive parody. The female pontiff gives way in the *Quart livre* to a male pontiff, Homenaz. However, the female pontiff of the *Cinquiesme livre*, with her mystagogues and her ceremonies, is intertwined in two passages where priests are called into question. On the one hand, the priests who are complicit in clandestine marriages, "pastophores taulpetiers," are compared to the pontiffs of Cybele in Phrygia; mentioned are their mysterious temples, the ceremonies and sacrifices of the "mystes" (from the Greek, "initiated in the mysteries of paganism," and used only in this chapter, just like the term "symmistes," "initiated with the other mystes").[18] The mystes of the *Tiers livre* correspond to the mystagogues of the *Cinquiesme livre.* On the other hand, Pantagruel says that in the gestures and words of Triboulet, the crazy fool, he has observed some remarkable mysteries, which explains why the Turks consider madmen as musaphiz and prophets (*TL* 45:393); the Magi believe that the movement of the head is the coming of the prophetic spirit; and given as examples are the Pythia and the "gelded Galli, priests of Cybele." (*TL* 45:393) *Pontiffe* and *cérémonie* seem to be privileged markers.

Rabelais uses the term *cérémonie* again on Sharper's Island (île de Cassade) in the *Cinquiesme livre* where a flask of *sang-vreal* appears, "a divine thing, known to few people." (*CL* 10:633) At Panurge's request, this object is shown with three times as much ceremony and solemnity as the Pandectes is shown in Florence or the veil used by Veronica to wipe away the sweat of Christ is shown in Rome—but what was revealed was only the face of a roasted rabbit! Duval has highlighted the critique of the Eucharist in the use of the form *sang-real* (Saint Graal) and shown how the last episodes of the *Quart livre* are part of a satire of "all that Erasmus, following Saint Paul, calls *human constitutions.*"[19] Such was already the meaning of Pantagruel's prayer in the first of Rabelais's books where human constitutions, false prophets, are denounced: "I will have thy Gospel preached pure, simple, and entire, so that the abuses of a bunch of hypocrites [*papelars*] and false prophets, who, by human institutions and depraved inventions, have envenomed the whole world, will be driven forth from around me." (*P* 29:227) This passage, with the pure, simple and

18. *TL* 48:398.
19. Duval, "La messe, la cène et le voyage sans fin du *Quart livre*," 131.

entire sermon of the holy Gospel, resonates singularly with the passage from the *Quart livre*'s dedication letter to one of its protectors,
to which we now turn.

ANAGNOSTE, GOSPEL, AND APOCALYPSE

The *Brief Declaration* accorded particular attention to the castigated
groups of glossators, diviners, and false prophets. Using an identical
device—a group with non-individualized members—Rabelais strikes
a blow against his detractors. Thus, in the *Quart livre*, at the beginning of his epistle to his protector, where he denounces the atrocious
slander by "certain cannibals, misanthropes, *agelastes*" (*QL* Liminary Epistle:422), three terms entitled to their own glosses:

> *Cannibales*: a monstrous people in Africa who have faces like dogs
> and who bark instead of laughing.
> *Misantropes*: hating men, fleeing the company of men.
> *Agelastes*: never laughing, sad, cross.[20]

In opposition to these three glosses (and the multiple entries of the
Brief Declaration concerning groups held in contempt), the following
four entries, corresponding to the text of Rabelais's dedication of the
Quart livre of 1552 to his protector, take on a singular relief, with two
references to Scripture:

> *Iota*: a point. It's the smallest letter of the Greeks. Cic. 3 *De Orat.*;
> Martial Book 2.92; in the Gospel, Matthew 5.18.
> *Theme*: position, subject. What someone proposes to discuss, prove,
> and deduce.
> *Anagnoste*: reader.
> *Evangile*: good news.[21]

In the face of slander, Rabelais asserts that he has been tempted not
to write an iota more. The gloss of the *Brief Declaration* refers among
other things to the Beatitudes (Matthew 5.17–18), where Jesus says
he has not come to abolish the Law or the Prophets, but to fulfill it:
not an *i*, not the dot of an *i* will be left out of the Law, lest it fail to be
accomplished.

For his defense, Rabelais next maintains that his book is full of
"joyous fooleries," which constitute the "sole subject and theme" of

20. *Brief Declaration* [In the Liminary Epistle]: 593.
21. Ibid.

these books. He praises the *Anagnoste* ("reader" in Greek) who presented it to the kings of France. Francis I, warned of attacks against
Rabelais "and having carefully heard and understood a distinct reading of these books of mine by the most learned and faithful reader
in the kingdom [. . .] had found no suspect passage whatever" (*QL*
Liminary Epistle:423). It had been the same with Henry II, who had
granted Rabelais a privilege and particular protection against slander-
ers through the intermediary of his protector who had this "gospel"
in Paris and at Saint-Maur. (At the beginning of the *Quart livre*, the
author will speak of God "whose sacrosanct word of good news I re-
vere, that's the Gospel") (*QL* Prol:425).

The passage from the dedication letter of the *Quart livre* echoes a
passage from *Gargantua* that offers the first of only two occurrences
of the term *Anagnoste* in Rabelais's work and that refers to realities
corresponding to the other glossed words of the *Brief Declaration*.
Upon Gargantua's waking up, and on the instructions of his preceptor
Ponocrates:

> While they were rubbing him down, there was read to him loud and
> clear some page of the Holy Scripture, with a delivery appropriate to
> the matter, and assigned to that was a young page, a native of Basché,
> named Anagnostes. According to the gist and argument of this lesson,
> he often gave himself up to revering, adoring, praying, and beseeching
> the good God, whose majesty and marvelous judgments the reading
> demonstrated. (G 23:55)

The *Anagnoste*, the reader, rises up in his singularity and the pu-
rity of the divine scripture, a simple word passer in the face of all the
interpreters, diviners, and abusers of all religions. As much in fiction
as in reality, kings, without the help of any intermediary explanation, were able to make their own interpretation. *Subject* and *theme*
at the beginning of the *Quart livre*, and *propos* and *argument*, are
synonyms and are to be taken in parallel with each other. Rabelais's
work is therefore comparable to divine scripture. It is the equivalence
that Duval has so well demonstrated, showing how *Pantagruel* is a
new Testament and how Jewish Law and Revelation are in opposition within it.[22] This religious book/profane book equivalence is a
constant in Rabelais's work. It is explicit from the first lines of *Pan-*

---

22. Duval, *The Design of Rabelais's* Pantagruel (New Haven: Yale University
Press, 1991), 4–11.

tagruel (lines that will be modified in 1542): "not long ago you saw, read, and came to know the *Great and Inestimable Chronicles of the Enormous Giant Gargantua*, and, as true faithful, you had the courtesy to believe them, *just like the text of the Bible or the holy Gospel*" (*P* Prol:133).[23] Rabelais's own book was then given as superior to these *Chronicles*, and then ended with an equivalence, "and myriad other little jollities, all true. *They are beautiful texts of the Gospel in French*" (*P* 34:244) present again in the *Quart livre*.

In the first edition, Alcofrybas, claiming to offer a book "a little more objective and trustworthy" (*P* Prol:134) than the *Chronicles*, added that he could never lie and that he was bearing witness to what he had seen, by speaking of it as Saint John speaks of the Apocalypse:

> For do not suppose (if you don't want to make a mistake knowingly) that I speak of it as the Jews used to speak about the Law. I was not born on such a planet, and it has never happened that I lied, or gave assurance of anything that was not truthful: *those who lack understanding of their actions are not culpable*. I speak as Saint John of the Apocalypse: quod vidimus testamur ["we testify to what we have seen," John 3.11]. (*P* Prol:134)

This reference to the Apocalyse disappears from the *Pantagruel* of 1542, but the Apocalypse appears again in Rabelais's work, in the episode of the *Chicanous* in the *Quart livre*, thanks to the same but somewhat altered expression. Two old *Chicanous* are weeping, for "two of the finest worthy people of Shystroovia [*Chiquanorroy*] had been given the monk by the neck at the gallows." Gymnaste points out that his pages "give the monk by the feet" to their sleeping companions (an allusion to the gag consisting of attaching to the toe of the sleeping person a string that you pull to wake him up), but that "to give the monk by the neck would be to hand and strangle the person." And Frère Jean points out: "you're talking about it like Saint Jean de la Palisse [Saint John of the Apocalypse]." The cause of such punishment is stealing "the instruments for Mass" and hiding them beneath the bell-tower. "That," said Epistémon, "is spoken in a terrible allegory" (*QL* 16:473–74). This passage gives rise to two long glosses in the *Brief Declaration*:

---

23. All text in italics here and in the following two passages is found in earlier versions removed in the 1542 edition and is my translation.

Comme sainct Jan de la Palisse: a colloquial way of speaking, by syn-
cope, instead of L'Apocalypse; like Idolâtre for Idololâtre [Idolatrous].

Les ferremens de la messe [*implements for Mass*]: so the Poitevin villagers call what we call ornaments; and "le manche de la paroece,"
[the parish handle] what we call "le clochier" [the bell tower], this by
a rather clumsy metaphor.[24]

Rabelais had already written "Thus you say *idolâtre* for *idololâtre*,"
in connection with the use of *Guaillardon* for *Guaillartlardon* (QL
40:522). The phonetic remark attracts attention to *Idolâtre*, a word
that could be applied to the Papimaniacs, Engastrimyths, and Gastrolaters. *Apocalypse* appears only in the altered form *la Palisse* and
in Epistémon's exclamation, "*Vivat, fifat! Pipat! Bibat! O what an
apocalyptic secret!*" (QL 53:554). It is again this character who speaks
of "the cunning and fantastical allegory"[25] for interpretation by Panurge who turns the black beasts that the poet Raminagrobis claims
to have hunted into mendicant friars, a passage whose importance
Duval has revealed.[26] The dreadful allegory is to be read in connection
with the allegory of the mendicant friars, and in light of the prologue
to *Gargantua* and Duval's interpretation of it.[27]

The *Brief Declaration* is invaluable for clarifying Rabelais's text
and its designs, for a reading between the lines. It offers two sorts of
words. At the head of an entry, the glossed terms are scholarly and
rare, terms that stop the reader and seem to function as toothing-
stones ["pierres d'attente"];[28] moreover, such is the case, throughout
Rabelais's work, of words like *Thélème* (*Gargantua*), *callöier des Isles
Hieres* (on the title page of the *Tiers livre*), or *Thalamege* of the *Quart
livre*. In the definitions of these obscure terms, Rabelais avails himself of more current terms which, repeated or in constellation, are, in
the same way, as many secret places designated by the master, like
pontife or *Apocalypse*, or elsewhere *murailles* in *Pantagruel*, *mes-
siers* (guardians of the vine), *prélude* and *travail* in *Gargantua*. Certain words are skillfully placed, others in their recurrence or their

24. *Brief Declaration* [Chapter 16]: 598.
25. "sophisticque et phantastique allegorie" (*TL* 22). Translation mine.
26. Duval, *The Design of Rabelais's* Tiers livre de Pantagruel, 200.
27. Duval, "Interpretation and the 'Doctrine absconce' of Rabelais's Prologue to
Gargantua," *Études rabelaisiennes* 18 (Geneva: Droz, 1985): 1–7.
28. Toothing-stones are stones that jut out from a wall, as needed, so that another
wall or edifice can be attached to the existing structure while maintaining a continuous surface.

arrangement are obvious signs of obsessions. The images call to each other from one book to another, and not from one book *after* the other, with each of the books of the Pantagrueline *geste* to be considered, in the wake of Duval's work, as a whole unto itself. In any case, Rabelais must be taken at his word, as attested by the *Brief Declaration*, his final pronouncement.

—Translated from the French by Mary Byrd Kelly

II. Italy and France: Identity and Boundaries

RICHARD COOPER

Praise and (More) Blame of Dante in Late Renaissance France

Dante is a key figure of cultural exchange between France and Italy in the Renaissance.[1] It is clear that he was relatively well known in certain fifteenth-century circles, when poets showed familiarity with the *Commedia*, and when the nobility collected his manuscripts, several of which were in the library of the Angoulême family in Cognac, and passed into the royal library at Blois.[2] Once on the throne, François I, with his sister Marguerite, showed a particular interest in the poet; he commissioned both illuminated manuscripts (such as the translation of *Paradiso* by François Bergaigne, with paintings inspired by cuts in Venetian incunable editions), and an incomplete manuscript of *Inferno* with important pen illustrations.[3] Poets at the Valois court, like Jehan Bouchet, and like Marguerite de Navarre herself, show knowledge of particular episodes. When printing his edition of Petrarch in 1545, Jean de Tournes acknowledged the French appetite

1. Paul Friederich Werner, *Dante's Fame Abroad, 1350–1850* (Chapel Hill: University of North Carolina Press, 1950); Deborah Parker, *Commentary and Ideology: Dante in the Renaissance* (Durham: Duke University Press, 1993); Dario Cecchetti, "Dante e il Rinascimento francese," in *Letture Classensi* 19 (1990): 35–63; Richard Cooper, "Dante sous François Ier: la traduction de François de Bergaigne" in *Pour Dante: Dante et l'apocalypse; lectures humanistes de Dante*, ed. Bruno Pinchard (Paris: Champion, 2001), 389-406; *Dante in France*, ed. Russell Gouldbourne, Claire Honess, and Matthew Traherne, special number of *La Parola del Testo* 17/1–2 (Pisa and Rome: Fabrizio Serra, 2013).

2. Edmond Sénemaud, "La bibliothèque de Charles d'Orléans, Comte d'Angoulême au Château de Cognac en 1496," *Bulletin de la Société archéologique et historique de la Charente*, 3e sér., II (1860): 48-83, 130–82 ; H. Michelant, *Catalogue de la bibliothèque de François Ier à Blois en 1518* (Paris: A. Franck, 1863).

3. Turin, Bibl. Naz., ms. L. III. 17; cf. Jules Camus, "La première version de l'*Enfer* de Dante" in *Giornale storico della letteratura italiana* 37 (1901): 70–93.

YFS 134, *The Construction of a National Vernacular Literature in the Renaissance: Essays in Honor of Edwin M. Duval*, ed. DeVos and Hayes, © 2018 by Yale University.

for literature written in Italian, "this language so highly esteemed today, especially in the Court of our great Sovereign," namely François I.[4] Recent studies have explored echoes of Dante in the poetry of his reign.[5] One letter of the period suggests that the Pisan diplomat, Gabriele Cesano, who accompanied Cardinal Ippolito d'Este to the French court in the early 1540s, had gathered around him a group of Dante enthusiasts: "Master Gabriello Cesano has virtually set up a Tuscan academy in France, where he reads Dante every day. And he says that all those lords and ladies are competing for who can best understand the language."[6]

But rather than the Court, it was Lyon, the most Italianate city in France, with its active colony of merchants, bankers, humanists, and assorted exiles, that sustained and developed this interest in Dante. Dante first appeared in print in Lyon at the beginning of the century, in a pirated edition of Pietro Bembo's Aldine octavo of 1502, printed by Baldassarre da Gabiano and Balthazar Troth.[7] The market for vernacular Italian in Lyon grew in the 1540s, thanks in part to the exiled humanist Lucantonio Ridolfi, who was commissioned as early as 1543 to do a manuscript translation into Italian of Boccaccio's *De mulieribus claris*, which would then be translated into French and published in 1551, a year after the *Decameron*.[8] However, the first of the three Tuscan crowns (Dante, Petrarch, and Boccaccio) to appear in print in Lyon was not Boccaccio but Petrarch. Using a new set of italic type that he had commissioned for poetry, the printer Jean de Tournes published the text in 1545 in the more affordable sextodecimo format to reach a wider public, illustrating it with a portrait medallion, headpieces, and initials. This initiative led two years later

4. *Il Petrarca* (Lyon: Jean de Tournes, 1545), 3. Unless otherwise indicated, all translations are my own.

5. Thomas Hunkeler, "Dante à Lyon: des 'rime petrose' aux 'durs épigrammes,'" *Italique: poésie italienne de la Renaissance* 11 (2008): 9–27; Gisèle Mathieu-Castellani, "Echos de Dante dans la poésie française du XVIᵉ siècle," *Littérature* 133 (2004): 40–53.

6. Letter of Bernardino Duretti-Cosimo I, Trento, 8 July 1545, in Archivio di Stato, Florence, *Carteggio universal di Cosimo I de' Medici*, III, filza 373, fᵒ 75; cited in Arturo Farinelli, *Dante e la Francia* (Milan: Hoepli, 1908), vol. I, 297.

7. *Le terze rime di Dante* (Venice: Aldo Manuzio, 1502), 8ᵒ; *Le terze rime di Dante* (Lyon : Baldassare Gabiano, n.d. and 1503); *Le terze rime con sito, et forma de lo inferno novamente restampito* (Lyon: s.n., 1515).

8. See the dedication to Maria Albizzi, 24 June 1543, in Boccaccio, *Des Dames de renom* (Lyon: Guillaume Roville and Thibauld Payen, 1551), 7–9.

to a similar pocketsize edition of the *Commedia*,[9] dedicated by de Tournes, like the Petrarch, to Maurice Scève (who may have been an editor at this press), and with the same ornaments of a medallion portrait, headpieces, and capitals, as well as a very short *summario* of Dante's life at the end.

The dedication to the "most ingenious and learned Maurice Scève" ("molto ingenioso et dotto M. Mauritio Sceva") announces the printer's commitment to the "the renewal of the vernacular Poets." Having offered his readers the "elegant, measured diction of M Francesco Petrarch," he is now venturing into a very different style, "the slightly more difficult and obscure language of the Florentine Poet, M. Dante Alighieri." He hesitated before venturing, conscious of the difficulty of interpreting the text ("shrouded in mist midst the dark woods of the infernal Abyss"), and of the controversy between older commentators ("old-fashioned professors") and more recent ones ("young new professors"),[10] and settling finally on a mixture of both. His summaries of each *canto* and his brief marginalia are scaled down from Landino's editions, but as he admits, they fail to clarify all the difficulties, and leave a lot to the "perspicacious reader."[11]

In the late 1540s, two Lyon publishers were competing for the vernacular market: de Tournes found a worthy rival in the merchant-bookseller Guillaume Roville. Roville, too, saw an opening for cheap editions of the "three luminaries" ("tre lumi") of Tuscany,[12] on which he worked closely with Ridolfi, whom he saw not just as a humanist scholar, but also as a man with the insights of a poet. Roville took advantage of a new commentary on Dante, "so accurate, corrected and annotated."[13] This new commentary—clearly a copy of Alessandro Vellutello's 1544 edition—was the basis of Roville's 1551 edition of the

9. *Il Dante con argomenti, & dechiaratione de molti luoghi* (Lyon: Jean de Tournes, 1547).

10. The merits of Landino and Vellutello's commentaries are discussed in *Ragionamento havuto in Lione da Claudio de Herbere gentil'huomo lionese, et da Alessandro de gli Uberti gentil'huomo fiorentino* (Lyon: Guillaume Roville, 1557), 37–49.

11. *Il Dante con argomenti*, 4: "chiarito havemo difficultade alquante: non che a entera sodisfatione d'il tutto: ma che giovato per noi in parte il lettor provido, da se stesso nel resto se guidi."

12   See the dedication of Roville's Boccaccio of 1555.

13. Roville-Ridolfi, *Il Petrarca con nuove et brevi dichiarationi* (Lyon: Guillaume Roville, 1550), 2.

Commedia, dedicated to Ridolfi,[14] and published in the same format as its rival from de Tournes, but with new woodcuts commissioned from Pierre Eskrich, including a portrait medallion and three full-page cuts copied from the eighty-seven illustrations to the quarto 1544 edition, one to accompany each *cantica*. While de Tournes's edition was not reprinted, Roville's had a considerable success, reappearing in 1552 with a new title page, with further editions in 1571 and 1575.[15]

Having cornered the market for Italian texts in France, Roville wanted to reach a potential national readership among "those who are lovers and promoters of the Tuscan language."[16] His 1555 edition of Boccaccio includes a letter by Jean-Baptiste Dufour, apostolic notary and secretary to the archbishopric of Lyon, encouraging Roville to publish more Italian authors, "the French nobility today being very keen on Tuscan."

This includes not only the French court, where "so many noble Ladies [. . .] and so many Princesses [. . .] not only delight in it, but have perfect knowledge of Italian," supporting his argument by a long list of the principal ladies at court, who constitute "rather than a Court, [. . .] a new heavenly choir of Muses."[17] Roville, having already printed Dante, Petrarch, and Castiglione, should not delay in publishing Boccaccio, where he will satisfy not only the court but also the Italophile circle of ladies in Lyon, whom he also lists at length, concluding that the presses of Lyon will now rival those of Venice, Florence, and Rome in their own language.

Evidence of the standing in Lyon of Dante, in company with his Tuscan fellows in the "three crowns," is manifest in the triumphal entry of Henri II in September 1548, where the court encountered the Italianate community in Lyon. The Florentine colony, together with the archbishop of Lyon, Cardinal Ippolito d'Este, had fitted out, to designs by Sebastiano Serlio, a pioneering Italianate theater in the archiepiscopal palace; it was adorned with statues of Tuscan worthies, includ-

14. Printed in Venice by Francesco Marcolini, 1544; *Dante con nuove, et utili ispositioni* (Lyon: Guillaume Roville, 1551). See Henri Baudrier, *Bibliographie lyonnaise* vol. 9 (Lyon: A. Brun, 1895–1921), 187.

15. Baudrier, *Bibliographie*, vol. 9, 196, 334, 353.

16. Roville to his readers in Boccaccio, *Decamerone*, 6–7.

17. Jean-Baptiste Dufour – Rigaud di Saint-Marsal, in Boccaccio, *Il Dicamerone* (Lyon: G. Roville, 1555), 927-32.

ing Dante, Petrarch, and Boccaccio. Their statues would reappear in the entry of Philip of Spain to Antwerp the following year.[18]

A degree of interest in Dante was sustained in France in the second half of the century, with the focus shifting to Paris. The exiled Florentine scholar, Jacobo Corbinelli, protected by Catherine de Medici, had laid his hands on a manuscript of the unpublished *De vulgari eloquentia* and opted to publish his discovery in Paris.[19] It was dedicated to Henri III, with liminary pieces by two luminaries of the Pléiade, Jean Dorat and Jean-Antoine Baïf. Dorat's eulogy compares Dante to Virgil and Lucretius, but shows no knowledge of the poet except his burial in exile.[20] Baïf praises Dante, "the first Tuscan (whom one can call Father / Wherever his vernacular tongue holds sway)," the first to regularize the "beautiful common speech" of Italian, the maternal language of the king.[21] The editor's own letter to Pierre Forget de Fresnes, the royal Secretary of State, gives the minister a short course on Dante's contemporaries and successors, before launching into a stout defense of Dante over Petrarch, the poet in favor at the Valois court. He allows Petrarch's poems a certain musicality; his sonnets and *canzoni* are "mellifluous [in] style and manner" and "replete with poetical sweetness, but these are not long poems." They cannot compare with the "most learned and high-sounding sayings" of Dante,

> who feeds us with strong and lasting delights, not only in graceful subjects, but in all others, as one who has spoken of everything, and is so consistent in himself, that no-one will hesitate to admit that he was not only the first maker and composer of all four elements of our native language, but also the first singer and Poet of our Tragedy and Comedy.[22]

Corbinelli's preference for the ambition of the epic, which surpasses Petrarch in its action, its structure, in its "richly intricate imagination," and in its bold metaphors, is quite exceptional at this time,

18. See Maurice Scève, *The Entry of Henri II into Lyon, September 1548*, text with an introduction and notes, ed. and trans. Richard Cooper (Tempe, Arizona: MRTS, 1997).

19. *De vulgari eloquentia libri duo* (Paris: Jean Corbon, 1577); see Farinelli, *Dante*, vol. 1, 462–63; Massimo Lucarelli, "Il 'De vulgari eloquentia' nel Cinquecento italiano e francese," *Studi Francesi* 176/LIX.II (2015): 247–59.

20. *De vulgari eloquentia*, 7.

21. Ibid., 9.

22. Ibid., f° G2.

when Petrarch was at his zenith, and Corbinelli's *editio princeps* of a text celebrating the "illustrious vernacular" failed to have the desired impact on Parisian readers.[23]

Nonetheless, new translations of Dante were being made.[24] The ones that are better known were produced in François d'Alençon's circle,[25] namely the last canto of *Paradiso* by Guy le Fèvre de la Boderie (1578), and brief extracts of all three *cantiche* by Jean de La Gessée (1583).[26] The first complete rendition into French of the whole poem, written in the second half of the century but never published, has escaped critical notice.[27] The translator hesitates over what meter to choose instead of *terza rima*, opting for the decasyllable in all of *Inferno*, except for alexandrines in the first two cantos, then for alexandrines in the whole of *Paradiso* and in all of *Purgatorio*, except for the first two cantos, which are in decasyllables, and for couplets with alternating masculine and feminine rhymes. This hesitation reflects the transition the Pléiade was facing in the 1550s and 1560s in regard to longer poems: decasyllables were used for Ronsard's *Franciade*, but the alexandrine replaced the decasyllable in his *Hymnes*, and dominated the *Discours*. Apart from the relative merits and demerits of this major undertaking, it is interesting to note two clues to the context in which the translator places his work. The first can be found in canto VI of *Paradiso*, where the name of Margaret of Provence, wife of Louis IX, is highlighted in larger letters.[28] This may perhaps be a flattering allusion to one of the Valois's princesses, but to judge by a liminary sonnet, it may be something more personal, which provides an interesting slant on how the *Commedia* is being presented:

23. Farinelli, *Dante*, vol. 1, 464; Isabelle Pantin, "L'édition Corbinelli du 'De vulgari eloquentia.' Un événement littéraire parisien?" in *Poètes, princes et collectionneurs. Mélanges offerts à Jean-Paul Barbier-Mueller*, ed. Nicole Ducimetière, Michel Jeanneret, and Jean Balsamo (Geneva: Droz, 2011), 367–84.

24. Turin, Bib. Naz., *ms.* L. III. 17, published by Camille Morel, *Les plus anciennes traductions françaises de la Divine Comédie* (Paris: Librairie Universitaire, 1897).

25. Jean Balsamo, "Dante, *L'Aviso Piacevole* et Henri de Navarre," *Italique* I (1998): 83.

26. See Pierre de Nolhac, "Un traducteur de Dante au temps de la Pléiade: Guy le Fèvre de la Boderie" in *Comité français catholique pour la célébration du Sixième centenaire de la mort de Dante, Bulletin du Jubilé* 5 (1922): 528–30; Jean de La Gessée, *Les premieres œuvres françoyses* (Antwerp: Christophe Plantin, 1583), 664–65.

27. Oesterreichische Nazionalbibliothek, *ms* 10201, published by Morel, *Les plus anciennes traductions*.

28. Morel, *Les plus anciennes traductions*, 499.

Thanks to Virgil Dante was able to see his lady,
And I am trying to see mine again through Dante,
Who may have similar powers over her,
Excellent as she is, holding the Muses dear.

His Lady was very beautiful and learned in spirit;
To see mine is to behold an unchanging beauty,
Who has the most exquisite knowledge of literature.
So the one well represents the other.

To see his Lady, Dante passed through hell,
And I desire to go through Auvergne to the land of iron;
He went through the approaches to Mount Purgatory,

And I seek to climb the thrice encircled mountain;
He had the good fortune to see her at the holiest summit,
And I aspire in a similar place to the same glory.[29]

In this rather opaque poem, the translator compares his situation
to that of Dante; he was hoping, like Dante, to be reunited with his
lady, but to do so he must cross the Auvergne to the "land of iron."
If the poet is starting from Paris, then crossing the Auvergne might
bring him to the iron mines of the Mâconnais; if starting from Lyon,
then he would come to the region of Berry, which had an important
iron industry. The latter seems a more plausible option because it
links directly with praise of Marguerite de France, duchesse de Berry,
a well-known patroness in the 1550s, whom some poets imagined living with the Muses on Mount Helicon.

The existence of this complete but unpublished translation both
belies and confirms Balthasar Grangier's statement in the introduction to his ambitious three-volume translation of 1596–97: "No one
I know of had turned their hand to it before." Grangier was the 32nd
abbé of Saint-Barthélemy de Noyon from 1573 to his death in 1606,
canon of Notre-Dame de Paris, and a royal counselor and almoner; he
came from an ambassadorial family (Grangier de Liverdis), close to
Pomponne de Bellièvre: he clearly had the social connections to allow
him to dedicate his translation to Henri IV, as Corbinelli had had in
dedicating to Henri III his edition of *De vulgari eloquentia*. Grangier
chose the smaller duodecimo or sextodecimo format like the one
used by Lyonnais printers, but the increasing copiousness of his commentaries meant that three volumes of increasing size were needed to

29. Ibid., 193 on last folio (228) of manuscript.

accommodate his material. Like the translator of the Vienna manuscript, he opted for the alexandrine and the six-line stanza. He commissioned a portrait of the royal dedicatee and a title page for each volume with a portrait of Dante from distinguished Dutch engraver Thomas de Leu; and he obtained a royal ten-year privilege for the edition, which was shared between two Paris publishers, the widow of Georges Drobet and Jehan Gesselin.

Grangier is fulsome in his praise of Dante, whom he extols as "a profound Philosopher, and a judicious Theologian, dealing with almost all the finest subjects within those two disciplines in a language which, although obscure, is more vigorous (*nerveux*) than precious (*mignard*)."[30] Building on the contrast of *nerveux* and *mignard*, he warns both the monarch and the reader to expect a style of poetry very different from contemporary post-Pléiade or Petrarchan fashion: "The Poetry you will find here is not the delicate, precious, smooth and easy style of almost all of our French Poets."[31] Dante is not only *sublime* but *unique*, with his "concise and difficult style, peculiar to [him] alone,"[32] and the reader should prepare to encounter a *satyrique* worthy of Persius, who, with his "Menippean or Milesian artistic licence,"[33] spares no one in society, not Popes, nor Emperors, nor Kings. This theme of Dante the satirist seeking to correct vices had been voiced by Gabriel Chappuis in his translation of Doni's *I Mondi*, where he described the aims of this "esprit unique" to "criticize his enemies and punish them for their crimes, making the wicked confess from their own mouth the evil they have done, for which they are being punished."[34]

This translation marks the high point of praise of Dante in Renaissance France, and yet the signs were already inherent of the poet's eclipse in France over the next two centuries. The essential difficulty of his poetry alluded to above (and which earned him comparison with Maurice Scève),[35] is one that Grangier tried to anticipate in describing the poet as "the most difficult, obscure and concise to be

30. *La Comedie de Dante*, vol. 1, trans. Balthasar Grangier (Paris: veuve Georges Drobet, 1596), f° Bv°.

31. Ibid., I, f° Ævº

32. Ibid., I, f° Bv°.

33. Ibid., I, f° B2v°.

34. Antonfrancesco Doni, *Les mondes celestes, terrestres et infernaux*, trans. Gabriel Chappuis (Lyon: Barthélemy Honorat, 1578): 334.

35. Guillaume Roville, *Seconde partie du Promptuaire des* Medalles (Lyon: Guillaume Roville, 1577), 251: "whose mind and understanding approached those of the very obscure and difficult poet, Dante"; cf. Hunkeler, "Dante à Lyon," ibid.

found, not only among the Italians, but even among Latin writers."[36] But Dante's complexity was not the main reason for the French reaction against him. Ronsard had seen him as essentially medieval, associating him with gothic gloom, whereas Petrarch was associated with the rising sun:

> Ever since your Petrarch had overcome the gloom
> Of Dante and Cavalcanti, and, bright like a Sun,
> Had strewn the Earth with his fame,
> And was made a citizen of Heaven.[37]

Ronsard's correspondent, Bartolommeo del Bene, conceded that Dante's poetry comprised "harsh rhymes," and Roville judged him to be a difficult poet. However, while this depreciation of Dante echoed contemporary Italian criticisms by Pico della Mirandola, Pietro Bembo, and Sperone Speroni, who identified Petrarch as a better model for the national language, the arguments used by French commentators were different and more specific to the political turmoil in France in the last half of the century.

In the Counter-Reformation context of a country long divided by religious war, Catholic opinion unfavorably viewed Dante's strictures against prominent clerics, including Popes and Cardinals. By contrast, Huguenots supported the poet in his criticism of the Roman Church, as seen in the anonymous *Aviso piacevole* addressed to Henri de Navarre that was published in London under a false imprint in 1586.[38] Written in response to Sixtus V's 1585 bull of excommunication against Henri de Navarre and Henri de Bourbon-Condé, *Brutum fulmen*, the numerous excerpts from Dante's poetry are chosen to show him as a severe critic of the papacy (the Antichrist), of Rome the new Babylon, and of the Mass, whereas Navarre and Condé are held up as worthy heirs of Emperor Henry VII.

While some French Gallicans sympathized with Dante's diatribes against the Roman or the Avignon Church, there was almost

---

36. Grangier, *La Comedie*, I, f° Æv°.

37. Ronsard, *Œuvres*, ed. Laumonier (Paris: STFM, 1967) vol. 18, 254, vv. 22–23; Isidore Silver, "Ronsard Comparatist Studies," *Comparative Literature* 6 (1954): 164–65; Jean Balsamo, "Note sur l'Elegie à Bartolommeo Delbene Florentin," *Revue des amis de Ronsard* 19 (1997): 145–62.

38. *Aviso piacevole dato alla bella Italia d'un nobile giovane Francese* (Monaco: Giovanni Swartz, n.d.) (London: John Wolfe, 1586), f° 13–27v°; see Balsamo, "Dante, *Aviso piacevole*," ibid.

universal condemnation of his aspersions against the legitimacy of the Capetian and Valois kings as the successors of Charlemagne, whose line Dante suggests had died out. Etienne Pasquier reports that when Luigi Alamanni was reading *Purgatorio* to François I, and came across the line (in Canto XX, 52) where Hugues Capet claims to be the son of a butcher, the King "was indignant at this imposture, commanded it to be removed, and was prepared to ban reading it in his Kingdom."[39] To judge by one of Villon's ballades, Capet's lowly origin was a standing joke among some medieval satirists.[40] The Poitiers poet and chronicler, Jean Bouchet, who, like François I, was broadly favorable to Dante, took pains to rebut this slur, first in his chronicle: "And because the poet Dante has written that the said Hugues came from a line of butchers, and Master François Villon after him, slanderer of the true History of France";[41] and again in his verse epitaph for the King:

> Truly descended from royal blood,
> And not from the butcher's trade,
> Whatever Dante the Florentine may have said.[42]

Dante's verse on Capet's origins enraged French patriots, especially at a time of national agonizing over who had the right to succeed the last Valois on the throne. François de Rosières, a historian of the Lorraine family, argued that the Lorraine family had a strong claim to the throne because they were descendants of Charles de Lorraine, ousted and imprisoned by Hugues Capet, who had invaded France and usurped the crown.[43] Two Italian exiles sought to defend the legitimacy of the Capet and Valois inheritance, but from different sides of the political divide. A Marchigiano jurist, Matteo Zampini, dedicated his detailed genealogical study of the Capetians and early Valois to

39. Estienne Pasquier, *Œuvres* (Amsterdam: Compagnie des libraires associez, 1723), I, col. 514 (book VI chap. 1).

40. François Villon, "Question au clerc du Guichet ou ballade de l'appel," vv. 8–9: "Se fusse des hoirs Hue Capel / Qui fut extraict de boucherie."

41. Jean Bouchet, *Les anciennes et modernes genealogies des roys de France* (Paris, [D. Janot], 1541): f° xcii v°.

42. Ibid., f° xciii v°.

43. François de Rosières, *Stemmatum Lotharingiæ ac Barri ducum tomi septem* (Paris: Guillaume Chaudière, 1580), f° 194v°–195, 200r°–v°. In 1583 the author was prosecuted for this passage; see Augustin Calmet, *Histoire de Lorraine* (Nancy: Antoine Leseure, 1757): VII, col. lxxxiii–lxxxiv.

Henri III in 1578;[44] following the death of the last Valois heir, François d'Alençon in1584, however, Zampini sided with Charles de Bourbon and the Ligue against Henri de Navarre, and he was obliged to leave France on his accession. By contrast, the Florentine exile, Alfonso del Bene, bishop of Albi, sided in his own treatise of 1595 with the incoming monarch, Henri IV, whom he saw as the instrument of national peace.[45] Neither of these Italian scholars actually brings Dante's aspersions into their argument, unlike French authors on the same subject. Pierre de Saint-Julien's 1585 treatise, which had sufficient success to warrant a second edition,[46] established that Hugues Capet was directly descended from Charlemagne, and that Dante's calumny was to be rejected.[47] For Saint-Julien, Dante's reputation had been ruined by his attack on the houses of Valois and Anjou: "Dante unworthily vented his anger and the spite he conceived against the House of France: but because he found no one to support what he had written in his fury, the shame has fallen on him alone."[48]

This notion of Dante's *cholere* (anger) is held up by both Saint-Julien and by Grangier, not as an excuse, but as an explanation for his animus against France; he vents "anger and spite" against Charles de Valois (brother of Philippe le Bel), "by whom Dante and his faction, the Whites, were banned from Florence."[49] Pasquier's firm view is that if Dante really believed that Capet was the son of a butcher, then he was "a most ignorant Poet" and an "inept man."[50] Grangier had briefly considered suppressing this line in his translation, but did not, for fear of destroying "the whole order and structure of so fine, ancient and venerable a work."[51] Another solution was simply to change the

---

44. *De Origine et atavis Hugonis Capeti, illorumque cum Carolo Magno, Clodoveo atque antiquis Francorum regibus, agnatione, et gente* (Paris: Thomas Brumen, 1578): 8°, with a ten-year privilege.

45. *De gente, ac familiae Hugonis Capeti origine, iustoque progressu ad dignitatem Regiam* (Lyon: Thibaud Ancelin, 1595).

46. *Discours et paradoxe de l'origine de Hugues Capet, extraict du differant d'entre Louys II Roy de France & de Marguerite de Bourgongne* (Paris: Guillaume Le Noir, 1585), 8°. Second edition in 1586.

47. Pontus de Tyard confirms this in his *Extrait de la genealogie de Hugues, surnommé Capet, roy de France* (Paris: Mamert Patisson, 1594), 4, 10–11.

48. Saint Julien, *Discours et paradoxe*, f° 2v°–3.

49. Ibid., f° 7vo; cf. Grangier, *La Comedie* f° B2v°–B3v°; Jean-Papire Masson, *Annalium libri quattuor* (Paris: Nicolas Chesneau, 1577), 211, 367.

50. Pasquier, *Œuvres*, I, col. 513–14.

51. Grangier, *La Comedie* f° B4.

translation. In the Vienna manuscript, the offending line "I was the son of a Paris butcher" was replaced with something blander: "My father was then the Count of Paris."[52] A third solution was to gloss the line to mean anything other than a real butcher. Pasquier suggests that the words *figluol* [. . .] *d'un beccaio* could be construed as a metaphor, which means "son of a great and valiant warrior" ("fils d'un grand et vaillant Guerrier"), which he shows Hugues le Grand to have been.[53] Grangier's extenuating arguments is that Dante is a satirist who spares no one, "Emperors, Monarchs and Kings, Dukes, Counts and Marquises," and he uses the word *beccaio* to mean "great dispenser of justice in his time over nobles and other evil doers and rebels, a butcher of Paris."[54] Both Pasquier and Grangier repeat an annotation in the 1551 Lyon edition by Roville, where the word is taken to mean "great dispenser of justice" who has carried out "great butchery of malefactors in Paris."[55] It is even seen as a Gallicism that Dante might have picked up during his study in Paris. Saint-Julien had refused to accept this gloss, asserting that Dante's slur had to be rejected "however much a certain commentator may seek to tone it down."[56] Contemporary chroniclers were nonetheless uneasy about the solidity of Capet's claim to the throne. Both Fauchet and Pasquier record that Capet descended from the Saxon *Witikind* (or *Widukind*),[57] and that he was one of three sons of Hugues le Grand.[58] Although Dante's remark about the son of a butcher would therefore be false,[59] Fauchet admits that the circumstances of Capet's taking the throne are so mysterious that one might wonder whether "Capet, or those who supported him, have suppressed the Authors who wrote the truth of this change of ruler."[60]

52. *Purg.* XX, 52; Morel, *Les plus anciennes traductions*, 432, v. 39.
53. E.g. Pasquier, *Œuvres*, I, col. 514.
54. Grangier, *La Comedie* f° B2, B3v°.
55. *Il Dante* (Lyon: Guillaume Roville, 1551): 360.
56. Saint-Julien, *Discours et paradoxe*, f° 7v°.
57. C. Fauchet, *Les antiquitez françoises*, in his *Œuvres* (Paris: Jean de Heuqueville, 1610): bk. XII, f° 352v°; Pasquier agrees in his *Œuvres*, book VI, ch. 1.
58. Fauchet, *Les antiquitez françoises*, bk. XII, ch. xiv, f° 461, clearly says Capet is one of three sons of Hugues le Grand.
59. Ibid., bk. XII, chap. xviii, f° 469v°: the chapter summary states "Error of those who say that Hugues le Grand was the son of a butcher," but this is not argued in the text.
60. Ibid., f° 465.

The allusion above to Dante's stay in Paris adds a new dimension to the controversy. Corbinelli's letter to Pierre Forget includes this hypothesis concerning the *De vulgari eloquentia*:

> [I]t is likely that he wrote this in Paris, where he moved in his last years, since he composed it close to his death: and that he opted for the literary language rather than the vernacular there, where more than anywhere else, and still today, letters were held in honor, and studies were pursued of the more serious and sacred areas of knowledge.[61]

French writers willingly accepted the evidence in Boccaccio and Villani on Dante's stay in Paris.[62] They also accepted Laurent de Premierfait's gloss on Boccaccio's *De casibus*,[63] where we read of the three marvels that struck Dante in Paris: the Université de Paris, symbol of the Earthly Paradise (whose stars he portrays in *Paradiso* X); the churches of Paris, symbol of the Heavenly Paradise; and the Palais de Justice, symbol both of Paradise and of the Torments of Hell. According to Premierfait, it was in the intellectual environment of Paris that he studied theology, acquired his ideas on the vernacular, and decided to resume writing in Latin. Dante's biographer Jean Papire Masson concluded that the poet had been able to return to Italy "more erudite and learned by far than before."[64]

But it was not to Paris alone that Dante was believed to be indebted: he had an intimate knowledge of medieval French and Provençal authors, but he refused to acknowledge this. Premierfait argued that it was in France that Dante had discovered the *Roman de la Rose*,[65] which had given him the inspiration for his *Commedia*: "[Dante,] who had received from God and nature the spirit of poetry, discovered that in the *Roman de la Rose* is described in French the paradise of the virtuous and the hell of sinners, which he wanted to put into a different verse form and to imitate in Tuscan."[66] With the rise of interest in Provençal culture in sixteenth-century France, a

---

61. Dante, *De vulgari eloquentia libri duo* (Paris, J. Corbon, 1577), in-8, f° Fii v°; Farinelli, *Dante*, I, 463.

62. E.g. Jean Papire Masson, *Annalium libri quattuor* (Paris: Nicolas Chesneau, 1577), 406.

63. Arsenal, *ms.* 5193; Farinelli, I, 198–202.

64. Jean Papire Masson, *Elogiorum pars secunda* (Paris: S. Huré, 1638), 18–19; previously printed in his his *Vitæ trium Hetruriæ procerum* (Paris: D. du Pré, 1587), f° 3.

65. Arsenal, *ms.* 5193; Farinelli, *Dante* I, 198–202.

66. BnF., *ms. fr.* 226, f° 396.

pioneer like Jean de Nostredame was keen to show how much Tuscan authors owed to this rich inheritance: "From where did Dante, Petrarch, Boccaccio and other old Tuscan Poets enrich their language and draw their inspiration, if not from the works of our Provençal Poets?"[67] In his text, which was also published in Italian for readers across the Alps to recognize their cultural debt, Dante is only credited with having drawn from Provence for his *De vulgari eloquentia*, and with having frequently cited Ramon Berenguer,[68] while Petrarch is more often seen as having borrowed from the troubadours. Henri Estienne went further when he suggested that Italian was merely a decadent form of French, and that the earliest Italian writers, like Brunetto Latini, Dante's mentor, had written in French or Provençal, whose influence Italians should acknowledge.[69] Pasquier said as much in a letter to Ronsard, arguing that "The Italians [. . .] are forced to acknowledge that they are wholly indebted for their Poetry to us alone," as can clearly be seen in the work of Dante, "who embellishes a part of his writings with a number of features, drawn as much from Provençal as from French."[70] Indeed, Italian poets before Dante "deserved the name of Rhymers rather than Poets,"—and if Dante—and Petrarch after him—were "the two fountainheads of Italian Poetry," they were "fountainheads which sprung from our Provençal Poetry."[71] In more polemical terms, Paquier wrote: "Dante and Petrarch dressed in borrowed plumes of our Provençal authors."[72] In the same way in which Petrarch himself had been accused of defamation and of animosity against France,[73] a culture to which he owed so much, so too Dante was guilty of hypocrisy and ingratitude when he railed against the French crown: "The Florentine poet Dante, ungrateful for all he had gained while studying letters in Paris, and oblivious of the warm welcome he had received in France."[74]

Despite the best efforts of a Dante apologist like Grangier, the Tuscan poet had fallen out of favor in France. Compared with the

67. Jean de Nostredame, *Les vies des plus celebres et anciens poetes provensaux* (Lyon: A. Marsilius, 1575), 12.

68. Ibid., 8, 105.

69. Farinelli, *Dante* I, 472.

70. Pasquier, *Œuvres* cit., II, col. 39.

71. Ibid., I, col. 696.

72. Ibid., I, col. 695.

73. Notably by Jean de Hesdin and Nicolas de Clamanges; see Franco Simone, *Il Rinascimento francese* (Turin: Società editrice internazionale, 1961), 47–54.

74. BnF, *ms fr.* 5794, f° 12.

divine Petrarch, his writing was seen as harsh and obscure, full of impenetrable allusions to past people and politics; and his slurs against France were thought outrageous and unworthy of a writer who owed so much to medieval French and Provençal culture. This eclipse in France was long-lasting, with no new editions appearing for over two hundred years, despite an attempt by Voltaire to rehabilitate the poet.[75] But even Voltaire, with his appetite for books, would have found it hard to lay hands on a recent edition of Dante, since, even in Italy, the *sommo poeta* was not reprinted between 1629 and 1716. Dante would have to wait until the Risorgimento to be restored to his rightful place as the voice of the aspiring Italian nation.

75. See Russell Goulbourne, "'Bizarre, mais brilliant de beautés naturelles': Voltaire and Dante's *Commedia*," in *Dante in France*, 31–43.

RICHARD E. KEATLEY

Intimacy and Public Display: Secretarial Design in Montaigne's *Journal de voyage*

As Montaigne and his "troop" headed toward Italy through the German-speaking Alps, passing through Western Switzerland to the Imperial city of Constance, they suffered their first misadventure, in what Montaigne's secretary describes as "a sample of the barbaric German unruliness and pride."[1] This incident began from an argument between a footservant and a guide they had hired in Basel, and wound up in the local courts:

> And because the thing came before the judges, to whom Monsieur de Montaigne went to complain, the provost of the place—an Italian gentleman who has settled and married here and has long had the right of citizenship—answered Monsieur de Montaigne, when he asked whether his servants would be believed in their testimony *on our behalf*, that yes, they would be believed, provided Monsieur de Montaigne discharged them; but that immediately afterward he could take them back in his service. This was a remarkable piece of subtlety.[2]

On its surface, the guide's complaint brings up a legal question regarding the fusion of a lord's interests with those of his hired help. The servants' words cannot be used as reliable testimony unless they are somehow disassociated from the interests of their employers. It takes an Italian "subtlety" to come up with the idea of dissolving this association for the purposes of litigation.

---

1. All citations of the *Journal*, except where indicated, are from *The Complete Works of Montaigne: Essays, Travel Journal, Letters*, ed. and trans. Donald Frame (Stanford: Stanford University Press, 1958), 889.
2. Ibid., emphasis mine.

YFS 134, *The Construction of a National Vernacular Literature in the Renaissance: Essays in Honor of Edwin M. Duval*, ed. DeVos and Hayes, © 2018 by Yale University.

Read more broadly, Montaigne's literary servant also appears to question the value of his own work as testimony for his lord, placing pressure on the idea of the secretary's words as a transparent representation of his lord's thoughts. Montaigne's secretary (the Secretary of the *Journal*) affirms his unique status by including himself among the "we" of the narration and separating himself from the body of "domestic" servants. This defense of status adds a social and political dimension to what François Rigolot calls a "relativité énonciative" that blurs the borders between the *Journal*'s indistinguishable voices.[3] As close readers, we might choose to untangle these alternating and mixing voices, attributing some pieces of text to Montaigne and others to his hired servant, as Craig Brush has done, as long as we follow the Italian provost's advice and put them back together when we are done.[4] A blurring of a quotation's meaning does not necessarily void the literary qualities of the *Journal de voyage* as a document meant to serve a rhetorical purpose.[5] Rather than identifying which passages belong to Montaigne, it is more important to understand the physical and social circumstances under which the *Journal* was produced so that we can assess the work's joint message and authorial intention.[6]

Viewing the first portion of the *Journal* as the literary production of Montaigne's servant may produce readings that deviate from the lost manuscript's original intentions while providing an overall meaning that is, like that of Jacques Amyot's translation of Plutarch according to Montaigne, "probable and well in keeping with what precedes and what follows."[7] This "fiction" of the Secretary's authorship deserves our attention, moreover, since Montaigne himself corroborates it as

3. Francois Rigolot, "La situation énonciative dans le *Journal de voyage de Montaigne*," in *Poétique et Narration. Mélanges offerts à Guy Demerson* (Paris: Champion, 1993), 477.

4. Craig B. Brush, "La composition de la première partie du *Journal de voyage de Michel de Montaigne*," *Revue d'histoire littéraire de la France* 71 (1971). See also, "The Secretary, Again," *Montaigne Studies, An Interdisciplinary Forum* 5/1- 2 (1993); Fausta Garavini, "Introduction," in *Journal de Voyage*, ed. Fausta Garavini (1983); Richard Keatley, "Le statut du valet dans le *Journal du voyage de M. de Montaigne en Italie, par la Suisse et l'Allemagne en 1580 et 1581*" (Master's Thesis, Université de Paris IV-Sorbonne, 1997).

5. Rigolot suggests that this blurriness results in a form of "discourse where the enunciation, in its flowing and diverse path, prevents quotation from having meaning." Rigolot, 477 (translation mine).

6. For Montaigne's use of secretaries in writing the *Essais*, see George Hoffmann, *Montaigne's Career* (Oxford: Clarendon Press, 1998), 36-62, 130-87.

7. *Works*, 951.

he claims to have had no hand in writing his journal until he took up the pen in Rome: "Having dismissed the one of my men who was doing this fine job, and seeing it so far advanced, whatever trouble it may be to me, I must continue it myself."[8] How does being forced to execute his servant's task affect Montaigne's writing about himself? What is the rhetorical message of the first portion of the *Journal* and how is Montaigne's secretary's presence essential to that message? Is there a "design" to the *Journal de voyage?*

INTIMACY, PUBLIC COMMUNICATION, AND THE SECRETARIAL ART

Recent research suggests that the rhetorical ambiguity of the *Journal* reflects the particular role secretaries played in the lives of late sixteenth-century noblemen. As participants in their lord's personal and public lives, secretaries worked at the fulcrum of noble identity, negotiating and expressing the intersections between their masters' public and private *personae.*[9] As servants of the mind, they lived in close physical and mental proximity to their lords in a way that blurred distinctions of individual and social identity.[10] Secretaries followed their masters, looking after their every need, eating with them, sleeping near them and, most importantly, communicating their lords' interests in writing. This practiced intimacy made the secretary the nobleman's closest and most important servant, as Gabriel Chappuys asserted in his 1588 adaptation of Francesco Sansovino's *Il Segretario* of 1573:

---

8. Ibid., 947.

9. On the role of the Renaissance secretary, see Chapter 6, "Open Secrets: The Place of the Renaissance Secretary," in Douglas Biow, *Doctors, Ambassadors, Secretaries: Humanism and Professions in Renaissance Italy* (Chicago and London: The University of Chicago Press, 2002), 155-76; Marcello Simonetta, *Rinascimento segreto: Il mondo del Segretario da Petrarca a Machiavelli* (Milan: Franco Angeli, 2004); Daniela Costa, "Dall'ideale del Cortegiano alla figura del segretario: metamorfosi del modello castiglionesco tra Italia e Francia nel Cinquecento," in *"Il Segretario è come un angelo": Trattati, raccolete epistolari, vite paradigmatiche, ovvero come essere un buon segretario nel Rinascimento* (Fasano: Schena, 2008); Salvatore Nigro, "Il segretario: precetti e pratiche dell'epistolografia barocca," in *Storia generale della letteratura italiana, VI Il secolo barocco* (Milan: Federico Motta, 2004).

10. As Biow writes, Machiavelli's secretary is "not a typical subordinate, but one able to stand on an equal footing with the prince in a fruitful, horizontal dialogue of exchange," Biow, 169.

[The secretary] is of such great importance, that Theologians have compared him to the Angels closest to God, because he is the closest to the Prince, in services not of the body, or means and faculties, but of the mind, taking all things of consequence in, a fact that renders this office truly worthy and honorable.[11]

The secretary is not a servant of the body, but of the "spirit/mind," who carries his master's interests "within himself" ("tire quand et soy"). He has an authority as close to that of his master as possible, indistinguishable in form and content from the original whose interests he represents.

Though narrowly defined as letter writers, secretaries were trained in all aspects of their lords' professional lives.[12] Much of this training was literary and linguistic, devoted to developing the ability to compose orders, privileges, edicts, and "other written acts."[13] Secretaries needed to be proficient in Latin and the "vulgar languages" (especially Italian), were students of history and "the means by which the ancient Princes were governed, and [...] should have seen and read the counsels of peoples, examples and laws, decrees and ordinances, and, finally, all the actions of great individuals who have ever lived."[14]

Beyond possessing these technical and epistemic skills, a secretary was also expected to act as a sort of psychologist and student of his master's identity, remaining physically and mentally near him at all times and studying his habits.[15] Through the study of poetry and familiar letters, he worked to create an intimate writing style that would allow him to reflect his lord's closest thoughts.[16] This intimate side of the secretarial art often takes on the Neoplatonic aspects of an ideal friendship, one in which the secretary serves his lord in

11. Gabriel Chappuys, Le Secrettaire (Geneva: Droz, 2014), 11 (translation mine).

12. Stefano Iucci, "La trattatistica sul secretario tra la fine del Cinquecento e il primo Seicento," Roma moderna e contemporanea III/1 (1995).

13. Chappuys, ibid., 18. See also Benedict Buono, "La trattatistica sul 'segretario' e la codificazione linguistica in Italia fra Cinque e Seicento," Verba 37 (2010); Biow, ibid.,169.

14. Ibid., 20.

15. "[...] they participate in their most intimate thoughts, and are like repositories of their honor and reputation." Stefano Guazzo, La civil conversatione del Signor Stefano Guazzo ... : divisa in quattro libri (Venice: Alaris, 1574), 116 v.

16. On the links between the rhetoric of intimacy and the epistolary genre, see Kathy Eden, The Renaissance Discovery of Intimacy (Chicago: University of Chicago Press, 2012).

a spirit of "love, respect, faith, vigilance, politeness and secrecy."[17] This relationship would allow the nobleman, moreover, to become more himself through the accomplishment of his own will that was unimpeded by the constraints of ceremony, so "that the lord (might) be master of himself" even as his secretary becomes "almost his (master's) own soul."[18]

If the idealism of this vision of the secretary's role supports the reading of a fusion of the interests of Montaigne and his servant, the tensions underlying the social conditions of secretarial work require us to question how far this concomitancy actually goes. If secretarial manuals encourage the letter writer to "think of his audience,"[19] the *Journal* poses the problem of having only one potential reader, the subject of the narrative himself, "M. de Montaigne." Thus, one possible interpretation of the Secretary's image of Montaigne is that it acts as a means for his master to better observe himself. Viewed in this way, the first portion of the *Journal de voyage* embodies the tensions underlying the master-servant relationship while becoming a crucible of authorial experimentation that prepares Montaigne's future writing about himself. Claims of cultural and intellectual equality, counterbalanced by the need for the servant to place all his thoughts and desires beneath those of his patron suggest that Montaigne's secretary "resists" anonymity even while practicing the voice of intimate servility.[20]

WRITING MONTAIGNE

In accordance with his duties, Montaigne's secretary clearly takes an interest in voicing his lord's concerns. Despite the alternation of voices in the *Journal*—the triangle of enunciation between the "il" of Montaigne, the secretary's first person "je," and the communal "nous" of the troop—it is clear from the outset that the narrative focuses on Montaigne. Even in passages where the servant asserts his own voice, his presence can be interpreted as a rhetorical means for better depicting Montaigne's actions and thoughts. The Secretary as-

17. Guazzo, 126 v.
18. Ibid., 248 v, 250.
19. Chappuys, 38.
20. See Biow, 176-224 ; and Marc Bizer, *Les lettres romaines de Du Bellay* (Montreal: Les Presses de l'Université de Montréal, 2001), 62-66.

serts himself less as an individual than as an observer of a subject he knew well enough to judge, confirm, and analyze.

One of the explicit themes of the Secretary's *Journal* is the importance of his lord's particular qualities: a passion for travel and an avid intellectual curiosity. The movements of the "troop," who appear to march along without any apparent will of their own, are punctuated and dictated by the whims of "M. de Montaigne," as he visits churches and monasteries, measures his arm against that of the supposed Ogier the Dane, consults with local officials, and delights in the landscape. Montaigne meets with local intellectuals in order to gain a better understanding of the places he visits, and his servant accurately portrays this quest for knowledge. While the troop moves along, generally arriving and departing as if on an established course, the Secretary records changes to the itinerary as a function of Montaigne's desire to see or experience something new. In Innsbruck, the troop made a trip to the Austrian Arch-Duke's pleasure palace at Hall, "just to see it."[21] In Augsburg, Montaigne "was very sorry, being only a day's journey from the Danube, to leave without seeing it or the town of Ulm."[22] Outside Markdorf, Montaigne is "lured by the fine day to change his plan of going to Ravensburg that day, and turned aside a day's journey to go to Lindau."[23]

Sometimes, his spoiled plans reinforce how determined Montaigne was to explore new things. We read how his wanderlust was foiled by circumstances beyond his control, leaving him disappointed that he had to alter his route. In the Duchy of Bar, Montaigne was hit by a bout of colic forcing him to give up "his" plans to visit Toul, Metz, Saint-Dizier and Donrémy-sur-Meuse, "in order to reach the baths of Plombières in all haste."[24] The troop could not visit Zurich because of the plague and had to put off seeing Loreto because of banditry in the Marche d'Ancona.[25] Leaving Padua, the Secretary records that Montaigne "headed straight for Abano," with the others scampering close behind. There the essayist inspected the famous baths while asserting his intention to return to explore Venice more thoroughly:

21. 906.
22. 903.
23. 890.
24. 871.
25. 887.

He would not go there [to Rome], considering that he was to revisit all
this region, notably Venice, at his leisure, and thought nothing of this
visit; and what had made him to undertake it was his extreme hunger
to see that city [Venice]. He said could not have stayed peacefully in
Rome or anywhere else in Italy without having a look at Venice and
for that purpose he had turned out this way.[26]

The Secretary's precise depiction of his lord's actions and desires provides psychological context for Montaigne's decisions. Montaigne's
resistance to Rome's call is motivated by his desire to see the city
his deceased friend Étienne de La Boétie would have preferred to call
home.[27] This "extreme hunger," moreover, helps explain the troop's
atypical itinerary leading from Paris through Switzerland, Bavaria,
and Austria.[28] The Secretary's narrative, in other words, allows us
to interpret Montaigne's entire German expedition as nothing more
than a topographical and mental detour in pursuit of his memories of
La Boétie.

It is hard to ignore the Secretary's role in underlining the differences between Montaigne and the rest of the travelers, the tracking of
details that separate his master's interests and tastes from that of the
troop, or the rhetorical refinement in the passage the *Journal's* first
editor, Meunier de Querlon, believed to be too eloquent to belong to
the Secretary's servile pen:

> I truly believe that if Monsieur de Montaigne had been alone with
> his own attendants he would rather have gone to Cracow or toward
> Greece by land than to make the turn toward Italy; but the pleasure
> he took in visiting unknown countries, which he found so sweet as to
> make him forget the weakness of his age and of his health, he could
> not impress on any of his party, and everyone asked only to return
> home. [. . .] If someone complained to him that he often led his party,
> by various roads and regions, back very close to where he had started
> (which he was likely to do, either because he had been told about
> something worth seeing, or because he had changed his mind accord-

26. 922.
27. Montaigne wrote of La Boétie that "he would rather have been born in Venice
than in Sarlat," adding "and with reason" in the first reprinting of his work after the
voyage to Italy. Frame, 144. Montaigne, *Essais*, ed. Pierre Villey (Paris: Quadrige/PUF,
1992), 194, note.
28. The standard itinerary for travelers departing from Paris was over the Mont
Cénis into Piedmont. See my book, *Textual Spaces: French Renaissance Writings of
the Italian Voyage* (Truman State University Press: forthcoming).

ing to the occasions), he would answer that as for him, he was not going anywhere except where he happened to be, and that he could not
miss or go off his path, since he had no plan but to travel in unknown
places.[29]

By capturing the spirit and logic that motivate Montaigne's behavior,
the Secretary participates in his master's travel discourse, giving form
to a diatribe against cultural myopia and making a spectacle of Montaigne's impatience with his less enthusiastic companions. He erects,
moreover, an image of his master *en voyage*, painting a portrait of
an avid, intellectually engaged traveler, an exceptional figure who
pushes himself on horseback even as he senses an oncoming attack
of his kidney stones, a naïvely curious wanderer following his fancy
and engaging with adventure following an aesthetic of *sprezzatura*.

BECOMING MONTAIGNE

One way to read this portrait is as a function of a secretary's duty to
represent his lord in the political context of their visit.[30] Had Montaigne been named ambassador, his *Journal* might have had a more
public presence, as part of a political memoir, such as that published
by Montaigne's contemporary and fellow Gascon Jacques-Auguste de
Thou, or as a *voyage d'Italie* of the type published by the French ambassador Duval de Fontenay-Mareuil some years later.[31] Montaigne's
Secretary is in fact attentive to political meetings and exchanges, recording how the lords Montaigne and d'Estissac were received during their journey, noting the exchange of social formalities and gifts
of wine that they received along their journey.[32] The noblemen are

29. Frame, 915. Querlon's comments can be found in his "Discours préliminaire,"
Michel de Montaigne, *Journal de voyage* (Paris: Gallimard, 1983), 38.

30. For a thorough analysis of Montaigne's political ambitions of being named in-
terim ambassador to Rome, see Philippe Desan, *Montaigne: Une biographie politique*
(Paris: Odile Jacob, 2014), 318-76.

31. Jacques-Auguste de Thou, *Memoires de la vie de Jacques-Auguste de Thou,
conseiller d'état et président à mortier au parlement de Paris* (Rotterdam: Reinier
Leers, 1711). Duval Fontenay-Mareuil, *Voyage faict en Italie par Monsieur le Marquis
de Fontenay-Marueil [sic] ambassadeur du Roy près de Sa Saincteté en l'année 1641...
ensemble la façon d'eslire les Papes, le tout recueilli par le S.r de Vologer Fontenay*
(Paris: L. Boulanger, 1643).

32. All told, Montaigne's secretary records about twenty of these encounters beginning with his meeting with the maître d'hôtel of the Duke of Nevers and ending
with Montaigne's attendance of festivities of the Captain of the Castel Sant'Angelo
(the Pope's son) on Fat Tuesday.

portrayed as representatives of France participating as tourists in an economy of political exchange. Montaigne seeks political authorities, such as the Burgermeisters of Schaffhausen, the Duke of Ferrara (a French ally), and the Pope in Rome, as well, most conspicuously, in Hall in Tirol, where he attempts at all costs to meet with the Austrian Archduke, only to be rebuffed with the explanation that "the house of France was hostile to his."[33]

The political discourse of the *Journal de voyage* nonetheless pales in comparison to the attention the Secretary pays to Montaigne's personal, mental, and medical needs. He tracks Montaigne, using a third-person pronoun that is off-putting until the reader understands this "il" to be Montaigne, tracking him in silence as he separates from the rest of the troop. The Secretary records many visits in which Montaigne was supposedly "alone" with a level of detail that implicates his own participation in the event. In Kempten, for example, his account begins with a characteristic description of the troop's lodging. The Secretary then comments on the food, records his efforts to obtain adequate bedding for Montaigne, and even highlights his master's particular need for extra napkins at dinner. Noting that the town is one of the first they had encountered where Protestants and Catholics lived together, the Secretary describes the Catholic mass, recording that "Monsieur de Montaigne went to the church of the Lutherans."[34] He describes the Protestant ceremony, the singing of a Psalm, the "very beautiful" responses of the organ, and how the people removed their hats with each verse, as well as Montaigne's meeting with "two old ministers."[35] A woman, "head bare and hair loose," says her prayers "in the mode of the country" and a young man arrives "with a sword at his side" to recite words we only then understand to be "certain rules for people who marry."[36] The Secretary then records details of Montaigne's interview with the minister, writing his questions and responses, all of which must have occurred in Latin, in direct quotations.

On several occasions, the Secretary hints that he was there even in moments when his narrative states that Montaigne set out alone. In Épernay, he writes that d'Estissac and Montaigne went to mass, "as

33. 907.
34. 894.
35. 895.
36. Ibid.

was their custom."[37] Épernay had been home to the Marshal of France Piero Strozzi, a man whom Montaigne admired for his military ability and whose tomb he longed to see, and while the Secretary does not mention accompanying Montaigne, he betrays his presence in his subsequent use of the pronoun "we," writing that "*we were told* that the queen had had him buried thus without pomp or ceremony because that was the will of the said marshal."[38]

In Meaux, the troop visited the city and its suburbs, the market and the abbey of Saint Faron before retiring to the hotel, when Montaigne "went to visit the treasurer of the Church of Saint Stephen."[39] The Secretary subsequently writes that "the most curious thing *we saw* there was a box-tree spreading its branches in a circle."[40] In Augsburg, too, as Montaigne goes to see several churches and attends a Protestant service, the Secretary writes, "*we* did not see one beautiful woman."[41] Finally, in Rome, where Montaigne spent his days wandering around the city on his own, the Secretary records his master's attendance at a circumcision, describing the traditional Jewish songs and clothing and writing of the rabbi's sermon again using "we": "the one *we* heard seemed to *him* to argue with great eloquence and wit."[42] Here the two different pronouns can leave no doubt that the Secretary attended the ceremony, while Montaigne judged the eloquence of the rabbi's Italian.

A strict interpretation of these passages gives an image of the Secretary working in close contact with his master, literally running behind him, as "he goes," exhibiting the "great effort" Stefano Guazzo advises servants take in looking after their masters, an effort that he compares to trying to make a wandering dog's bed.[43] During the communal experience expressed through the pronoun "we," the Secretary steps into the background, leaving space for his lord's communication and interaction with the outside world, exercising the silence for which he was paid. Even in the free and open spaces of Venice, where "everyone goes around by himself," the Secretary inscribes himself within his master's identity, writing: "a train of valets *is of no use to*

37. 868.
38. Ibid., emphasis mine.
39. 868.
40. Ibid.
41. 898, emphasis mine.
42. 945, emphasis mine.
43. *Civil Conversatione*, 251 v.

us at all here."[44] Montaigne, it appears, is alone when he is with his secretary.

WATCHING MONTAIGNE

The most unusual aspect of the Secretary's journal, however, is the attention he pays to Montaigne's personal habits, his tastes and needs, his medical conditions and treatments. The Secretary mixes the form of a *voyage d'Italie* with the note-taking of a medical log. Was this a part of his contracted duties? Did he have some sort of rudimentary medical training? Why was this non-domestic servant so attentive to his master's most intimate, painful bodily experiences?

In Plombières, the Secretary describes the baths, their location, the various waters, and the lodging they received. He takes pains to copy the lengthy tablet of laws governing the baths' usage and appears to have followed Montaigne into the baths, where he writes,"we saw men who had been cured of ulcers, and others of red spots on the body."[45] He observes Montaigne experimenting with the waters, pouring hot water from one glass to another, commenting on the water's effects on his master's appetite, urination, sleep, and delicate stomach. He also records the details of a painful attack of colic: "On the sixth day he had a very violent attack of colic, worse than his ordinary ones, and had it in his right side, where he had never felt any pain except a very slight one at Arsac."[46]

This passage illustrates two important points. The first is that Montaigne obviously communicated the details of his sickness to his servant, describing the workings of his bowels, ureters, kidneys, and bladder, the feelings of pain shooting down his right side, as well as details of his medical history. The second is that the Secretary pays close attention to these details, perhaps even jotting them down while in the baths. He not only watches Montaigne, but also watches others watching Montaigne, noting how the bathers in Plombières "found strange" his master's method of drinking and bathing without any previous experience there.

It is in this complex game of looking, writing, tasting, and experimentation that the Secretary records his first "I do not know" that

44. 921, emphasis mine.
45. 873.
46. 875.

distinguishes him from his master. The Secretary notes Montaigne's subjective perception of the water's taste, writing: "it seemed to Monsieur de Montaigne that if paid special attention, you could detect a faint taste of iron" ("il sembloit à M. de Montaigne qu'elle rapportoit *je ne sçay quel* goust de fer").[47] He repeats this same expression in Baden. Are these judgments, like Montaigne's assessment of the likeness of the bust of Bembo,[48] signs of the limitations of secretarial acquiescence? Are they signs that the Secretary controls the veracity of his master's opinions? A literal reading would tend to answer in the affirmative, since the observation recorded shortly thereafter that "the ordinary dress of the women seems *to me* as neat as our own" passes subjectivity back to the narrator (that is, the Secretary).[49] Is it the intimacy of pain and the subjective experience of watching an old man bathe that provokes this separation of the Secretary's *moy* from that of his lord, or the young man's interest in women's bathing clothes?

The Secretary's insertion of himself into these small details both reinforces and undercuts his master's account, making what Brush calls a "circumstantial description of the essayist" an object for further contemplation by its future readers.[50] The Secretary takes pains to offer his own version of Montaigne, capturing not only his master's particular way of experiencing and testing reality, but also his interpretation of this.

One further example will help show just how close this cooperation of acting, thinking, and observation between Montaigne and his servant was. Well before his famous exposition of Montaigne's wanderlust, Montaigne's Secretary observes his master's interest in the landscape around him, tracking his reactions as they pass through the most beautiful landscape Montaigne had ever seen. He continues, as he had done elsewhere, to summarize Montaigne's comments using subjective verbs in the imperfect:

47. Frame, 872. Michel de Montaigne, *Journal de Voyage*, ed. François Rigolot (Paris: Presses universitaires de France, 1992), 9. Emphasis mine.

48. In Padua, "There are many rare sculptures in marble and bronze. He looked with a kindly eye at the bust of Cardinal Bembo, which shows the sweetness of his character and something indefinable on the elegance of his mind." (919) ("Il y regarda de bon œil le visage du Cardinal Bembo qui monstre la douceur de ses moeurs et *je ne sçay quoy* de la gentillesse de son esprit.") (Rigolot, 67, emphasis mine)

49. 884, emphasis mine.

50. Brush, "The Secretary, Again," 135.

Monsieur de Montaigne said ("disoit") that all his life he had dis-
trusted ("il s'estoit mesfié") other people's judgment on the matter
of the conveniences of foreign countries, since every man's taste is
governed by the ordering of his habit and the usage of his village; and
he had taken very little account ("avoit fort peu d'estat") of the information that travelers gave him; but in this spot he wondered ("il
s'esmerveilloit") even more at their stupidity, for he had heard, and
especially on this trip, that the passes of the Alps of this region were
full of difficulties, the manners of the people uncouth, roads inaccessible, lodgings primitive, the air insufferable. As for the air, he thanked
God ("il remercioit Dieu") that he had found it so mild, for it inclined
rather toward too much heat than too much cold; and in all this trip
up to that time we had had only three days of cold and about an hour
of rain. But that for the rest, if he had to take his daughter, who is
only eight, for a walk, he would as soon do so on this road as on any
path in his garden. And as for the inns, he had never seen a country
where they were so plentifully distributed and so handsome, for he
had always lodged in handsome towns well furnished with victuals
and wine, and more reasonably than elsewhere.[51]

The Secretary describes Montaigne's words as they are being produced: "Monsieur de Montaigne said (disoit)," or that "this valley
seemed to Monsieur de Montaigne."[52] The effect of these indirect
progressive quotations is to recount, not Montaigne's exact words or
actions, most of which the Secretary observed during the day as they
rode on horseback over a rugged countryside, but the spirit of his
enthusiasm and crux of his argumentation. The Secretary provides a
portrait of Montaigne's discursive interaction with society and landscape, explaining his reactions through vivid descriptions of the context that inspired them. He reads his master and then, when needed,
fills in useful details and even confirms Montaigne's observations
about himself. One apparent aberration in Meunier de Querlon's
original punctuation, in fact, shows just how difficult untangling the
servant and master's voice can be. We are nearing the end of the Alpine detour and entering Italian territory, when Montaigne begins to
express his displeasure at leaving "Germany" and entering a space
that reminds him too much of home. The Secretary had been recording Montaigne's enthusiasm since the Inn valley, remarking how he
became increasingly enchanted with the Alpine landscape until they

51. 910.
52. 905-06.

arrived in Bolzano, when "Monsieur de Montaigne exclaimed that he clearly recognized that he was beginning to leave Germany: the streets narrower, and no handsome public square."[53]

This passage shows why we need a critical edition of the *Journal de voyage*, since modern versions of Montaigne's text all gloss over Meunier de Querlon's amusingly ambiguous punctuation. Querlon practiced a sort of double, direct and indirect quotation that (appropriately) confuses the travel narrative's melded voices. In this particular passage, Querlon complicates this back and forth with a punctuation that communicates the passing of voice from one author to the other: "M. de Montaigne cried out that he could see that he had begun to leave Germany:" the streets narrower, ..."[54] Following Montaigne's cited words, Querlon uses a colon that invites the Secretary to speak. In other words, Montaigne expresses his thoughts about the changing cultural landscape and pauses as if to invite his servant to complete his thoughts and continue his ongoing narrative. In keeping with the theory of Francesco Sansovino, the journal's ideas (*inventio*) belong to Montaigne, while its words (*elocutio*) often fall under the purview of his servant.[55] We also get the impression, as the troop crosses the Alps and draws closer to Rome, that Montaigne talks constantly, reacting to the landscapes he sees, summing up his ideas, exclaiming as he sees a new place and attempting to communicate his enthusiasm to the troop. We imagine him saying all these things, aloud and to his secretary.

CONCLUSION

Montaigne's *Journal de voyage* is a unique case of collaborative writing that provides an example of how secretaries worked in the late sixteenth century. The Secretary's sense of his own identity, his powers of observation, and his proximity to his lord allow him to present a strong image of Montaigne *en voyage*, in the baths and during his daily routine. As Montaigne continued to write the *Essais* after

---

53. 911.

54. Querlon's edition reads: "M. de Montaigne s'ecria "qu'il connoissoit bien qu'il commançoit à quiter l'Allemaigne:" [colon inside the quotations] les rues plus estroites, et point de belle place publicque." Michel de Montaigne, *Journal du voyage en Italie, Par la Suisse et l'Allemagne en 1580 et 1581* (Rome: Le Jay, 1774), I, 183.

55. Viviane Mellinghof-Bourgerie, "Introduction," in Chappuys, *Le Secrettaire*, xlvii.

returning from his journey through Italy, he also continued to build on what Pierre Villey first labeled as the *peinture du moy*, applying the Socratic maxim to "know thyself" not only in a philosophical sense, but also in literal and even painstakingly physical terms that record his ongoing struggle with sickness, mortality, and depression. The ability to look at himself in detail, to imagine his *moy* as if he were another, should, at least in part, be attributed to the experience of his collaboration with his still anonymous secretary.

III. Women and the
Fashioning of Poetic Legacies

BROOKE D. DI LAURO

"Idol of my life": Idolatry and Poetic Immortalization in Scève's *Délie*

Maurice Scève has long been recognized as an extremely innovative poet whose work greatly influenced the Pléiade poets who followed him.[1] Indeed, he seems to anticipate that group's exhortation to write in the vernacular and to create poetry inspired by, but superior to, its models, and which would consequently grant immortality to the poet and his or her subject. Moreover, Scève's *Délie* is renowned for its erudition and for the complexity of its allusions; rather than simply paraphrasing and borrowing from his literary models to support his arguments, Scève instead reworks classical and biblical texts to give them a new meaning that is the opposite of its original one. For Gérard Defaux, the poet's much-touted idolatry of his beloved is one such example; for although Scève's idolatry was inspired by Jean Olivier's *Pandora*, everything that the latter considered sinful was exalted by Scève.[2] Furthermore, Scève's unabashed idolatry allowed him to distance himself from his two most prominent Christian models, Marot and Petrarch.[3] In fact, Edwin Duval claims that the *Délie*, the first true French *canzoniere*, can be considered an "anti-*canzoniere*" due to the poet's conversion, which occurs in the first poem and mirrors that of the *Rime Sparse*'s opening sonnet, but

1. "All of the Pléiade (or the poetic movement affiliated with the group) owes a lot to Scève, whom they often imitated without admitting it," according to Enzo Guidici, "Joachim Du Bellay et l'École lyonnaise," *L'esprit créateur* 19/3 (1979): 68.
    2. Gérard Defaux, introduction to *Délie: Object de plus haulte vertu*, ed. Gérard Defaux (Geneva: Droz, 2004), lxxiv.
    3. "For it is indeed against these two [Marot and Petrarch] that Scève desires and proclaims himself idolatrous, that he proclaims the eternity, the indestructible continued existence of love, its sufferings and its deaths, that he claims the imperishable beauty, the inexhaustible and confusing spirituality of humans" (Defaux, lvi). Unless otherwise noted, all translations are my own.

YFS 134, *The Construction of a National Vernacular Literature in the Renaissance: Essays in Honor of Edwin M. Duval*, ed. DeVos and Hayes, © 2018 by Yale University.

suggest[s] something entirely different. Scève has turned not from Laura to God, but from all the other ladies of Lyon to his own Laura, Délie. He has not been transformed from an idolater into a penitent, but from a skirt chaser into an idolater. For Délie is indeed for Scève an object of idolatry, just as Laura was for Petrarch. Scève states as much in his last line: "Constituée idole de ma vie." But whereas idolatry was an obstacle to conversion in Petrarch, it is the result of conversion in Scève, and is accordingly given a positive, sacramental value in the last four lines of Scève's poem.[4]

Scève's unabashed celebration of his idolatry allows him to both acknowledge and transform his models and to present a love that is more human, more complex. Rather than juxtaposing the spiritual and the sensual or the Judeo-Christian and the pagan, Scève combines the two models.

Defaux astutely recognized the centrality of idolatry to the *Délie* as a whole, but in insisting on the *inventor idolatriae*, he downplays the importance of the idol herself.[5] After all, Délie's status as "idol of [his] life" (D1:10) and Scève's position as her idolater who "idolize[d] in [her] divine image," (D3:1–2) are the foundation of their relationship and the reason for "the deaths which [she] renews in [him]" (huitain: 3). In addition to the verb "idolize" mentioned in the third poem, the verb "adore" appears fifteen times in the *Délie*. Moreover, in the very first poem, the word "idol" is mentioned twice, followed by "fatal Pandora" in the second poem, and "divine image" in the third. From the very outset of the *Délie*, the poet selects specific vocabulary that serves both to forcefully situate his work within the traditions that inspired it and to simultaneously distance himself from them,

4. Edwin Duval, "Wresting Petrarch's Laurels: Scève, Du Bellay, and the Invention of the Canzoniere," ed. William J. Kennedy, *Annals of Scholarship* 16/1–3 (2005): 55. I would like to take this opportunity to thank Ned Duval for instilling in me the importance of close readings and of returning to the original texts. I came to graduate school with a love of Renaissance literature and the challenges it presented for the modern reader—for me each text was a puzzle to be solved—but I was not particularly familiar with the Vulgate, Classical philosophers, or Petrarch. Early on I would make casual, somewhat superficial references to those texts and Ned would consistently push back, insisting that I look deeper, read more carefully. It was in following his advice that I went beyond my initial understanding of Scève as a "traditional" Renaissance poet and learned that with Scève nothing is quite what it seems.

5. Defaux first dedicated an article to the topic in his "L'idole, le poète et le voleur de feu: Erreur et impiété dans *Délie*," *French Forum* 18/3 (1993): 270; he later expanded the argument in the introduction to his 2004 critical edition of the *Délie* noted above.

alluding to various texts only to subvert their original meaning. More than a rewriting of specific models, Scève's idolatry highlights the poet's distance from the Neoplatonic and Petrarchan traditions more broadly and allows him to dramatically change the role of the lady in love poetry.

Just as Scève's idolatry underscores his antithetical love, which is interpreted both in secular and spiritual contexts, so too does Délie's role as idol highlight her dual nature. Although the poet often employs the typical vocabulary of courtly love to describe his relationship with Délie ("service," "servitude," "homage," "agreement," "lady"), Délie is not merely the beloved of the courtly romances whose unattainability inspired the lover's ultimate allegiance and devotion in the hope of receiving the *don du mercy*. Nor is she solely a Beatrice or Laura. For despite frequently being praised for her ability to lead to the poet's ascension through her "lofty" example and being described as "angelic," "celestial," "saintly," and "divine," Délie is not presented as an idealization of virtue who would lead the poet to a superior existence. As Defaux has succinctly concluded, Délie is neither exclusively the source of the poet's suffering nor the key to his salvation: "For the Lover, Délie is not only the dangerous and irresistible Pandora, she is also the holy and pure, the immaculate Mary" (cll). Although Defaux's Pandora/Mary dichotomy accurately points to Délie's dual nature, it falsely presents Délie as a figure who is, at least in part, a redemptive figure. While Scève at times presents her as a virtuous and elevating force as per the Platonist tradition, he categorically rejects the idea of salvation from the very first poem. Ultimately, Scève transforms his beloved into a lady who is far more than cold and demanding; in the *Délie* she becomes an idol who requires that the poet sacrifice his life to her. However, the voluntary self-sacrifice and self-destruction needed to appease Délie also allows the poet to create a new self through poetry. At the same time that the poet is transforming Délie into an idol, he is transposing their love story into the *Délie*, and it is his beloved's insistence on his death that allows for his rebirth in poetry.[6]

---

6. For Jerry Nash, Scève's poetry has intrinsic therapeutic value: "For one who certainly experienced and yet struggled against such feelings of great despair and anguish caused by love, Scève discovered in the therapeutic value of poetic art a means of escape and consolation. Through the poet's struggle with the stylized and especially

The Latin "idolum" and the French "idole" are both derived from the Greek εἴδωλον (eidolon), "an object of sight, a thing which is seen," and the relationship between idol and idolater is necessarily a visual one. In fact, as Lance Donaldson-Evans suggests, Délie is an approximate anagram for εἴδωλον, "she who is seen."[7] It is no coincidence that the poems describing Délie as an idol are constructed around a visual representation: "eye," (D1:1, D24:1, D297:2); "to see" (D182:7); "view" (D24:9); "her two suns" (D235:5)). In particular, the first poem of the *Délie* begins with the word "Eye" and ends with the transformation of Délie into an idol. In many ways, the first dizain is merely a description of the *innamoramento* central to all love poetry. However, by transforming his beloved into an idol Scève revolutionizes this first encounter by making it one of sacrificial violence:

> The Eye, too fiery with my youthful errors,
> Spun like a weathervane, imprudent, aimlessly:
> When suddenly (oh fear of delightful terrors)
> My Basilisk with its sharp gaze
> Piercing Body, Heart, and devoid of Reason,
> Penetrated into the Soul of my Soul.
> Great was the blow, which without sharpened blade
> Kills the Spirit though the Body survive,
> Pitiful victim in your eyes, Lady,
> Nominated Idol of my life. (D1)

Although fickle in his youth, the poet has fallen victim to Délie's magical, bewitching power. The process is entirely visual: Délie's gaze alone ("its sharp gaze," l. 4; "in your eyes," l. 9) arrests Scève's wandering eye ("eye too fiery," l. 1) and she, in turn, becomes the sole object of his gaze, "idol of my life" (l. 10). As the poet later explains to his beloved, he lives and sees (the French word "vis" that he uses could be either) with the sole purpose of adoring her (D24: 10). Scève's *innamoramento* is a violent one in which the lover becomes the beloved's victim just like he is later her "immolated offering" (D163:10). The alliteration of plosive initial consonants—"peur" ("fear") (l. 2), "poignant" ("sharp")

---

metaphoric reality of art, he was able to transcend the anguished confines of his existential dilemma and to relieve, or at least lessen, his feelings of rejection and despair." See Jerry Nash, *Love Aesthetics of Maurice Scève: Poetry and Struggle* (Cambridge, Cambridge University Press, 1991), 142.

7. Lance K. Donaldson-Evans, *Love's Fatal Glance: A Study of Eye Imagery in the Poets of the École lyonnaise*, vol. 39 (University of Mississippi: Romance Monographs, 1980), 94-95.

(l. 4), "perçant" ("piercing") (l. 5), "penetrer" ("penetrate") (l. 6), "piteuse" ("pitiful") (l. 9)—insists on the violence of this sacrifice. Even if
the body survives intact ("vivant"), the soul is divided ("dévie") from it,
or lifeless ("dé- vie"). By expressing his fear before indicating the source
of that fear (line 4), the poet intensifies the effect that that object has
on the reader—the suspense is in fact maintained until the ninth line,
when the significantly revised courtly beloved or "lady" is revealed to
be the subject of all of the violent actions inflicted on the poet in lines
2-10. In fact, the basilisk of the fourth line, and the lady of the ninth
line are one in the same. The basilisk, the mythological serpent capable of killing with a single glance (and an allusion to Alain Chartier's
"belle dame sans merci" capable of the same), is also a symbol for the
Antichrist (Psalm 91:13) and evocative of the poet's blasphemy. Finally,
the use of the Latin sacrificial term "constituere" further highlights
the violence of the process in which Délie becomes an idol.

Although still a courtly "dame" (l. 10) demanding the service of
her vassal, Délie here also embodies a pagan goddess who demands
sacrifices.[8] In the *Délie* the poet himself is sacrificed and is entirely
at the mercy of Délie who "kills the spirit" (l. 8)—"devoid of Reason"
(l. 4), the poet is but a "pitiful victim" (l. 9). "Hostia," which in Latin
has meaning as both a Christian (Communion host) and a pagan (sacrifice), points to the juxtaposition of the two traditions that is crucial
to our understanding of the relationship between idol and idolater.
Furthermore, Scève's systematic reversal of elements borrowed from
biblical passages continues with the Latinism "au conspect de toy" in
the ninth line and again allows the poet to highlight his irreverence:

> Return to your rest, O my soul,
> For the Lord has dealt bountifully with you.
> For you have delivered my soul from death,
> My eyes from tears,
> And my feet from falling.
> I will walk before the Lord
> In the land of the living. . . .
> *Precious in the sight of the Lord (Pretiosa in conspectu Domini)*
> Is the death of His saints.
> O Lord, truly I am *Your servant;*
> I am *Your servant*, the son of Your maidservant;

---

8. Specifically, she is reminiscent of her namesake, the chthonian deity, Hecate,
to whom black puppies and she-lambs were sacrificed.

You have loosed my bonds.
I will offer to You the sacrifice (hostiam) of thanksgiving,
And I will call upon the name of the Lord.
(Psalms 114:7–9, 115:15–17)[9]

The semantic similarities between the above passage and the first dizain of the *Délie* highlight the way in which Scève paraphrases the biblical text only to place it in a context with the opposite meaning. The believer is the Lord's servant whereas Scève is serving his lady, his idol. Scève has moved beyond the feudal model whereby he, as servant, would grant favors to his lord in return for protection. The relationship of which the poet speaks is not a reciprocal one, but rather one in which he is a literal victim rather than the figurative victim of the *Rime Sparse* where Petrarch claims "I am born and die one thousand times a day" (164:13). Although Scève displays signs of possession (*"my* basilisk") and of devotion (10), unlike the speaker in the Psalms, he does not declare his willingness to offer sacrifices to his Lord as a sign of his gratitude. Furthermore, the poet declares that his *domina*, or "lady lord" regards his death as that of a helpless victim ("Piteuse hostie au conspect de toy, Dame," l. 10) rather than as a valued sacrifice of a saint ("Pretiosa in conspectu Domini.")

The third dizain extends the sacrificial imagery presented in the first dizain, continuing the notion of the beloved as idol and of the poet as victim but in much more explicit terms. Most interestingly, the victim here seems to participate in his own sacrifice; it is he who immolates his own heart and sacrifices his life and soul:

Your sweet venom, your grace, makes me
Idolize your divine image
Due to which my credulous eye ignorantly errs
By not foreseeing my future harm.
Immolating for you my heart in homage,
Sacrifices with the soul life.
So you were, o freedom, ravished,
Given in prey to all ingratitude
So I hope with deceptive desire
In low Hells to find beatitude. (D3)

Whereas the first dizain describes Délie's aggressive gaze and the poet's defenselessness against it, the poet's death in the third dizain is much more certain: he "sacrificed with his Soul, his life" (6). The

9. Unless otherwise noted, all emphasis is mine.

poet embraces his role as obsequious lover and hopes that such an oblation to Délie will win her favor. The sacrifice, however, is unsuccessful because his sacrifice has no effect on his beloved (7-8). The poet loses his freedom and his life for naught. In contradistinction to traditional lyric sequences, both Petrarchan and Neoplatonic, where the beloved leads the lover to heaven or a transcendent state, the poet of the *Délie* can hope for nothing more than to find happiness in the pagan underworld (10). Despite the explicitly religious terminology of the poem—"idolize" (2), "divine" (2), "homage" (5), "sacrificed" (6), "hope" (9), "beatitude" (10)—Scève's newly conceived love relationship is neither Christian nor Neoplatonist. As Duval has pointed out, "the *Délie* glorifies idolatry in a way that subverts any possibility of transcendence except through and within the experience of loving an *earthly* lady" (Duval, 55).

Scève's treatment of idolatry is evidently far removed from traditional views, both biblical and classical. For Plato, for example, the worshipping of the beloved as an idol is not the blasphemous act of a heathen as in the Christian tradition, but, on the contrary, permits a spiritual transcendence whereby the soul may ascend from human to divine love:

> Now he whose vision of the mystery [contemplation of true being] is long past, or whose purity has been sullied, cannot pass swiftly hence to see beauty's self yonder, when he beholds that which is called beautiful here; wherefore he *looks upon it with no reverence, and surrendering to pleasure* he essays to go after the fashion of a four-footed beast, and to beget offspring of the flesh, or consorting with wantonness he has no fear nor shame in running after unnatural pleasure. But when one who is fresh from the mystery, and saw much of the vision, beholds a *godlike face or bodily form* that truly expresses beauty, first there come upon him a shuddering and a measure of that awe which the vision inspired, and then *reverence as at the sight of a god*, and but for fear of being deemed a very madman he would *offer sacrifice to his beloved, as to a holy image of deity*. [. . .] by reason of the stream of beauty entering in through his eyes [. . .] his soul's plumage is fostered, and [. . .] the stump of the wings swells and hastens to grow from the root over the whole substance of the soul, for aforetime the whole soul was furnished with wings.[10]

10. Plato, *The Collected Dialogues of Plato including the letters*, ed. Edith Hamilton and Huntington Cairns, trans. Lane Cooper et al., Bollingen Series, vol. 71 (Princeton, New Jersey: Princeton University Press, 1961), *Phaedrus* 250e–251b.

Human love is presented here as precisely the opposite of idolatry insofar as it shows no reverence and is merely an act of succumbing to physical temptation. For Plato, idolatry and the desire for sacrifice that accompanies it are the first steps toward the transcendence of the physical person. For Scève, however, they are the end. Scève does not go beyond Délie; he loves her for what she is, in the flesh, body and soul—not a means to an end but an end in itself. In Augustinian terms, the poet has passed immediately from using to enjoying, from Christian love to blasphemous idolatry and his idolatry, in turn, seems to inspire his sacrifice.[11]

Dizain 275 is yet another example of this process. The poem demonstrates that despite the superficial connections to Plato's love theory as laid out in the *Symposium* and *Phaedrus*, Scève's depiction of love and sacrifice to the beloved is distinctly anti-Platonist:

> To prostrate myself often before this image
> Of your beauty an admirable Idea,
> I pay homage to you as many times
> As every law favorably decided
> Can give you. Whereas my faith guided
> By reason, which comes to me dying,
> Whether I leave, or remain,
> Reverently, seeing you, I salute you,
> As one who offers, with what is left of it,
> My life at the feet of your high value. (D275)

Although the first two lines describe a meditation that appears Neoplatonist in nature, the poet explains that mere rational contemplation of the "idea" that inspired Délie's "beauty" is not sufficient. Despite the numerous lexical and semantic similarities between Scève's dizain and the passage from Plato's *Phaedrus* cited above, each author's ultimate goals are quite distinct. Having transformed his Délie from a traditional "lady" who is to be served and adored into a pagan goddess and idol in the very first poem, here Scève goes even further, suggesting that "service" or "homage" to this idol must consist in

---

11. Although Perry believes death to be of primary importance in the *Délie*, he explicitly dismisses its relation to idolatry that, in turn, he declares deviant: "in 3.6 the poet 'Sacrifia avec l'Ame la vie.' Rather than a true unbinding of spirit from body, however, such esthetic ecstasis is a deviation (1.8) leading to idolatry (1.10, 3.2)." T. Anthony Perry, "Délie! And Old Way of Dying (A New Hypothesis on Scève's Title)," *French Forum* 1/1 (1976): 8.

acts of self-immolation and human sacrifice. Scève's offering is an attempt to earn the favor of his lady whom he has transformed into an idol. His oblation is not a Platonistic gesture aimed at transcending this world for a higher realm, but rather is a desperate act intended to appease his implacable pagan goddess. Like a courtly lover, the poet has paid repeated "hommage" (D3:5, D275:3) to his beloved, but there is no sign of reciprocity. As in the first dizain, his only chance to reach her in her superior abode is to sacrifice his life in her honor. What is essential is not that she is an "Idea," a model of creation, but that she is an "idol," a simulacrum and object of worship.

For Scève, idolizing Délie is fundamental to their relationship, and he defends his idolatry in dizain 75. More than merely a declaration of his preference for Délie ("I prefer to all Gods my Mistress, / Just as Love had commanded me," D 16), this poem allows Scève to justify his worship of Délie as an idol. Here it is particularly clear that Délie, although she is incontestably the object of Scève's contemplation, simply does not correspond to a Platonic Idea. Rather than presenting Délie as an eternal exemplar, Scève focuses instead on his particular relationship with his beloved. Délie is not a Platonic idea, an archetype, but rather a very specific and inimitable creature whose effect on Scève is unique:

> In devoting myself to such happy service,
> I have succeeded in being comparable to the Gods.
> Can this therefore be held against me,
> Establishing in her my high Heavens?
> Assure only, Lady, that from your eyes
> To me is always all harm slow.
> So you, Harmful Gods of the silent shades,
> (She will preserve me from adversity)
> Do not take from me by violent force
> Even one Iota of my happiness. (D75)

The poet is making, creating, ordaining, and establishing as a ritual, his own personal Paradise within his Lady (l. 4). If Delie is "nominated ("constituée") idol of my life" (D1:10), the poet, in turn, responds by "establishing ("constituant") in her [his] high heavens" (l. 4). The poet unhesitatingly affirms his right to worship Délie-idol as the ultimate god, and hopes that he will be forgiven for such idolatry since his devotion to serving Délie puts him in a situation analogous to the gods.

The poet's unabashed blasphemy is again made stronger by his use of biblical language to describe the protection and happiness his idol provides him. Scève, in describing how his goddess-turned-idol assures his complete happiness despite significant opposition, modifies a line from Matthew 5:18: "iota unum" becomes "non un iota" (10). The gospel passage follows the Beatitudes of Jesus's Sermon on the Mount and encourages steadfastness in the face of persecution. Jesus explains that ignoring even "the smallest" law can hurt one's chances of being granted access to Heaven. Complete dedication is required in order to be considered among the blessed. Scève, on the other hand, declares Délie his own Heaven and claims that his devotion to her will protect him from any danger so that not even Virgil's Stygian gods (l. 7) can take away "the smallest bit" (l. 10) of his happiness.

A metaphysical or spiritual transcendence as described by Plato or by Augustine is completely absent from the *Délie*. Instead, Scève devotes his life on earth to idolizing Délie and is willing to sacrifice his life in oblation to his beloved. The offerings mentioned so far ("pitiful victim" [D1:9] and "immolated offering" [D161:10]) and even the more explicit instances of self-sacrifice (D3, D275) have not been particularly violent, but in dizain 194, Scève's description of the sacrifice required to appease his beloved demonstrates clear affinity with rituals of pagan sacrifice:

> Does it suffice for you, oh lady, to make golden
> With your virtues our blessed age,
> Without attempting to have the World adore
> So fervently the holiness of your image,
> So that many must, through shared damage,
> Die at the hands of your great cruelties.
> Are you not horrified, being on all sides
> Surrounded both by corpses and by tombs,
> To see thus smoking on your altars
> To appease you, thousands, and thousands of Hecatombs? (D194)

The poem may begin as a fairly typical description of the virtuousness and divine nature of the beloved (lines 1–4), but its tone abruptly changes: this poem, more than any other in the cycle, is dominated by images of death and pagan sacrifice, most notably in the last three lines. Délie here embodies Hecate, the triune goddess to whom sacrifices are made—the connection is explicit in the reference to the etymologically similar "hecatombs" (the sacrifice of one hundred bulls). Although the fifth and sixth lines of transition could be read as a euphemism for the extreme respect Délie deserves, the profusion of macabre imagery that follows ("mortz," l. 8, "tombes," l. 8, "fumer," l. 9, "hecatombes," l. 10) alerts the reader that Scève is introducing a new topos. The ambiance Scève creates in dizain 194 is remarkably similar to one that Virgil describes in the *Aeneid* (VI:243–54). Rather than a Christian or Platonist vision of a lover whose sacrifice leads to immortality, Scève's vision replaces the Christian God with his own idol and initiates a transfer from the Christian realm of symbolic sacrifice to the pagan world of violent human sacrifice.

Keeping in mind that Scève's translation of the *Deplourable fin de Flamete* included the motto "Souffrir se ouffrir," it is also possible to read the *Délie's* motto as "S'ouffrir non souffrir" where, according to Edmond Huguet, "s'ouffrir" is "to offer oneself to death," "to offer oneself in sacrifice," or "to offer one's service to someone."[12] Scève is entirely at the mercy of love or, more specifically, at the mercy of Délie. His new beloved *qua* idol commands not only the utmost respect—the poet "admires," "adores," "honors," and "reveres" her—but she also demands the ultimate sacrifice: the poet's own life. The hyperbole of the last line is particularly striking since, in the Petrarchan tradition, "mille, et mille" refers to the strength of life-granting love whereas Scève instead employs the phrase to refer to the overwhelming number of life-extinguishing sacrifices needed to appease his lady, his self-made idol. Scève has pushed the Petrarchan notion of service and suffering in love to such an extreme that he celebrates death in a way the Pléiade does not, making it difficult to accept Dorothy Coleman's claim that his poetry illustrates "the whole problem of death as seen by a poet who was not like the Pléiade (poetry vanquished death) but [who] was simply affirming that love for Délie conquers death."[13] For Scève, it is the creative process that liberates him from the confines of his mortal existence, and his art depends on his idolatry and its mandate of self-obliteration.

12. *Dictionnaire de la langue française au XVIᶜ siècle*, 7 vols. (Paris: Champion-Dider, 1925–67), ed. Edmond Huguet, Vol. 5, 505.
13. Dorothy Coleman, *An Illustrated Love "Canzoniere": The* Délie *of Maurice* Scève (Geneva: Slatkine, 1981), 21.

Délie rarely appears as a person in this work, but rather is presented as an object, a simple inventory of body parts (eyes, hands, ligatures, nose, mouth, face, feet, and hair)[14] or a work of art (effigy, statue, portrait, column) described by its visual appearance (polished, marble, stucco, enamel, bronze, or chiseled). What is curious in the *Délie*, however, is that Délie's reification, her transformation into an object, an idol who demands worship and sacrifice as violent as any pagan goddess, correlates directly to the poet's destruction through self-immolation (D1, D3, D163, D194); as the idol is being reconstructed, he is being destroyed. The theory of authorial effacement, prominent since the fourteenth century, contends that an author loses a part of himself when creating his work. Indeed, while the lady is being redefined and recreated, the poet is reduced to ashes, to dust; he melts like wax in fire or like snow in sun, or he dissolves into streams of tears. By participating in his own bodily death, Scève's poetic persona redefines itself, thereby providing the author with material for the verse that will assure both the viability of their legacy and that of the beloved. Thomas Hunkeler sees such self-effacement as central to Scève's *Blasons* and the *Fiametta* translation as well, and claims that the poet's erasure or sacrifice of his own voice was essential to building a monument to the lady that would revitalize both their corpses: "Through the poet's pen, this textual truth takes the form of a poetic corpus the creator of which endeavors to cut himself off—to 'die'—to better give it life."[15]

In particular, in dizain 418 the poet describes Délie as a caryatid. This poem's presentation of Délie-object is an extremely detailed hyptyposis, a verbal picture of a column more detailed than any single description the poet offers of Délie the person. Here, despite her divine nature ("lofty" 4, "angelic" 7), Délie is merely an earthly object. It should be noted that the description of Délie as a column is a reminder, too, of the significance of her name. Délie, named after the mythical figures of Diana / Persephone / Luna / Hecate, has been transformed first into a Corinthian column that, according to Scève (*Microcosme* III:2743–2749), is sacred to Diana, and second into a

---

14. Scève was always fascinated with the body and anatomizing it through writing. In 1536 he won the prize for best blazon, a descriptive poem on a part of the human body. In the *Délie*, his beloved is often represented through synecdoche.

15. Thomas Hunkeler, *Le vif du sens: corps et poésie selon Maurice Scève* (Geneva: Droz, 2003), 275.

hecataea, a pillar found at crossroads and in doorways that is thought to keep away evil and death.

> Beneath the square of a black abacus covering
> Her Capital with Nature's hand,
> And not by art's crude work,
> Perfect was such lofty Architecture,
> Where chiseling each flute,
> Volutes with leaves of gold
> With soft features deeply Angelic,
> Sitting upright on her Base, and followed well
> Above her plinth with hollow, and round edges
> To erect her Column of my life. (D 418)

Scève moves systematically from top to bottom, detailing the column with architectural precision. Just as Délie is "nominated idol of my life" (D1:10), here the poet has succeeded in "erecting her column of my life" (l. 10). By implicitly relating "idol" and "column," Scève stresses their similar function—to memorialize the love experience. The repeated emphasis on "life," however, serves to draw attention to its opposite, death. Furthermore, Scève's use of "column" is a clear allusion to and rewriting of *Rime Sparse* 268, 269, and 360. What was for Petrarch a symbol of a disconsolate lover lost after the death of his lady becomes, for Scève, a way to overcome death.[16]

If we consider that according to Song of Songs 14.15–21, idolatry is caused by images made in memory of the dead that in the course of time became objects of worship, Scève's transformation of Délie into an idol can be considered a preemptive assurance of what Jerry Nash has called a "literary afterlife" as laid out in the final dizain of the sequence.[17] In the case of *Rime Sparse* 269, Petrarch laments the loss of his "double treasure" of column and laurel, of his beloved

16. A previous version of this argument on the role of memory and memorial in the *Délie*, "M'en souvenant, je m'oblie moymesmes": *Délie* as *Memento Mori*," appeared in *Memory and Community in Sixteenth-Century France*, ed. David P. LaGuardia and Cathy M. Yandell (Farnham, MA: Ashgate, 2015), 37–54.

17. In the preface to his collection of essays dedicated to Scève, Nash astutely notes that: "[the future tenses] clearly are a projection of the poet's intense desire of a literary afterlife. [. . .] Scève was indeed a poet very much concerned with Délie's place, his place, and his work's place in the future. [. . .] There can be little doubt that a significant part of this Renaissance love poet's purpose was to create a 'living virtue' in which to embody his art for future generations." Nash, "Préface: Scève's 'vertu, qui viue nous suyvra,'" in *A Scève celebration: Délie 1544–1994*, ed. Nash, *Stanford French and Italian Studies* 77 (Saratoga, CA: Anma Libri, 1994): 1–2.

and his poetry, both of which were taken from him by Death. But by transforming Délie into an idol without adopting the transcendence afforded to idolatry by Augustine and Plato and instead sacrificing his life to submit to his earthly beloved's demands, Scève was inspired to transpose his love into a work of poetry: a monument resistant to death.

CATHY YANDELL

Ronsard's *Discours* for Two Queens: The Poetics of Political Pamphlets

Poetry and politics: While these oddest of bedfellows come together in both predictable and surprising ways throughout Pierre de Ronsard's work, the collected *Discours des misères de ce temps* undoubtedly constitute the most compelling example of their interaction. Most of the poems appear in the chronological order of their composition in the *Œuvres* of 1567,[1] but Ronsard highlights the *Discours à la Royne*, written on the eve of the French Wars of Religion in 1562, by placing it first in the collection.[2] As the editors of the Pléiade edition note, these verses dedicated to Catherine de Medici could well have figured first for reasons of protocol,[3] but more than any other poem in the collection, this *Discours* captures a pivotal, crucial moment, both in the development of the Wars of Religion and in Ronsard's poetic evolution.

Rather than juxtaposing the *Discours à la Royne* with the pieces that follow in the collection, I have found it illuminating to read the poem in conjunction with another of Ronsard's *Discours* written some fifteen months earlier, the *Discours à elle-mesme* (dedicated to Mary Stuart).[4] Penned shortly after the young widow's departure

---

1. *Œuvres de Pierre de Ronsard* (Paris: Gabriel Buon, 1567).
2. The *Discours à la Royne*, addressed to Catherine de Medici in 1562, thus appears before the *Institution de l'adolescence du Roy tres-chrestien Charles IXe de ce nom* (1561) as well as the *Discours* dedicated to Guillaume Des Autels and Louis Des Masures (both of 1560). Pierre de Ronsard, *Œuvres complètes*, 25 vols, ed. Paul Laumonier, Raymond Lebègue, and Isidore Silver (Paris: STFM, 1914–75), hereafter Laum.,11:19-32; *Œuvres complètes*, 2 vols, ed. Jean Céard, Daniel Ménager, and Michel Simonin, Bibliothèque de la Pléiade (Paris: Gallimard, 1993-94), 2:991–96, hereafter Pl.
3. Pl. 2:1572.
4. Laum. 12:277-84; Pl. 2:657–60.

YFS 134, *The Construction of a National Vernacular Literature in the Renaissance: Essays in Honor of Edwin M. Duval*, ed. DeVos and Hayes, © 2018 by Yale University.

for Scotland in February of 1561, the *Discours à elle-mesme* was published for the first time in the *Trois livres du Recueil des nouvelles poësies* of 1564. An analysis of these two poems will foreground a paradoxical development: as the kingdom of France is undergoing turmoil, instability, and widespread anxiety, Ronsard's authorial persona gains ascendency; and although the court poet represents the Catholic position of the crown, he subtly asserts his independence, ultimately affirming his commitment to the primacy of literary engagement over political proclomation.

Given both the consonances and the important distinctions between the *Discours à elle-mesme* to Mary Stuart and the *Discours à la Royne* to Catherine de Medici, it is surprising that (to my knowledge) the two poems have not been read in tandem. The poems contain a few striking similarities: both are called *Discours*—not an extensive genre in Ronsard's work— and both are dedicated to queens who have lost their status as "Roynes de France" through the deaths of their husbands, François II and Henri II respectively. While Mary Stuart remains "Queen of Scots" until 1567, that fact is understated in the *Discours à elle-mesme* as the poet privileges her lost relationship to France. When the *Discours à la Royne* first appeared, Catherine, as the mother of the young king Charles IX, had been appointed "Gouvernante" rather than Regent by the Conseil Privé.[5] Both Mary and Catherine were foreign, both were widows

---

5. As Jean-H. Mariéjol has observed, the États-généraux would have preferred to give the title of Regent to the King of Navarre: *Catherine de Médicis* (Paris: Hachette, 1920), 88, n.1. See also Robert J. Knecht, *Catherine de' Medici* (London and New York: Longman, 1998), 73–74. In their introduction to Catherine's writings, Leah Chang and Katherine Kong underscore the equivalency in power between "Gouvernante" and "Régente." See Catherine de Médicis and others, *Portrait of the Queen Mother: Polemics, Panegyrics, Letters*, trans. Chang and Kong, Other Voice Series (Toronto: University of Toronto Press, 2014), 14. In 1562, *de facto*, Catherine held a powerful position as "Gouvernante" and mother of the King—but *de jure*, she was not accorded the title of Regent. See also Seong-Hak Kim, *Michel de L'Hospital: The Vision of a Reformist Chancellor during the French Religious Wars* (Kirksville: Sixteenth Century Journal Publishers, 1997), 61–62. On Catherine's political capitalization of her maternal role, see Katherine Crawford, "Catherine de Médicis and the Performance of Political Motherhood," *Sixteenth Century Journal* 31/3 (2000): 643–73, and Sheila ffolliott, "Catherine de' Medici as Artemisia: Figuring the Powerful Widow," in *Rewriting the Renaissance: The Discourses of Sexual Difference in Early Modern Europe*, ed. Margaret W. Ferguson, Maureen Quilligan, and Nancy Vickers (Chicago: University of Chicago Press, 1986), 227–41.

in the Valois dynasty, and both were beleaguered by outside forces. Both poems begin with an insistence on temporality and history, and both employ human bodies as signs. However, in other ways the poems could scarcely be more different, notably in Ronsard's depiction of the tensions between time and memory, between cosmic forces and human agency, and between distinct visions of the role of the court poet.

THE TEMPORALITY OF TURMOIL

Reflecting Ronsard's perennial obsession with time,[6] both poems include in their opening lines the words "le jour que," situating Mary's departure from France in the first instance and establishing the moment of humanity's fall into vice in the second. The different perceptions of time in the two poems illustrate an evolution both in the political landscape and in Ronsard's rhetorical approach:

> The day when your sail was swelled by the Zephyrs
> [Le jour que vostre voile aux Zephyrs se courba]
> And from our weeping eyes your eyes taken away
> That day, the same sail carried far from France
> The muses who were accustomed to dwelling there.
>   (Discours à elle mesme, lines 1-4 [my emphasis])[7]

> We must confess that ill-favored vice
> Is not victorious but retains the same form
> That it received the day when man was arrayed,
> [Qu'il receut dés le jour que l'homme fut vestu]
> Like clothing, in vice and vertu.[8]
>   (Discours à la Royne, lines 7-10 [my emphasis])

6. See, among others, Neil Kenny, *Death and Tenses: Posthumous Presence in Early Modern France* (Oxford: Oxford University Press, 2015), 200–204; Emmanuel Buron and Julien Gœury, *Lectures de Ronsard. Discours des misères de ce temps* (Rennes: Presses Universitaires de Rennes, 2009); Anne-Pascale Pouey-Mounou, *L'imaginaire cosmologique de Ronsard* (Geneva: Droz, 2002), 351–59 ; Cathy Yandell, *Time and Gender in Early Modern France* (Newark, DE: University of Delaware Press, 2000), 48–84; Malcolm Quainton, *Ronsard's Ordered Chaos: Visions of Flux and Stability in the Poetry of Pierre de Ronsard* (Manchester: Manchester University Press, 1980), 92–130; and Isidore Silver, *Three Ronsard Studies* (Geneva: Droz, 1978), 94–107.

7. All translations are mine.

8. Laum. 11:19 (lines 7-10)

The *Discours à elle-mesme* opens with two synecdochic images—one of the sail of Mary's ship as it slips away, and another of the poet's weeping eyes as he is deprived of the young queen's eyes. "Le jour que" inscribes a nostalgic moment simultaneously denoting past and present, both the memory of the young queen's departure and an admission of the poet's dearth of subject matter because the Muses, too, have departed with her. The *Discours à la Royne*, on the other hand, is situated in a postlapsarian temporality. In this passage, Ronsard critiques the pessimism of such Reformers as Pierre Viret who insist that vice is progressively taking over the world. The poet counters with a reply reminiscent of Castiglione: virtue and vice will always coexist in the world.[9] Ronsard thus begins with a trope frequently exploited by such contemporaneous artists and emblematists as Lorenzo Lotto, Paolo Veronese, and Barthélemy Aneau.[10] The poem opens with a refusal to see human history as a continual degeneration, as evidenced by the glorious annals of France and its kings, which Ronsard briefly recites:

> Ah, what will the souls of so many valiant kings say from beneath their dusty tombs below? / What will Pharamond say? Clodion and Clovis? / Our Pepins, our Martels, our Charleses, our Louis? / . . . What will so many dukes and men of war say, who were the first to die from wounds in combat? / And who suffered so many extreme hardships for France / Seeing it destroyed today by us? (lines 55-58; 61-64)

The *Discours à la Royne* unfolds in a temporal space between the past ("le jour que") and the future ("que diront[-ils]"), but not quite in the present: no verbs in the present tense appear in this passage. The frontispiece of the first edition of the *Discours* seems to echo Ronsard's recourse to history, yet without a clear future to apply it to, like the Greek sage Bias at the origin of this motto: "Omnia mea

9. Men are "alwayes coverynge a vyce with the name of the next vertue to it, and a vertue with the name of the nexte vice." See *The Courtyer of Baldessar Castilio . . . , done into Englyshe by Thomas Hoby* (London: Wyllyam Seres, 1561), n.p. https:// scholarsbank.uoregon.edu/xmlui/bitstream/handle/1794/671/courtier.pdf.

10. Lorenzo Lotto, *The Allegory of Virtue and Vice* (1505), http://www.nga.gov/ content/ngaweb/Collection/art-object-page.297.html; Barthélemy Aneau, *Picta poesis* (1552), "Virtutes ingenitas vitia erumpentia expellunt," http://www.emblems.arts.gla .ac.uk/french/emblem.php?id=FANa094; and Paolo Veronese, *The Choice Between Virtue and Vice* (ca. 1565), http://collections.frick.org/view/objects/asitem/items $0040:276.

mecum porto"—"All that is mine I carry with me"—or, as it might be said in the humanist tradition, "We are what we remember." As Edwin Duval notes, "[Ronsard's] purpose is [. . .] to impress upon his contemporaries the momentousness of the moment."[11] At the same time, the present in these verses lacks determinacy, suspended between the ancient kings' gaze and Ronsard's exhortations to Catherine for the future, much like the poet's own ambivalence about the decision either to seek peace or to wage war.

The rhetorical questions posed by Ronsard in this passage evoke rulers of France's monarchical past, without however ventriloquizing them, thus advancing both the poet's continuing political alignment with the Valois dynasty and his own oratorical dexterity. Yet the accusatory tone directed at Protestant adversaries in the later *Discours* is here absent: instead, Ronsard insists on France's internal self-destruction, castigating both sides of the conflict through his use of the word "nous" (us): "Seeing [France] destroyed today by us." Ronsard affirms his allegiance to the kingdom by bemoaning its current state, which he allegorizes in the form of a hybrid body.

ANATOMY AND HYBRIDITY

Contemporaneous readers of the *Discours* might have imagined that their literary culture had moved well beyond the *Blasons anatomiques du corps féminin* of the 1530s and 40s, but if so, they were mistaken. Much like musical *contrafacta*, love songs whose melodies were retrofitted to become Protestant hymns, so the amorous images of Ronsard's early sonnets take on a new political purpose in the *Discours*. As Malcolm Smith has noted, Ronsard's praise of Mary between 1558 and 1561 probably stems from his desire to cultivate the patronage of her uncle, the cardinal de Lorraine.[12] Although the two *Discours* to Mary and Catherine embody different political aims, both include anatomical blazons—in the first poem, a blazon of the body of the addressee Mary:

11. Edwin M. Duval, "The Place of the Present: Ronsard, Aubigné, and the *Misères de ce Temps*," in *Baroque Topographies: Literature/History/Philosophy*, Yale French Studies 80 (1991): 15.

12. Malcolm Smith, "Ronsard and Queen Elizabeth I," *Bibliothèque d'humanisme et Renaissance* 29 (1967): 98; rpt. *Renaissance Studies: Articles 1966–1994*, ed. Ruth Calder (Geneva: Droz, 1999), 15. See also John D. Staines, *The Tragic Histories of Mary Queen of Scots, 1560–1690: Rhetoric, Passions, and Political Literature* (Farnham, UK: Ashgate, 2009), 73–74.

When your beautiful lip where Nature placed a beautiful garden . . . /
When your starry eyes, two beautiful dwellings of Love . . . / When
your alabaster forehead and the gold of your hair . . . / When this
white ivory fills your breast / When your long and slender and delicate
hand . . . / When your beautiful waist and your beautiful figure/ Alas,
are no longer here! . . . / How could the voices of poets sing / When,
because of your parting, the Muses are silent? (*Discours à elle-mesme*,
lines 17-40)

The description of Mary conforms to the tradition of head-to-toe
anatomizing, and the anaphoric repetitions lend a litany-like quality
to the poet's description: "Quand vostre belle lévre . . . / Quand vos
yeux estoilez . . . / Quand votre front d'Albastre . . ." The temporally-
charged anaphora "quand," one of the two most frequently employed
words in the poem, evokes Mary's past presence. A detailed enumera-
tion rehearses the particular parts of her body that will be missed,
thus inscribing them in the poet's—and the reader's—memory. Concluding the sequence of "quand, quand . . . ," Ronsard queries whether
poets will ever be able to sing again in her absence. And yet, while
Mary's body parts appear to be scattered on distant shores (reminiscent of Petrarch's *Rime sparse*), at the end of the *Discours*, God *ex
machina* brings about a reassuring conclusion:

Thus God who cares for your Majesty / Brought about —a great miracle—the birth of your beauty / On a foreign shore, as something left /
Not for the eyes of man, but for his thoughts. (*Discours à elle-mesme*,
lines 17-39)

While nothing in the anatomical blazon explicitly distinguishes
Mary's body from those of the poet's other muses, the lyrical and the
political unite in the concluding verses of the poem, implicitly educ-
ing the queen's "two bodies" in the epithet "your Majesty."[13] The
young Scottish Queen will thus remain present in France—if not in
body, then in the poet's remembering. By extension, as long as Mary
remains alive in memory, the reader is invited to imagine that she
will also live on the page.

No such reassurance of the power of memory can be found in the
Discours à la Royne. Here the blazon of Mary's body is replaced not

13. Ernst Kantorowicz identifies the concept of a king's two distinct bodies in medieval thought: the body politic and the body natural. *The King's Two Bodies: A Study
in Medieval Political Theology* [1957] (Princeton: Princeton University Press, 2016).

by Catherine's body (which is most decidedly absent from the poem), but by that of allegorized "Opinion." Luc Racaut points out that the word "Opinion" does not signify a judgment or an idea in the context of sixteenth-century polemical pamphlets, but rather an entrenched view, belief, or doctrine.[14] Randle Cotgrave's 1611 dictionary also furnishes the translations "censure, sentence, doome."[15] The blazon of "Opinion" predictably serves quite a different purpose from that of Mary—but how does it function? Anne-Pascale Pouey-Mounou notes the composite nature of the personification of Opinion as it combines vegetal, animal, human, and meteorological elements, evoking the hybridity of a siren. In this "être de division"[16] (divided being), she argues, interiority and exteriority of the elements are inverted: the head is full of wind, for example, and its legs are lacking flesh and bones.[17] This amalgamated character in fact emblematizes the kingdom's disintegration and the upheavals described throughout the poem.

Personified Opinion's anatomy unfolds as follows:

She had the gaze of a haughty beast
With wind and smoke her head was filled
Her heart was steeped in vain affection [. . .]
Her face was beautiful, like a siren's
With sweet speech her mouth was filled,
Light, she had wings on her back,
Her legs and feet were neither of flesh nor of bone,
They were made of wool and tender cotton [. . .]
This monster I described sends France to war,
Begging help from Savoy and Spain,
And from the nation that, quick to sound the drums of war,
Drinks the wide Danube and the waves of the Rhine. (*Discours à la Royne*, lines 139–41, 143–47, 153–58)

The blazoned figure of Opinion seems to represent the monster of heresy, and by extension the Protestants. Opinion has arrived quietly

---

14. Luc Racaut, *Hatred in Print: Catholic Propaganda and Protestant Identity during the French Wars of Religion* (Aldershot, UK: Ashgate, 2002), 49.

15. Randle Cotgrave, *A Dictionarie of the French and English Tongues* (London: Adam Islip, 1611).

16. Anne-Pascale Pouey-Mounou, *L'imaginaire cosmologique de Ronsard* (Geneva: Droz, 2002), 405.

17. Ibid., 410.

and unexpectedly, like gods with woolen feet.[18] Yet in this first reference in the *Discours à la Royne*, the nature of the monster is not entirely clear: the poet rues foreign presence in the French conflict, yet he cites Savoie and Spain, both of which contributed Catholic forces, and Germany, whose citizens were engaged in both sides of the French civil war. Had the poet sought to indict uniquely Reformist foreigners, a reference to Geneva would have been unmistakable, but that city is nowhere evoked in the poem. Thus this "monstre" causing the breakdown of society seems to originate simply from elsewhere. A later reference attributes France's destruction to "l'erreur d'un estranger" (the error of a stranger [Luther]), thus clarifying which foreigner has contributed most egregiously to the conflict, without however naming him. "Le monde à l'envers" (the world upside down) ensues:

> L'artizan par ce monstre a laissé sa boutique,
> Le pasteur ses brebis, l'Advocat sa pratique,
> Sa nef le marinier: sa foire le marchand,
> Et par luy le preudhomme est devenu meschant.
> (*Discours à la Royne*, lines 167–170)

> [Because of this monster, the artisan has left his shop,
> The pastor his sheep, the lawyer his practice,
> His ship the mariner, his market the merchant,
> And because of him, the gentleman has become wicked.]

Although partially inspired by Virgil, this depiction clearly bears Ronsard's poetic imprimatur: not only does the passage portray an upside-down world in which the responsible figures—the artisan, the lawyer, the shepherd—have abandoned their posts, but a chiasmus records this upending in which subjects and objects are syntactically reversed. Given the syllepsis omitting the verb "laisser" in lines 168 and 169, the poem could be read as follows: the pastor has left his sheep, the lawyer his practice, the ship has left the mariner, the market the merchant. Thus the upheaval is not only described but also inscribed in these verses. While in the earlier blazon Mary Stuart's body is intact (both politically as reigning Queen of Scotland

18. This image comes from Porphyrion (a commentator of Horace) and also figures in Erasmus's *Adages*. See Emmanuel Buron, "L'Opinion dans les *Discours*," *Lectures de Ronsard: Discours des miseres de ce temps*, ed. Emmanuel Buron and Julien Gœury (Rennes: Presses universitaires de Rennes, 2009), 128.

and literarily as a "reconstructed" poetic memory), in the *Discours à la Royne*, Opinion's body—a monstrous composite—wreaks havoc in the kingdom. But significantly, the poem does not end there; instead, the poet intervenes.

NATURE AND FORTUNE, AGENCY, SUBJECTIVITY

The *Discours à elle-mesme* and the *Discours à la Royne* provide a treasure trove for vital materialists and the human-nonhuman assemblages they examine.[19] For the purposes of this study, I am particularly interested in the poet's rhetorical position as he faces the "confederate agency" of such forces as storms, shipwreck, hideous comets, driving rain, a monster, a wild pony, a swarm of bees, snakes, dust, thunder, and falling rocks. How does Ronsard's rhetorical response to these forces reveal his shifting political and poetical stance?

The two juxtaposed poems provide a microcosm of Ronsard's developing attitudes toward Nature and Fortune, and by extension, toward authority and subjectivity. Mary Stuart's departure is brought about most immediately by the sail that carried her away—in the vocabulary of vital materialism, the sail serves as an actant. No other agents or "operators" can be found at the beginning of the poem. Similarly, as the poet imagines parting the seas to visit her, he admits that "It is impossible to force Nature / . . . the Sea must enclose us in the waves" (lines 107–108), giving his full allegiance to natural phenomena. Finally, the "pointe" concluding the poem, as we have seen, holds that God has created Mary's beauty not to be seen, but to be contemplated and remembered. While the narrator regrets her departure, no rhetorical attempt is made to change the course of events. He praises Mary for her generous heart and indomitable courage, but ascribes the events to Fortune, who took the life of her young husband. The poem thus ends on a note of peaceful resignation.

In contrast, Catherine's authority, or lack thereof, is central to both the text and the subtext of the *Discours à la Royne*. As in the *Discours* to Mary Stuart, the forces of nature appear to be insurmountable, threatening the very existence of France:

Alas! My Lady, in this time when the cruel storm
Is threatening the French with such a pitiful shipwreck,

---

19. For a contemporary reading of nonhuman agency, see Jane Bennett, *Vibrant Matter* (Durham and London: Duke University Press, 2010), 20–38.

When the hail and the rain, and the fury of the heavens
Have disturbed the sea with seditious winds [. . .] (lines 43–46)

In this passage, the storm, hail, wind, and rain preside over the impending disaster of the shipwreck of France. But in contrast to the *Discours à elle-mesme*, here the poet urges Catherine to fight the forces of nature as helmswoman of the ship: "Take the rudder of this poor ship [. . .] and steer it safely to the harbor" ("Prenez le gouvernail de ce pauvre navire [. . .] et conduisez-le à bon port" [lines 48–50]). Projecting once again into the future in order to look back on the present, the poet bemoans the fact that historians will be forced to write "l'histoire monstrueuse" (the monstrous story/history) of the tumultuous times (lines 115–20).

Contemporary evidence corroborates the precariousness of Catherine's perceived authority. In a letter dated July 2, 1561, the Duc de Guise convinces Catherine that the Reformers are usurping her authority: "And these wretched men don't hesitate to fish in troubled waters, and furthermore, they dare to take advantage of your name and authority."[20] Ronsard is of course cognizant of these threats to Catherine's sovereignty from several opposing forces, but in this *Discours*, he still adheres to her and Chancellor Michel de L'Hospital's position that a peaceful solution should be found, and that the Valois will be stronger if the warring factions can reach an agreement.[21] To this end, nowhere in the *Discours* does the poet use the word "Huguenot," an injurious term that had been forbidden by the Royal Edict of 19 April 1561.[22] The word does, however, surface for the first time in Ronsard's *Remonstrance au peuple de France* of December 1562.[23] Moreover, as Isabelle Garnier has shown, not until the *Remonstrance* does Ronsard challenge Protestants on their own linguistic terrain,

20. François de Lorraine, duc de Guise, "A Monsieur le duc de Wirtemberg," *Bulletin de la Société de l'histoire du protestantisme français* 24 (1875): 72.

21. See Yandell, "Rhetorics of Peace: Ronsard and Michel de L'Hospital on the Eve of the French Wars of Religion," *Itineraries in French Renaissance Literature*, ed. George Hoffmann, Jeff Persels, and Kendall Tarte (Leiden: Brill, forthcoming 2018).

22. See Sylvie Daubresse, *Le parlement de Paris, ou, La voix de la raison: (1559–1589)* (Geneva: Droz, 2005), 81, and Linda C. Taber, *Royal Policy and Religious Dissent within the Parlement of Paris 1559-1563* (Palo Alto, CA: Stanford University Press, 1982), 147–59.

23. *Remonstrance au peuple de France*, lines 212–14, Laum. 11:75; Pl. 2:1025.

using what she calls a *parler protestant*—such terms as "L'Eternel" to designate God and "Christ" instead of "Jésus-Christ."[24]

Another corroboration of Ronsard's attempt to shore up Catherine's power and to promote a peaceful solution can be seen in the fact that Ronsard never uses the term "religion" in the *Discours à la Royne*. His position echoes the perspective of Michel de L'Hospital, who argued in his speech to the Estates General in August of 1561 that the state's interest should not be in curbing religious differences, but rather in maintaining peace and allegiance to the crown: "I do not wish to debate the controversies of religion, by appropriating the judgment of said people of the Church [. . .] but only what pertains to policy, to keep the people in peace and tranquility."[25]

Finally, Ronsard buttresses Catherine's early position of uniting the kingdom under a single faith by insisting on the political rather than on the religious nature of the uprisings. The Edict of January 1562 forbids the destruction of images and crosses and other "scandalous and seditious acts."[26] Note that iconoclastic acts are described as seditious and not sacrilegious. In the quatrain cited above, Ronsard, too, insists on mutiny and sedition rather than on heresy by referring to the seas being troubled by the "seditious winds." This hypallage stands in for rebellious citizens, who are also described in the poem as "the mutinous people." Given these political threats to royal power, the poet urges Catherine throughout the poem to assume her rightful authority: "by your authority calm the maleficence"; "the sole dignity of [. . .] your authority."

Despite the poet's exhortations to the Queen, Daniel Ménager argues that in this poem humans are dwarfed by the forces of nature: "History does not belong to men, because it is subject to a determinism whose model is found in nature."[27] In Ménager's defense, the threat of a metaphorical shipwreck of the kingdom of France does

24. Isabelle Garnier, "Héritage marotique et parler protestant dans les *Discours des misères de ce temps*," *Ronsard, poète militant. Discours des misères de ce temps*, ed. Véronique Duché (Paris: Presses universitaires de France, 2009), 68.

25. Michel de l'Hospital, *Œuvres complètes*, ed. P.J.S. Duféy (Paris: Boulland et Ce, 1824), 1:449.

26. http://elec.enc.sorbonne.fr/editsdepacification/html/editsdepacification.html#edit_01.

27. Daniel Ménager, *Ronsard: le roi, le poète et les hommes* (Geneva: Droz, 1979), 202.

suggest a deterministic reading. However, in this *Discours* we see that the poet's position has shifted away from the reverence for *natura naturans* of the *Hymnes*,[28] away from the nostalgic acceptance observed in the poem to Mary Stuart, and toward a clearer expression of human agency faced with nature, as the following lines suggest: "But you, wise Queen, in seeing this conflict / Can, by commanding it, make them all agree" (lines 197–98).

The poet's urging of divine intervention serves paradoxically as another example of human agency. "Donne" (grant) in the second-person imperative constitutes the most repeated verb in the *Discours à la Royne*. At first glance, calling for God's intervention would seem to denote a dearth of human power, yet the poet exhorts God to enact a very specific program, with nine anaphoric instances of "donne que": make it so that the Queen becomes powerful, make it so that the two camps are appeased:

> Grant (I beg you) that this Queen mother / May appease the anger of the two camps / Grant me that henceforth her powerful scepter / Flourish in arms, despite the discord. . . . / Grant that this monster's barbarous fury / Retreat far from France to the shore of the river Tartar. (lines 215–20)

The poet's insistence on the Queen's dominion is of course more prescriptive than descriptive, more aspirant than accurate, but the poet fashions for her in these verses a "powerful scepter." The figure of hypallage functions further to bestow sovereignty on the Queen through the metonymy of the scepter. But the Queen's agency is not the only potentially powerful force evoked in the *Discours à la Royne*: the poet's own ability to intervene is at stake in his pronouncements, entreaties, and pleadings throughout the poem.

---

28. An anonymous fourteenth-century text, translated from the Latin and printed by (and sometimes attributed to) Philippe Le Noir and republished three times in the 1520s and 30s, succinctly defines "Natura naturans" as the controlling force of the sublunar universe: "*Natura naturans* is of such a nature that all natures are made and sustained by it." *Sensuit le cueur de philosophie: contenant plusieurs demandes et questions proposees par le saige Placides au philosophe Tymeo, et les responces co[n]tenuz en icelluy* . . . (Paris: Philippe Le Noir, 1530). Ronsard describes nature's powers in similar terms, as in this passage from "Le tombeau de Marguerite de France" of 1574: "For Nature and God are almost the same thing: / God reigns everywhere as an absolute Prince / (Nature) executes what God intended / His order is a strong, solid oak" (Laum. 17:80; Pl. 2:904).

The nostalgic poet who resigns himself to Mary Stuart's departure as Nature's course in the *Discours à elle-mesme* has given way to a determined counselor of Catherine de Medici in the *Discours à la Royne*. Certainly the circumstances motivating the two poems examined in this study are remarkably different. Nonetheless, Ronsard makes a rhetorical shift from a sense of natural order to a recognition of social chaos, from nostalgia to pragmatism, from resignation to resolve, and from an acceptance of Nature's immutable force to the positing of human ability to act (even against overwhelming odds). Within the space of these two *Discours*, Ronsard addresses royal figures who textually mediate the poet's political and poetic positions as he moves from the relatively uncomplicated lyric clarity of a past moment to the challenging indeterminacy of the present.

Ronsard, the self-described "chantre de tant de roys,"[29] had clear political motives for writing "occasional" verses to these Queens. Yet his poetic authority glimpsed in the *Discours à la Royne* adumbrates the rhetorical tour de force of the *Response aux injures et calomnies* (written in April 1563) in which Ronsard demolishes his critics and illustrates both explicitly and implicitly his poetic virtuosity ("You are my subjects, I am your only Law; you are my streams, I am your fountain."[30]). This authorial turn may also account for the circumscription of the poet's allegiance. after the Saint Bartholomew's Day Massacre of 1572, Ronsard never praised the Catholic "victory," nor did he write any other pugilistic poems on behalf of the Catholic cause. On the contrary, Ronsard's notable silence on the matter serves to underscore his claim in the *Franciade* that, unlike the historian, the poet writes not to record but "for beauty, for the splendor of the verses."[31] The evolution of Ronsard's authorial voice and the marshaling of rhetorical strategies in these poems addressed to Mary and Catherine uncover a greater design: polemics in the service of poetry.

29. "Elegie à Mylord Robert Du-Dlé," Laum. 13:73, line 250; the verse containing this expression was excised in the edition of 1584.

30. Ronsard, *Response aux injures*, Laum. 11:169, line 1039; Pl. 2:1066, line 974.

31. Posthumous preface to *La Franciade*, Laum.16:332; Pl. 1:1162.

JESSICA DeVOS

Ronsard's Poetic Progeny: Fashioning Madeleine de l'Aubespine's Literary Persona

Shortly after Madeleine de l'Aubespine's death in 1596, François Le Poulchre, seigneur de La Motte-Messemé wrote of how she "was esteemed even by Ronsard, Prince of our Poets, for her learning."[1] While l'Aubespine and Ronsard's personal and poetic affinity was widely-known among their contemporaries, their friendship and mutual admiration had been largely forgotten by modern scholars until Anna Klosowska's 2007 publication of a bilingual edition of l'Aubespine's poetry.[2] My examination of the poetic exchange between l'Aubespine and Ronsard is greatly indebted to and builds upon Klosowska's study of these poems. I share with her the belief that l'Aubespine's corpus challenges modern preconceptions regarding the forms of lyric expression available and permissible to Renaissance women authors and forces us to reconsider many of the differences we assume existed between the roles accorded to male and female poets within literary culture. However, while Klosowska has astutely examined questions of sex, gender, and subjectivity in l'Aubespine's verse from the theoretical perspectives of queer and cultural studies, in this article I examine the ways in which l'Aubespine's Petrarchism (or, rather, anti-Petrarchism) and poetic persona are influenced by her personal and poetical relationship with Ronsard. I begin by briefly analyzing how both poets entered into

1. "Cette de l'Aubespine [...] estoit estimée mesmes de Ronsard Prince de noz Poëtes pour son sçavoir." François Le Poulchre de La Motte-Messemé, *Le passe-temps*, ed. Brigitte Lourde (Paris: Champion, 2008), 103. Unless otherwise noted, all English translations of verse and prose are my own.
2. *Madeleine de l'Aubespine: Selected Poems and Translations*, trans. and ed. Anna Klosowska (Chicago: University of Chicago Press, 2007). All English translations of l'Aubespine's verse are Klosowska's. Page numbers after citations from l'Aubespine are to this edition.

YFS 134, *The Construction of a National Vernacular Literature in the Renaissance: Essays in Honor of Edwin M. Duval,* ed. DeVos and Hayes, © 2018 by Yale University.

an intertextual dialogue with the opening sonnet of Petrarch's *Canzoniere* in order to establish their distinct authorial identities and highlight how l'Aubespine's adaptation of the famous opening sonnet is mediated by Ronsard's 1560 *Élégie to* Cassandre. I then focus on the final decade of Ronsard's life and career, in order to better appreciate his transfer of specific key *topoi* (which he had previously reserved for himself and other members of the Pléaide) to his *fille d'alliance*.

RONSARD AND L'AUBESPINE, ANTI-PETRARCHISTS

One cannot overemphasize the widespread influence of the word "error" throughout the Renaissance world. As François Rigolot reminds us:

> Error belongs to all ages, but has perhaps never mobilized as much energy, sparked as much passion, and seen as many manifestations, in the end, as during a time that we continue to call, somewhat arbitrarily, the Renaissance. [...] The Renaissance was to take great pleasure in cataloging this hodgepodge before the philosophical status of error was nailed down by rationalist discourse.[3]

The word dominates both the sermons of Calvinist preachers ranting against the teachings of Rome and the retaliatory invective of Catholic priests. It is used to describe the navigational mistakes of ships sailing vast uncharted waters, as well as the misplaced inquiries of Rabelais's *sophistes* and *curieux*. Wherever one ventures in the Renaissance world, one encounters a very specific verbal reminder that *errare humanum est*.

Yet while the *topos* of error is omnipresent in Renaissance writings, its source in sixteenth-century French sonnet sequences can be traced to one man: Petrarch. Renaissance readers understood Petrarch's *Canzoniere* as a retrospective narrative tracing the poet's initial *innamoramento*, followed by his introspection and struggle to regain psychological self-mastery before finally sublimating his earthly attachment into Christian devotion. The initial apology of the first sonnet served as both a spiritual confession on the part of the poetic persona and a *captatio benevolentiae* on the part of the author. Petrarch begins by addressing an anonymous and eternal audience—"Voi, ch'ascoltate"

---

3. François Rigolot, *L'erreur de la Renaissance: Perspectives littéraires* (Paris: Honoré Champion, 2002), 7-8.

(You who hear).[4] This simple introduction has become so closely associated with Petrarch's opening sonnet that it is often used as a shorthand for the entire poem. His descriptions of the organization and content of the collection have also become exemplary signifiers both of the *Canzoniere* and of Petrarchan poetics—the poems are "rime sparse" (scattered rhymes) (I.1) that recount his "primo giovenile errore" (first youthful error) (I.3). The error to which he refers was his amorous attachment to Laura, who received the devotion that should have been directed to God. In the retrospective opening sonnet, however, Petrarch seeks to distance himself from his adolescent ways by emphasizing that these events took place "quand'era in parte altr'uom da quel ch'i' sono" (when I was in part another man from what I am now) (I.4). The second quatrain presents examples of what we now refer to as Petrarchan opposition—the simultaneous existence of conflicting sentiments or sensations. The author also expresses his desire to locate an indulgent audience that might forgive his youthful transgressions. In the tercets, he traces the humiliation he now feels upon realizing that his previous behavior made him the talk of the town. This public shaming contributes to his conviction that the pleasures of this world are a "breve sogno" (brief dream) (I.14).

In addition to popularizing the sonnet as a poetic form, the *Canzoniere* introduced a fiction, a framework, and a vocabulary that innumerable writers across Europe imitated and innovated. Although much more can and indeed has been said about the opening sonnet of the *Canzoniere* and its influence on French verse,[5] I wish to limit my present analysis to a brief summary of an early instance in which Ronsard forged his own literary persona through an intertextual dialogue with Petrarch's poem. I will then situate Madeleine de l'Aubespine's "Mon cœur, c'est trop langui sans espoir d'allegence" within this same context of poetic self-fashioning.

4. All English translations of the *Canzoniere* are from *Petrarch's Lyric Poems: The* Rime Sparse *and Other Lyrics*, trans. and ed. Robert M. Durling (Cambridge: Harvard University Press, 1997).

5. While there are many excellent studies on this topic, I am particularly indebted to Edwin Duval's "Wresting Petrarch's Laurels: Scève, Du Bellay, and the Invention of the *Canzoniere*" in *Renaissance Transactions and Exchanges*, ed. William J. Kennedy, special issue, *Annals of Scholarship* 16/1-3: 53-73 (2005), in which Duval examines how Scève and Du Bellay imitate and challenge Petrarch in their opening poems as well as in the ordering of their collections.

One of Ronsard's most direct responses to Petrarch's opening sonnet concludes the 1560 edition of *Les amours*. It is a poem in which themes of nationalism are interwoven with traditional lyric elements as Ronsard seeks to "domesticate" his Italian predecessor. The elegy can be divided into two distinct movements. Ronsard begins by exhorting Cassandre to find another poet willing to sing her praises. Although he evokes Cassandre's ungratefulness in line sixteen, the main cause of Ronsard's poetic struggle in the first half of the poem is the relative inferiority of French verse compared to the Latin works of Rome. He explains that the inadequacy of his verse is due to the fact that France was not "planté" (sown) (l.6) with a bountiful crop of poetic models that he could harvest. Cassandre must instead be content with local fame, like Petrarch's beloved in Tuscany. The irony is, of course, that Petrarch's "Laura" had already eclipsed the previously privileged Latin models of female beloveds, including Tibullus's Delia: "Tu serois tant leüe / Que si Tibull' t'avoit pour sienne esleue" (You would be as widely read / as if Tibullus had elected you his own) (ll.7-8).

Line nineteen, the mid-point of the poem, marks a rupture with the preceding half signaled by the adverb "toutefois" (nevertheless). Throughout the second half of the elegy Ronsard evokes and reworks elements of Petrarch's opening sonnet. Like Petrarch, "celui qui scait que nostre vie / N'est rien que vent, que songe, et que folye" (He who knows that our life / Is but wind, illusion, and folly) (ll.35-36), Ronsard realizes that our time on earth, when governed by worldly attachments, is but a "songe" or "sogno" (I.14). Ronsard also confesses that the remnants of his spent youth are scattered "Deça delà dedans ce livre icy" (Here and there in this book) (l.33). This line echoes Petrarch who prepares his readers to hear the "rime sparse" (I.1) about his "primo giovenile errore" (I.3).

Yet in this second half of the elegy Ronsard enters into conversation with his predecessor in order to alter the fundamentals of Petrarchan poetics. Ronsard further underscores how he inverts his Italian model by placing his most direct response to Petrarch's opening sonnet at the end of his collection. The French poet's attention shifts from recounting his own past defeats to predicting the future of his beloved. As time takes its toll on Cassandre (as it has already done on the beleaguered poet), she will regret the suffering she inflicted on her admirer:

> Et toutefois je m'asseure, quand l'age
> Aura donté l'orgueil de ton courage,
> Que de mon mal tu te repentiras
> Et qu'à la fin tu te convertiras.
>
> [And nevertheless, I am certain, that when age
> Subdues the pride of your fortitude,
> You shall repent of my pain
> And in the end you shall change.] (ll.19-22)

Until Cassandre realizes the error of her ways, however, she will continue to take sadistic pleasure in his amorous affliction:

> Et ce pendant je souffriray la peine,
> Toy le plaisir d'une liesse veine
> De trop me veoir languir en ton amour[.]
>
> [And in the meantime, I shall suffer the pain
> You, the pleasure, of vain happiness
> Of watching me languish in love.] (ll.23-25)

Ronsard then describes details the sympathetic reaction his verses will receive from readers who have experienced similar trials in love:

> Ceux qui amour cognoissent par espreuve,
> Lisant le mal dans lequel je me treuve,
> Ne pardon'ront à ma simple amytié
> Tant seulement, mais en auront pitié.
>
> [Those who know love through experience,
> Reading my current suffering,
> Will not only pardon my honest affections
> But will also pity my situation.] (ll. 27-30)

This translation of Petrarch's "ove sia chi per prova intenda amore, / spero travar pietà, non che perdono" (where there is anyone who understands love through experience, I hope to find pity, not only pardon) (I.7-8) differs in one significant aspect from its source. While Petrarch merely hopes to find forgiveness from an indulgent public, Ronsard uses the future indicative tense to confirm that his readers will both pardon him and pity his fate. This elegy was added eight years after the initial publication of *Les amours*. Ronsard had indeed been vindicated as his verse had earned him renown and he asserts that it is now Cassandre who has committed an "error" for which she will be punished. Instead of humbly supplicating his beloved, or expressing remorse to his audience, Ronsard turns the tables on Petrarchan poetics. Such inversions appealed to Ronsard's poetic protégé, Madeleine de l'Aubespine, whose own verse continues the transformations introduced by her "père Apollon."

L'Aubespine's response to Petrarch's opening sonnet, "Mon cœur, c'est trop langui sans espoir d'allegence," is highly mediated by the second half of Ronsard's elegy in which the poet critiqued his beloved for her aloofness. L'Aubespine writes:

Mon cœur, c'est trop langui sans espoir d'allegence,
C'est bannir trop longtemps les plaisirs gratieux,
C'est trop suivre un ingrat sans raison et sans yeux,
Qui de tes beaux desirs n'eust jamais cognoissance.

Retire toy, mon coeur, pers en toute esperance,
Et ne te genne plus, pensant forcer les cieux.
Sans perdre ainsi le temps, tu feras beaucoup mieux,
D'une plus doulce vie ayant la joyssance.

Adieu donc pour jamais, doux attraictz mes vainqueurs,
Qui m'avez faict souffrir tant d'amaires langueurs:
De vostre ingrattitude enfin je me rebelle.

Un jour de cest erreur vous vous repentirez.
Et ce pendant, mon coeur, heureux vous joyrez
D'une ame obeissante, amoureuse et fidelle.

[My heart, too long you've languished without hope of relief,
You've banished for too long pleasurable delights,
You have followed too long a senseless, blind ingrate,
Who was never aware of your lovely desires.

Draw away, O my heart, abandon every hope,
Distress yourself no more, thinking you'll change your fate.
Don't squander time, you'll be much better off
If you choose to enjoy a sweeter life than that.

Adieu forevermore, sweet attractions, my foes,
Who caused me to endure so many bitter pains;
Against your ingratitude at last I have rebelled.

A day will come when you will regret having erred.
And meanwhile, you, my heart, will happily enjoy
The pleasure of a docile, loving, and faithful soul.

The conventional *belle dame sans merci*, whom the male poet implores to return his affections, is here replaced by a masculine "ingrat." By remaining aloof and withholding his favors, this man is playing the role traditionally attributed to the ungrateful and inaccessible lady. And like her male Petrarchan counterparts, the female speaker laments that an unreciprocated passion has caused her to languish.

In the first tercet, she evokes her beloved through the "doux attraictz" that have conquered her. This identification is further reinforced by the rime between *traictz* and *attraictz*, which suggests Cupid's arrows issuing forth from the eyes of the beloved. Line twelve serves as the poem's rhetorical *pointe*, privileging the main *point* of the poem: "Un jour de cest erreur vous vous repentirez," where the "vous" who will repent refers to the preceding plural "attraictz."[6] Like Ronsard's reproach of Cassandre, it is once again the beloved, not the poet, who will some day repent of his or her error, and when l'Aubespine employs the shorthand by which French Renaissance poets designated all things Petrarchan ("erreur"), she simultaneously rejects unrequited passion as well as its Petrarchan expression. The final four lines of her sonnet contain a series of three independent clauses, all held together through their *rime embrassée*. Any one of these clauses would suffice to forcefully conclude a sonnet. Yet the brusque, almost brutal, tone of lines eleven and twelve bring the poem to a fatalistic culmination. One can envision the poet slamming the door on Petrarch before walking away from courtly tradition.

"Mon coeur, c'est trop langui sans espoir d'allegence" only circulated in manuscript form during l'Aubespine's lifetime; thus we cannot know with any certainty the position she would have liked it to occupy in a published collection of her works.[7] Its placement

---

6. An interpretative challenge arises in the final two lines of the sonnet when it becomes unclear to whom the poet is speaking. Throughout the poem, l'Aubespine addresses her own heart with the informal pronoun "tu." In line thirteen, she adopts the formal "vous" when promising her "cœur" that it will enjoy "une ame obeissante, amoureuse et fidelle" (14). Perhaps l'Aubepsine intended to frame her sonnet with addresses to two separate hearts—one with which she is familiar (her own) and one from which she has been estranged (her beloved's)—thus underscoring the fragmentation and ambiguity that blight ideal Petrarchan and Platonic love. While it is beyond the scope of the current study, these two lines certainly invite a Duvalian decoding.

7. Klosowska's edition of l'Aubespine's collected works follows the order established in Biblioteca Nazionale MS M.IV.12, a posthumous collection that was held

within extant manuscripts, however, contributes to the meaning of the collection as a whole and to the formation of a poetic persona that is quite distinct from that of Petrarch. In both the Turin manuscript and BnF MS 1718, the poem appears toward the beginning of the collection. It is preceded by sonnets that express the poet's repentance and her Christian struggle to renounce earthly pleasures. Deprived of divine intervention when the fever she hoped would end her life and suffering lifts, the poet takes matters into her own hands, declaring "c'est trop langui sans espoir d'allegence." L'Aubespine will henceforth celebrate corporeal pleasures without the slightest misgiving. Instead of progressively striving to sublimate earthly attachments, l'Aubespine begins her mini-*canzoniere* by renouncing a particularly Petrarchan psychological and spiritual struggle.

In his 1926 edition of l'Aubespine's works, Roger Sorg places these religious poems in a separate section at the *end* of the collection under the title "Sonnets Chretiens." Adopting Ann Rosalind Jones's theory of "bad press,"[8] Klosowska explains Sorg's editorial practice in the following manner:

> The arrangement of l'Aubespine's poems into a narrative of a love affair (with Desportes, Sorg suggests) ending in spiritual redemption (pious poems) is not accidental. Instead, it reflects a pervasive editorial practice in the nineteenth and twentieth centuries among scholars editing early modern women. In the title of one of her essays, Ann Rosalind Jones calls this practice "bad press," because it detracts from the content of the poems and their literary value and emphasizes the putative biography of the woman author. The fact that these biographies are identical for every woman author across

---

in the Turin Library. The manuscript was destroyed in a 1904 fire, but the library's former director, Bernardino Peyron, had compiled a nine-page description of the volume, a copy of which is now held in France at the Bibliothèque Nationale. While this description provides an index of l'Aubespine's works, it does not contain the poems themselves. Klosowska therefore takes the actual text from several manuscripts held in France, the florilegium BnF MS fr. 1718 being the most comprehensive. When Peyron's index to the posthumous volume provides no information, she follows the order of BnF MS fr. 1718.

8. Anne Rosalind Jones, "Bad Press: Modern Editors Versus Early Modern Women Poets (Tullia d'Aragona, Gaspara Stampa, Veronica Franco)," in *Strong Voices, Weak History: Early Modern Women Writers and Canons in England. France, and Italy*, ed. Pamela Joseph Benson and Victoria Kirkham (Ann Arbor: University of Michigan Press, 2005), 287-313.

geographic and time divides—they always involve love, rejection and pious repentance—almost certainly means that they do not reflect reality.[9]

Klosowska is correct. These poems do not "reflect reality," but neither do they reveal a uniquely feminine sensibility, as Jones often suggests. Rather, they reflect (and refract) Petrarchan poetics.

In addition to the "bad press" explanation proposed by Jones and Klosowska, I would like to suggest another, literary motivation for Sorg's editorial choice. By placing the spiritual sonnets of repentance at the end of the collection, Sorg is not dismissing the literary value of l'Aubespine's poems; he is transforming her into a Petrarchan poet—an identity that she firmly renounces throughout her collection. Moreover, these editorial practices were not solely imposed upon the works of women authors. By fashioning a love affair between Desportes and l'Aubespine, Sorg *also* reduces the male author's poems to an autobiographical narrative.[10] Nor are Sorg's editorial practices exclusive to the nineteenth and twentieth centuries. Petrarch's own sixteenth-century editors reordered his *rime sparse* in an array of constellations in order to create various literary personae. Much like Sorg's approach, Alessandro Vellutello's 1525 *Il Petrarcha* separated the love poems from the others and rearranged the sequence to fit a biographical narrative. This version of Petrarch's persona was clearly appreciated by l'Aubespine's contemporaries, as it was the most frequently reprinted commentary during the sixteenth century.[11]

The presumed ordering of l'Aubespine's own sonnet sequence suggests, however, that she was moving away from certain Petrarchan fictions at a moment when aesthetic preferences were also shifting toward new forms of poetic expression. Her poems do not necessarily prove that women poets were obliged to "invert" Petrarchan poetics in order to speak in a female voice. Rather, these literary innovations provide evidence that she shared the widespread ambivalence regarding the potency and purpose of language that characterized late

9. Klosowska, Introduction to *Madeleine de l'Aubespine: Selected Poems and Translations*, 12.

10. Roger Sorg, Introduction to *Les chansons de Callianthe, fille de Ronsard* (Paris: Léon Pichon, 1926), 12-17.

11. William J. Kennedy, *The Site of Petrarchism: Early Modern National Sentiment in Italy, France, and England* (Baltimore and London: Johns Hopkins University Press, 2003), 3.

sixteenth-century poetry. I would now like to turn my attention to l'Aubespine's poetic exchanges with Pierre de Ronsard, in which Ronsard recognizes her literary talents and awareness of these contemporary aesthetic preferences.

THE SON AND DAUGHTER OF FRANCE'S *PRINCE DES POÈTES*

In 1584, the sixth edition of Ronsard's *Œuvres*, the last to be published during his lifetime, appeared in print. In this massive tome, Ronsard prefaces the section containing his *Amours diverses* with a dedicatory epistle to l'Aubespine's husband, Nicolas de Neufville, Lord of Villeroy. Thomas Greene once described this complex poem published a year before the author's death as "a valedictory farewell to poetry, to love, and more broadly to the active life at court the poet had spasmodically pursued throughout most of his mature career."[12] Although Ronsard had been bemoaning his old age and graying hair for much of his poetic career (he published his elegy to Cassandre, in which he mentions his "cheveus gris," at the ripe old age of thirty-six), his friendship with Villeroy and l'Aubespine did coincide with the autumn of his life and his laments take on a new urgency in these verses. If we accept the poet's claim in the second line of the dedicatory epistle that he is writing at age fifty-six, it is 1578 and the "guerres, debats, tantost tréves et paix," (wars, disputes, at times truces and peace) (l.15) evoked throughout the poem describe the nearly two decades of violent civil war that had racked the French nation. Emphasizing that his own end is near, Ronsard explains that the *Amours diverses* are his swan song and his final gift to a man—Villeroy—who remains a unique light of virtue in war-torn, apocalyptic France.

In a subsequent sonnet, Ronsard entrusts Villeroy with *La Franciade*, the unfinished national epic that should have extolled a unified French identity, but that never came to fruition. Punning on his patron's last name, Ronsard explains that Villeroy is worthy of serving as custodian of his poem since he too is "royal": "Mon livre plein de Rois, tout Royal comme luy, / C'est à son nom de Roy donner les Rois de France" (My book filled with Kings, royal like him, / To his name

---

12. Thomas Greene, "An Overshadowed Valediction: Ronsard's Dedicatory Epistle to Villeroy" in *Distant Voices Still Heard: Contemporary Readings of French Literature*, ed. John O'Brien and Malcolm Quainton (Liverpool: Liverpool University Press, 2000), 171.

of King I give the Kings of France) (II.13-14). This acknowledgment of Villeroy's nobility is preceded by a juxtaposition between the maca-bre fate awaiting France and the city ("Ville") over which his patron virtuously "governs." Ronsard thus evokes in this sonnet a political and geographical space that serves as an alternative to the French court of Henri III. The *Amours diverses* also contain a sonnet praising Villeroy's personal estate and residence, which Ronsard describes as a "chasteau fée" (fairy castle) (VII.9). Indeed, Ronsard's close alliance with the couple seemed to provide a harbor in the tempest of the Wars of Religion, their home serving as "un rempart, un fort contre le vice, / Où la Vertu maistresse se retire" (a rampart, a fortress against vice, / Where mistress Virtue resides) (VII.5-6).

If creating an imaginary space where Ronsard can seek physical and political refuge provides a partial resolution to his dilemmas, what re-mains of the poetic ambitions he once pursued at court? When Ron-sard declares "Il est temps de laisser les vers et les amours, / Et de prendre congé du plus beau de mes jours" (It is time to abandon poetry and love, / And to take leave of the most beautiful of my days) (ll.3-4), Greene rightly wondered "what status a poetic text could claim which begins by renouncing poetry."[13] Although Ronsard alluded to a possible solution: "J'ay couru mon flambeau sans me donner esmoy, / Le bail-lant à quelcun s'il recourt après moy" (I carried my torch while running without worry / Handing it off to someone who might follow after me), the torch is not passed until three years later, in the sonnet "Madelene ostez moy ce nom de l'Aubespine," which was included among the *Gayetez* in the posthumous 1587 version of Ronsard's *Œuvres*. This is where Ronsard designates l'Aubespine as his poetic successor.

One might initially wonder why this sonnet was not included alongside the poetic panegyric to her husband in the 1584 version. The absence of verses to l'Aubespine in the *Amours diverses* might be explained by their inclusion in another collection: the aforemen-tioned posthumous volume of l'Aubespine's complete works held in the Turin Library. In this manuscript, the sonnet from Ronsard was a *proposta* initiating a poetic exchange with l'Aubespine. In addition to her *risposta*, there was a final concluding poem by Ronsard, a tercet of which Anna Klosowska rediscovered and included in her 2007 edition of l'Aubespine's works. In her introduction to this edition, Klosowska

13. Greene, 172.

explains that the volume contained similar poetic exchanges with other authors, typical of other sixteenth-century collections of poetry. For example, when presenting Tullia di Aragona's poetry, Julia L. Hairston suggests that such collaborative poetic production "is perhaps best described by the term 'choral anthology' because it contains both sonnets and other forms of verse by d'Aragona as well as poems addressed to her by other poets. [...] This chorality emblematizes the social nature of Petrarchism[.]"[14]

When discussing French Renaissance women and lyric poetry, our first step is usually to articulate whether we are examining women *authors* speaking as "subjects of desire"—as Deborah Lesko Baker once labeled Louise Labé—or female beloveds, the silent objects of male representation, modeled on Petrarch's Laura. However, as Hairston suggests and Marina Zancan has shown,[15] this binary opposition becomes destabilized when we consider collaboration between male and female poets. For example, in the case of Vittoria Colonna and Michelangelo, the Marchesa di Pescara successfully promoted an idealized and ideological representation of herself by serving simultaneously as both the object of Michelangelo's poetic portraits as well as the subject of her own spiritual verse. Similar examples can be found in the works of dozens of Italian female *petrarchiste* and it is within such a framework that it is most useful to approach l'Aubespine's collaborative work with Ronsard.

Ronsard begins their poetic exchange by celebrating l'Aubespine's poetic talent and praising her verse:

> Madelene, ostez moy ce nom de l'Aubespine,
> Et prenez en sa place et Palmes et Lauriers,
> Qui croissent sur Parnasse en verdeur les premiers,
> Dignes de prendre en vous et tiges et racine.
>
> Chef couronné d'honneur, rare et chaste poitrine,
> Où naissent les vertus et les arts à milliers,
> Et les dons d'Apollon qui vous sont familiers,
> Si bien que rien de vous, que vous-mesme n'est digne,

14. Julia L. Hairston, introduction to *The Poems and Letters of Tullia d'Aragona and Others* (Toronto: Center for Reformation and Renaissance Studies, 2014), 48.

15. Marina Zancan, "La donna," in *Letteratura italiana: le questioni*, ed. Alberto Asor Rosa (Turin: Einaudi, 1986), vol. 5, 803–811.

Je suis en vous voyant heureux et malheureux:
Heureux de voir vos vers, ouvrage genereux,
Et malheureux de voir ma Muse qui se couche

Dessous vostre Orient. Ô saint germe nouveau
De Pallas, prenez cueur: les Soeurs n'ont assez d'eau
Sur le mont d'Helicon pour laver vostre bouche.

[Madeleine, for my sake, shed the name of hawthorn,
And accept in its place both palms and laurels
That grow on Mount Parnassus, first in greenness and bloom,
Worthy to take their stalk and their root in you.

Head crowned with honor, O rare and chaste breast,
Where arts and virtues are born by the thousands,
And the gifts of Apollo, so familiar to you
That nothing is worthy of you but yourself,

Seeing you, I am both happy and unhappy;
Happy to see your verse, generous work,
And unhappy to see my muse who's setting

Beneath your Orient. O holy new seed
Of Athena, take heart: the Sisters don't have enough
Water on Mount Helicon to moisten your mouth.][16]

One can easily envision Ronsard's poem as a prefatory sonnet to l'Aubespine's own collected works had she chosen to publish them. In the first quatrain, he urges l'Aubespine to shed her family name of "hawthorn." She should instead be crowned with the exemplary palms and laurels that grow on Mount Parnassus, the residence of the Muses. It is a commonplace of Renaissance poetry to select a poetic model by evoking the botanical crown to which it is related allegorically. Consider, for example, the opening sonnet of Du Bellay's *L'Olive*:

Je ne quiers pas la fameuse couronne,
Sainct orenement du Dieu au chef doré,
Ou que du Dieu aux Indes adoré
Le gay chapeau la teste m'environne.

Encores moins veulx-je que l'on me donne
Le mol rameau en Cypre decoré:

16. Klosowska, 56–57.

Celuy qui est d'Athenes honoré,
Seul je le veulx, et le Ciel me l'ordonne.

[I do not seek the famous crown
The holy vestment of the golden-haired god,
Or from the god worshipped in the East
To wear his merry hat.

Even less do I wish to be given
The limp branch that adorns Cyprus
That which is honored in Athens
Is all I want, and the Heavens ordain it.]

After rejecting the most famous crown shared by Apollo and Petrarch, Du Bellay proceeds to decline the ivy of Bacchus and the myrtle associated with the cult of Venus on Cyprus, before finally adopting the olive and composing erudite verse worthy of Pallas Athena. This seemingly paradoxical activity of "collaborative self-crowning" was much more than mere promotion. As Edwin Duval reminds us:

> The purpose—or at least the effect—of all this jockeying was not simply to share a common stage and erect a monument all one's own in a new poetic landscape, but also to broaden the landscape itself, and demonstrate the manifold potential of a new poetics so rich that it could allow France to have its own Horace *and* its own Pindar, its own Petrarch *and* its own Ovid, all at the same time.[17]

When Ronsard extends to l'Aubespine the most famous crown awarded to poet laureates, he is including her in the elite coterie of French Renaissance writers whom Pontus de Tyard praised for contributing to the "mutation du stile Poëtique" (evolution of poetic style) and "le progrez et avancement qu'a fait nostre langage François" (the progress and advancement that our French language has made).[18] In order to rival contemporaneous Italy, the French poetic landscape must expand to also include women poets. Toward the end of his life, Ronsard would surely have noticed how far the French had

17. Edwin M. Duval, "Rival Laureates and Multiple Monuments: Collaborative Self-Crowning in France" in *Laureations: Essays in Honor of Richard Helgerson*, ed. Roze Hentschell and Kathryn Lavezzo (Newark: DE: University of Delaware Press, 2012), 187.

18. Pontus de Tyard, *Erreurs amoureuses*, ed. John A. McClelland (Geneva: Droz, 1967), 90.

fallen behind their cisalpine competitors who could count scores of published *petrarchiste*.

In addition to coronation, Ronsard also borrows the theme of cultivation that runs throughout the Pléiade's manifesto, the *Deffence et illustration de la langue françoyse*. In this treatise, which was first published alongside *L'Olive*, Du Bellay frequently employs botanical metaphors when explaining how French poets will graft their own verse on the models of classical predecessors in order to grow a new national poetry. When Ronsard tells l'Aubespine that the laurels of Parnassus are worthy of taking root in her, she becomes the veritable site of poetic renaissance. This combination of botany and topology is reinforced in the final tercet when Ronsard portrays l'Aubespine as a seed (Ô saint germe nouveau) whose potential talent has surpassed all that the Muses could cultivate.

In the first tercet, Ronsard concedes that his poetic prowess is waning while l'Aubespine's is rising. In the opening sonnet of *Le second livre des sonnets pour Hélène*, contemporaneous to his epistle to Villeroy, Ronsard laments that he has lost his laurels and now has only a "chef grison (graying head)." As long as an amorous ember kindles his heart, however, he will continue to compose verse. Having sworn off Platonism, he likewise renounces youthful ambitions and foolish aspirations:

> Lecteur, je ne veux estre escolier de Platon,
> Qui la vertu nous presche, & ne fait pas de mesme:
> Ny volontaire Icare, ou lourdaut Phaëton,
>
> Perduz pour attenter une sottise estrême:
> Mais sans me contrefaire ou Voleur, ou Charton,
> De mon gré je me noye, & me brusle moymesme.
>
> [Reader, I do not want to be a disciple of Plato,
> who preaches virtue to us, but does not practice it,
> nor a headstrong Icarus or a dull-witted Phaethon,
>
> who perished because they attempted acts of extreme folly;
> but without imitating the Flier or the Charioteer,
> of my own free will I am both drowning and burning myself.][19]

---

19. *Pierre de Ronsard: Selected Poems*, trans. and ed. Malcolm Quainton and Elizabeth Vinestock (London: Penguin, 2002), 49.

While Ronsard now wishes to distance himself from the failed en-
terprises of Icarus and Phaethon, l'Aubespine responds to Ronsard's
poem by adopting the role of both characters, whom her mentor recently renounced:

Tant de flame et d'amour, dont tu vas allumant
La nuict de mes escripts que ta muse eternise,
Font que je me tiens chere et me plais et me prise,
Car je ne puis faillir, suyvant ton jugement.

Mon esprit, qui devant se trainoit bassement,
Pretend voller au ciel si tu le favorise [sic].
Donc, ô divin Ronsard, ayde à mon entreprise:
Je scay bien que sans toy j'ozerois vainement.

Ainsy que Phaeton, d'une audace nouvelle,
Puisque, ô mon Apollon, ta fille je m'apelle,
Je te demande un don, gaige de ton amour:

Monstre moy le chemin et la sente incongnue
Par qui tant de lumiere en la France est venue
Et qui rend ton renom plus luysant que le jour.

[So much fire and love, with which you come to light
The night of my writing, which your Muse makes eternal,
Make me treasure myself, please and value myself,
Because I cannot fail, according to your judgment.

My mind that heretofore was dragging low, presumes
To fly to the skies, if you will favor it.
So, O divine Ronsard, help in my enterprise:
I know well that without you I would dare in vain.

Like Phaeton, with new audacity,
Since, O my Apollo, I call myself your daughter,
I ask you for a gift, a token of your love:

Show me the way and the untrodden path
Through which so much light came into France
And that makes your renown more brilliant than day.][20]

20. Klosowska, 58–59.

After expressing her gratitude for Ronsard's encouragement, which endowed her with a new sense of self-worth, the female poet adopts the role of Icarus in the second quatrain. Like her predecessor, she wishes to fly to the heavens. However, she seems less likely to be guided by hubris, emphasizing instead that she is dependent upon Ronsard's assistance and that she will follow his guidance. The mythological relationship between a father and his child suggested in the quatrains is made explicit in the tercets. L'Aubespine casts herself as Ronsard's *fille d'alliance* ("ta fille je m'apelle" l. 10), while simultaneously constructing a male poetic persona (Phaethon) who is the son of Ronsard's literary avatar (Apollo). When describing herself as both Ronsard's son and daughter, l'Aubespine does not renounce her female sex. She does, however, distinguish between her identities as author and poetic persona. Ronsard inscribed the historic author Madeleine de l'Aubespine in the first line of his sonnet, which initiated their poetic exchange (Madelene, ostez moy ce nom de l'Aubespine). L'Aubespine likewise first engraves the historic author Pierre de Ronsard in her apostrophe for aid (Donc, ô divin Ronsard, ayde à mon entreprise). She then proceeds to present a scrambling of identities. Within her address to Ronsard, in which she preserves her sexual identity as a woman, she inserts the mythological poetic identity wherein she is the son of the sun god. Like Phaethon's request to drive his father's chariot, l'Aubespine's wish for "a gift" from the French god of sun and verse signals her desire for an acknowledgment of poetic paternity. While she undoubtedly intends to aim high, her audacity is tempered by her reliance upon Ronsard's guidance and approval. L'Aubespine appears reluctant to follow the example of Apollo's male child who was ultimately unwilling or unable to follow his father's instructions. In a cautious and repentant version of the Ovidian archetype, she requests supervision from her poetic father, recognizing that, without his help, her efforts could be fatal.

Working from Peyron's index to the posthumous manuscript, Anna Klosowska identified what she believes to be three lines from Ronsard's now lost response to l'Aubespine's sonnet:

Si vollant vous tombez pour me vouloir trop croire
Au moings vous acquerez pour tombe ceste gloire
Qu'une femme a vaincu les plus doctes françois.

[If you fall in your flight, too willing to believe me,
At least you will have earned this glory for your tomb
That a woman surpassed the most learned French men.][21]

In this excerpt, the mythological figure of Phaethon has been replaced by his Ovidian double, Icarus, who was evoked by l'Aubespine in the sixth line of her own sonnet, when she expresses her spirit's desire to "fly *to* the skies" (my emphasis). It was Icarus who wished to ascend vertically to the heavens, while Phaethon requested to drive his father's chariot *across* the skies. Both figures, however, remind us that while falls and failure may be inevitable, audacious aspiration is required of all those who strive to earn renown by emulating their poetic fathers. This is one of the reasons Phaethon and Icarus are the privileged personae of Renaissance poets. When Ronsard promises l'Aubespine that, should she fall, she will nevertheless receive a glorious tomb proclaiming her the nation's premier poet, he is not simply declaring a victor in a battle of the sexes. While he states that she will have surpassed the most erudite French men, more importantly, he acknowledges poetic paternity. Indeed, in these three lines he bequeaths to his *fille d'alliance* the destiny of poet laureate that he had once reserved for himself. The reprise of elements from the opening poem of *Sonnets et madrigals pour Astrée* is particularly striking:

Dois-je voler emplumé d'esperance,
Ou si je dois, forcé du desespoir
Du haut du Ciel en terre laisser choir
Mon jeune amour avorté de naissance?

Non, j'aime mieux, leger d'outrecuidance,
Tomber d'enhaut, & fol me decevoir,
Que voler bas, deussé-je recevoir
Pour mon tombeau toute une large France.

Icare fit de sa cheute nommer,
Pour trop oser, les ondes de la mer:
Et moy je veux honorer ma contree

De mon sepulchre & dessus engraver,
RONSARD VOULANT AUX ASTRES S'ESLEVER,
FUT FOUDROYÉ PAR UNE BELLE ASTREE.

21. Ibid.

[Must I fly winged with hope,
Or must I, compelled by despair
Let fall away from the Heavens to earth
My young love aborted from birth?

No, I prefer, transported by overconfidence,
To fall from up high, and foolishly deceive myself,
Than to fly low, even if I might receive
All of France for my tombstone.

Through his fall, Icarus had named,
Having dared too much, the waves of the sea:
And I wish to honor my country

By my tombstone upon which engraved,
RONSARD, ASPIRING TO CELESTIAL RENOWN
BY A BEAUTIFUL STAR, WAS STRUCK DOWN.]

When we situate Ronsard's exchange with Madeleine de l'Aubespine alongside his roughly contemporaneous *Sonnets et madrigals pour Astrée* and *Sonnets pour Hélène*, we see how he bequeaths key poetic elements to his *fille d'alliance*—the personae, the aspirations, the fall, even an epitaph commemorating the poet who strove to honor his country. The masculine sex of Icarus and Phaethon clearly did not prevent l'Aubespine or Ronsard from selecting a male figure as a suitable mask for the female author. This collaborative intertextual fashioning of Madeleine de l'Aubespine's poetic persona is an impressive example of literary prosopopeia. When cast as Ronsard's literary progeny, l'Aubespine is granted the most prestigious poetic paternity imaginable in sixteenth-century France, one that firmly situates her within literary tradition as a French poet, not as a woman who wrote verse in French.

IV. Politics, Religion, and Propaganda During the Wars of Religion

DORA POLACHEK

From Affinity Groups to Partisan Narratives: Brantôme, Pierre de L'Estoile, and the Guises

> [F]acts do not speak for themselves [. . .] the historian speaks for them, speaks on their behalf, and fashions the fragments of the past into a whole whose integrity is—in its *representation*—a purely discursive one.[1]

In a century filled with so much violence and bloodshed, the assassination of the Guise brothers represents a pivotal moment in the Wars of Religion. On December 23, 1588, Henri de Lorraine, third Duc de Guise, was stabbed to death by multiple assassins who had been ordered to do so by Henri III in the king's chateau at Blois, during a meeting he had called of the Estates General. On December 24, 1588, the Duc de Guise's brother, Louis de Lorraine, Cardinal de Guise, met the same fate. These facts are undeniable, but this article aims to examine how the social affinity group, formation, and political alignments of two contemporary sixteenth-century chroniclers color their account of "the facts." The analysis that follows of the related writings of Pierre de Bourdeille (better known as Brantôme) and of Pierre de L'Estoile is informed by Hayden White's insistence, as the opening epigram states, that "facts do not speak for themselves." White's observation reminds us that there is more similarity than difference between the writing of history and the writing of fiction, for in each case we are dealing with narratives and discursive practices that necessitate our awareness of the viewpoint that is incarnated by the narrator, whether historian, novelist, or chronicler. For a story to cohere, it needs to be shaped, and that shaping inevitably requires

---

1. Hayden White, "Fictions of Factual Representation," in *Tropics of Discourse. Essays in Cultural Criticism* (Baltimore: Johns Hopkins University Press, 1978), 125.

YFS 134, *The Construction of a National Vernacular Literature in the Renaissance: Essays in Honor of Edwin M. Duval*, ed. DeVos and Hayes, © 2018 by Yale University.

facts to be organized, that is, formed into a pattern that relates each element to the other. The author's intentions determine the organizational pattern.

As we shall see, Brantôme and Pierre de L'Estoile both portrayed members of the same clan—the Guises—and the same period of time—the aftermath of their assassination—but from entirely different vantage points and they arrived at strikingly divergent interpretations of the history they record. Because it is crucial to know where Brantôme and L'Estoile position themselves on the social and political spectrum, a short portrait of each follows. These sketches will facilitate an understanding of the narrative practices each writer adopts in his rendition of the key Guise players and the events that transpired after the Guise assassinations. Included in the analysis of differing vantage points will be how each chronicler describes and evaluates the role of key women in the narrative: Anne d'Este, mother of the murdered brothers, and Catherine-Marie de Lorraine, their widowed sister.

There are several crucial questions we must ask: As a clear supporter of the Guises, how do Brantôme's characterizations of the Duc de Guise and of the Guise women's campaign to defame the king reflect his own personal biases? How do Pierre de L'Estoile's radically different education, social position, and political proclivities color his portrayal of the same players and of the same event? The larger questions concern the kinds of issues that arise whenever we talk seriously about, for want of a better term, "historical writing." Can chroniclers ever be objective? How much faith can we put into what we are reading? Or hearing? Without a doubt Brantôme's and L'Estoile's accounts offer invaluable insights into sixteenth-century France, particularly when the very nature of French polity was at stake. However, once we read both viewpoints, what does our personal preference for one perspective over another tell us about what we ourselves choose to identify as "true"? What can we learn about our own personal biases when it comes to our intrepretations of historical chronicles?

CONTEXTUALIZING THE CHRONICLERS

At first glance, Pierre de Bourdeille (Brantôme) and Pierre de L'Estoile seem to be uncannily evenly matched. They share the same first name, were born a mere six years apart (1540 for Brantôme; 1546 for de L'Estoile), and died at almost the same time (1614 for Brantôme and 1611 for L'Estoile). They both lived during the Wars of Religion in France, and, as we shall see, both chronicled what they saw and heard. The similarities end here. Their differing social and political positions explain much about what drove one to describe the Guises with such admiration and the other with such derision.

Those familiar with Brantôme's work know that in addition to his ability to titillate readers with racy tales about the goings-on in the Valois court, he can also fascinate us through his historically significant portraits of the important figures of his time (portraits that fill more than six volumes).[2] He always makes clear his personal connections to these powerful and influential figures, and demonstrates much pride in these connections:

> I have been, thank God, always well-loved, known, and welcomed by the kings my masters, by the noble seigneurs and princes, by my queens, my princesses, in short by each and all, who held me in such great esteem that I can say, in all modesty, that the Brantôme name was of great renown there.[3]

Besides being a regular at the royal court, Brantôme's career involved travel and military expeditions. His connection to the Guises was longstanding. While in Rome in 1559 when Pius IV was installed as the new pope, Brantôme met the Cardinal de Guise and François de Lorraine, Duc de Guise (father of Henri de Lorraine, the Duc de Guise who was assassinated in 1588) with whom he traveled to Naples. In 1562, he joined the Catholic side in the French Wars of Religion. He fought at Blois, participated in the siege of Rouen with the Duc de Guise, and fought in the Battle of Dreux. In 1563, Brantôme was present when Guise was mortally wounded by the Protestant Jean Poltrot de Méré. A falling out with Henri III over the king's failure to honor a promise of an important political position most likely intensified his

2. For the complete works, see the eleven-volume *Œuvres complètes de Pierre de Bourdeille, seigneur de Brantôme*, ed. Ludovic Lalanne (Paris: Jules Renouard, 1864; New York: Johnson Reprint Corporation, 1968). For ease of reference and accessibility, unless otherwise noted, I use the Etienne Vaucheret edition, *Recueil des Dames, poésies et tombeau* (Paris: Gallimard, 1991). Because of space limitations, I offer only the English translations of the passages in question. However, directly after the English translation, I indicate within parentheses the page of the French citation in the Vaucheret edition. All translations are mine.

3. *Œuvres complètes de Pierre de Bourdeille, seigneur de Brantôme*, vol. 5, *Discours sur les couronnels de l'Infanterie de France*, ed. Ludovic Lalanne, 396.

loyalty to the Guise clan as the divisions between the king and the Guises grew wider.[4]

Pierre de L'Estoile's situation was strikingly different. Born in Paris into a bourgeois family, he came from a long line of service in the judiciary branch of the government. One of his professors at the Université d'Orléans, Matthieu Béroalde, later became a Calvinist minister in Geneva. When L'Estoile studied law in Bourges, his tutor was Alexander Arbuthnot, who would later play an instrumental role in the Scottish Reformation. L'Estoile was Catholic, but given his family background, education, and mentors, it is not surprising that he sympathized with the plight of the Protestants. Returning to Paris in 1566, he settled there for the rest of his life. He married the daughter of the head of the royal treasury, and purchased the office of *grand-audiencier* in the royal chancery, which included bringing cases for the Parlement to hear.[5]

L'Estoile's *Registre-journal* begins in 1574, with the death of Charles IX, and ends in 1611, offering an important chronicle of the period. The multi-volume work was first published in 1621. Even though subsequent volumes had different titles, it is significant to note that the two manuscripts that remain are both titled *Register-journal of a Curious Man* (*Registre-journal d'un curieux*).[6] This title immediately prepares us for a hybrid genre. Whereas a register can be construed as a factual recording of dates and events, a journal opens the way for commentary, and as can be expected, the commentary here is biased. His affinity group, educational background, and choice of profession would make it highly unusual for L'Estoile to be anything other than a *politique* who preferred stability to the chaos he was witnessing virtually on a daily basis, and who consequently opted

4. For comprehensive details about Brantôme's life and works see Madeleine Lazard, *Pierre de Bourdeille, seigneur de Brantôme* (Paris: Fayard, 1995); Anne-Marie Cocula-Vaillières, *Brantôme. Amour et gloire au temps des Valois* (Paris: Albin Michel, 1986). For a summary of Brantôme's biography and writings, see Dora E. Polachek, "Brantôme," *Dictionary of Literary Biography 327: Sixteenth-Century French Writers*, ed. Megan Conway (Farmington Hills, MI: Thomson Gale, 2006), 53–60.

5. To my knowledge, only one biography of Pierre de L'Estoile exists; see Eugène Vallée, *Notice sur Pierre de L'Estoile* (Paris: Lemerre, 1888). For a cogent summary and bibliographical information, see Frederic J. Baumgartner, "Pierre de L'Estoile," *Dictionary of Literary Biography 327: Sixteenth-Century French Writers*, ed. Megan Conway, 256-61.

6. For the publication history of L'Estoile's chronicles, see François Marin, "The Editorial Fortunes of the *Registres-journaux des règnes de Henri III et Henri IV* by Pierre de L'Estoile," *Nouvelle revue du seizième siècle* 20 (2002): 87–108.

for moderation and toleration in the religious disputes that were tearing the country apart.[7]

As a member of the judiciary class with *politique* views, as early as 1576, shortly after learning about the formation of the League and of the Guise leadership, L'Estoile wrote that he refused to take the Guises' militant ultra-Catholic fervor at face value; he doubted their objections to the king's efforts to arrive at an equitable solution with the Protestants. When a defamatory broadside posted throughout Paris accused the judiciary of exposing the country to destruction by promoting toleration of the Huguenots, L'Estoile saw this as yet another example of the League's propaganda machine at work. For L'Estoile, the League's leaders, at the head of which were the Guises, "would have been willing for all the world to be Huguenot on the condition that they [the League] could rule" (*Registre-journal* II, 53).[8]

ASSESSING THE ASSASSINATIONS

With this information about Brantôme's and L'Estoile's affinity groups, we can now turn to how each writer recounts the aftermath of the Guise assassinations. Brantôme spends two entire pages focusing on the murders from the vantage point of Anne d'Este, Duchesse de Nemours, the mother of the Guise brothers. He chooses to focus on the aftermath of the double death, when the Duchesse is immediately imprisoned by the king, who hopes to delay the return of the Guise women and their supporters to Paris for as long as possible. Paris is a Guise stronghold already hostile to the king and, as history makes clear, the city would grow devastatingly turbulent once word was received there of what transpired at Blois. In his third-person omniscient narration, Brantôme includes the mother's words. Using

7. For an introduction to the *politiques* and their beliefs, see Arlette Jouanna, "Politiques," in *Histoire et dictionnaire des guerres de religion*, ed. Arlette Jouanna et al (Paris: Robert Laffont, 1998), 1210–1213; for an in-depth study of the Parlement, see *Politiques de la parole. Le Parlement de Paris au XVIe siècle*, ed. Marie Houllemare (Geneva: Droz, 2011), in particular Chapter 12, "Le Parlement comme forum pendant les guerres de Religion," 525–56.

8. Pierre de L'Estoile, *Registre-journal du regne de Henri III*, ed. Madeleine Lazard and Gilbert Schrenck (Geneva: Droz, 1992–2003), vol. 6 (1588–1589), 86. This six-volume edition spans the years 1574–1589: volume 1 (1574–1575), volume 2 (1576–1578), volume 3 (1579–1581), volume 4 (1582–1584), volume 5 (1585–1587), volume 6 (1588–1589). Unless otherwise noted, all references will be to this edition, and hereafter will appear in the body of the article, in parentheses after the citation as *Registre-journal*, followed by the volume number and page number. All translations are my own.

both direct and indirect discourse he details how, contrary to her usual calm and controlled nature, she spewed out thousands of insults and curses against the king, repeatedly using the word "tyrant" (Brantôme 705).

When she calmed down, she said that if the king would only kill her as he had killed her sons, and in this way rid her of her misery, she would call him a good and clement king. Finally, quieting her words and cries, she circles back to the following refrain, which Brantôme cites in direct discourse, and then adds an editorializing detail designed to vivify those words: "'Ah! My children! Ah! My children,' regularly repeating these words along with her beautiful tears which would have melted a heart of stone" (Brantôme 705).

Narrating the event from such a close range, and from such a sympathetic vantage point, makes it virtually impossible to side with anyone except the grieving, traumatized mother. Brantôme expects the reader to condone the human response of cursing the culprit king. To guarantee this response, Brantôme interjects his personal evaluation within a parenthetical remark, forcing the reader to see Anne d'Este's virulent outburst as a normal reaction: "[. . .] for what would one not say or do given such intensity of loss and pain!" (Brantôme 704–05). Brantôme's use of "one" universalizes Anne d'Este's response, with the exclamation point intensifying this evaluation, serving not only as a figuration of his own emotion, but also functioning as a sort of dare to anyone who would disagree. Her begging the king to grant her the same death is Brantôme's next step in creating sympathy for her plight. Then he concludes with her fragmented, tearful lament, transcribed in direct discourse—"Oh! my children! Oh! My children!" (Brantôme 705). These words return the reader to the human dimension of a personal tragedy, in a manner clearly designed to provoke horror and sympathy.

Brantome's narrative strategies to garner sympathy for Anne d'Este are far from subtle; in the span of two pages, for example, the word children (enfans) is mobilized six times, and we find seven uses of exclamation points. Clearly, he aims to win the reader over to her side. After his lengthy description of the mother's heart-rending reaction to the death of her sons, Brantôme offers his own response to their demise, linking his sympathy for Anne d'Este to his own feelings about the Guise family. Again, there is no subtlety here: "Alas! She could indeed cry and lament them, for they were so good, so generous, and valorous, but above all was the great Duc de Guise, true elder and true paragon of virtue and generosity" (Brantôme 705).

Encomiastic adjectives proliferate, underlining the exceptional qualities of these two men, particularly extolling the merits and force of character of the Duc de Guise. When Brantôme adds his own evaluation, the impact of this loss extends beyond personal grief: these exemplary figures of virtue and valor, especially the Duc de Guise, have been lost to the world, and thus the greater good has sustained an enormous blow.

When we turn to Pierre de L'Estoile's description of the assassination, the differences in vantage point and personal assessment are noteworthy. Unlike Brantôme, L'Estoile devotes numerous pages to the king's carefully thought-out planning of the assassination. As he recounts it, the Duc de Guise represents a distinct contrast to the cautious, consensus-seeking king, for on the very morning of his assassination, Guise received numerous written warnings about what lay in store for him. Pocketing the last message, he said out loud: "Here's the ninth one from today" (Registre-journal, VI, 86).

That Guise could not or would not imagine that the king wanted to trick him is ascribed by L'Estoile to the Duc de Guise's heedlessness to what was as plain as day: "So blind was this great mind to the most obvious things, God having blindfolded him just as He usually does to those He wishes to chastise and punish" (Registre-journal, VI, 86). Instead of exclamation points and alases, L'Estoile employs sarcasm to emphasize Guise's brash recklessness and stupidity. This is evident in his use of the epithet of "great mind" to describe the Duke. Furthermore, L'Estoile emphasizes the providential nature of the Duke's demise as a way of exonerating the king of wrongdoing by insinuating that the king's decision was an act of God. According to L'Estoile, the punishment was warranted, and he further clarifies this point in the section devoted to the detailed description of each killing.

This particularly remarkable section is entitled *The bodies of the Guisards dismembered and reduced to wind and ashes*. L'Estoile begins the entry in a seemingly matter-of-fact style, first describing when the bodies of the Duke and Cardinal were dismembered by order of the king; where in the chateau this was done; how they were disposed of, "so that nothing remained of them, neither relic nor memory" (Registre-journal VI, 90).

The straightforward reportorial tone then gives way to a personal evaluation that, like Brantôme's, is meant to ensure that readers see the details from L'Estoile's point of view. Just as Brantôme wanted to defuse Anne d'Este's maledictions against the king by underscoring their justifiability from a human point of view, so does L'Estoile engage in strategies to avert what might possibly be construed as a horrific act on the part of a king. Allotting space for a grieving mother's lament would defeat his purpose. Instead the only perspective we have is L'Estoile's, who begins by clearly stating his own opinion. Then, by putting himself in the place of the reader, he gives the reasons why we should see the grisly deaths as he does:

> An ordeal worthy of their ambition, which, though at first glance may seem iniquitous, even tyrannical, is the secret judgment of God, hidden under such a ruling and its execution, and thus, obliges us to receive it as the hand of God. It is furthermore certain (and is seen in *all* histories) that in *all* great examples there is some injustice which is nevertheless compensated by public utility. (*Registre-journal* VI, 90; emphasis mine)

The first sentence identifies the punishment as fitting the crime: extreme aspirations merit extreme punishments. Next, L'Estoile shifts agency, and thus responsibility, from the king to God. In a deft reconfiguration of the trope of the king as God incarnate, possessing extra powers and qualities that are concomitantly bestowed on him, Henri III is described as actualizing God's will on Earth.[9] Thus, it is the hand of God that is writing and carrying out the death sentence. The implication is that we are obligated to accept what we cannot understand because it emanates from a higher realm: God's. L'Estoile's third argument also alludes to a higher order, but this time of a diachronically political nature, as borne out by the lessons that past histories always teach: all great actions contain an element of injustice that nonetheless serves the greater good.[10] This totalizing summation through the repetition of "all" is another way that L'Estoile's nar-

---

9. For the history and importance of this belief, see Marc Bloch, *Les Rois thaumaturges. Étude sur le caractère surnaturel attribué à la puissance royale particulièrement en France et en Angleterre* (Strasbourg: Librairie Istra, 1923).

10. See the encyclopedic work of Florence Greffe and José Lothe, *La vie, les livres et les lectures de Pierre de L'Estoile. Nouvelles recherches* (Paris: Champion 2004), 290–91, which bears out L'Estoile's familiarity with and interest in this Machiavellian slant on *realpolitik*, as evidenced by the inventory of books in his personal library.

rative aims to normalize what at first risks being perceived as egregiously ghastly. Under the guise of objective reportage, L'Estoile succeeds in metaphorically shredding the Duc de Guise, accusing him of an outsized ambition that is fittingly punished by the hand of God.

Thus, as was the case in Brantôme's description, the narrative elements at work lead us to perceive an event the way the writer wants us to. Specifically, Brantôme zooms in on the double assassination by means of an intimate viewpoint (that of Anne d'Este, the inconsolable mother) and then zooms out to a personal evaluation and the invocation of a higher good that has been compromised by the loss of the Guise brothers. L'Estoile, on the other hand, zooms in on the gory details, but then zooms out to justify the demise of the Guises by appealing to a higher order—God's—which cannot be questioned, and then to the lessons of history where the end has always justified the means, no matter how shocking and unjust the means may appear.

CATHERINE-MARIE DE LORRAINE: REVILED OR RESPECTED?

These markedly different descriptions of the aftermath of the Guise assassinations have demonstrated how affinity group and political predilections influence a chronicler's vantage point. The following section focuses specifically on one woman—Catherine-Marie de Lorraine—one of the most powerful women of the League. Here perhaps is the best example of how bias operates in creating a narrative that conforms to a narrator's particular version of events and of its key players: she is denigrated by L'Estoile and venerated by Brantôme.

L'Estoile's chronicles leave no doubt that Henri III may have become the most maligned king in French history, but L'Estoile's support remained constant, and he fervently affirmed the king's inalienable right to continue to rule. As we have seen, he directed his venom at the ultra-conservative Catholic League, led by the Guises. Most certainly, L'Estoile was an avid collector of pamphlets, broadsides, books, and yes, his journal and these items are important primary sources of information about the extraordinary upheaval that Paris experienced, particularly during the war being waged between the Guises and the king. Yet he is not even-handed in his account. In his introduction to a new edition of the illustrated broadsides collected by L'Estoile, entitled *Les belles figures et drolleries de la Ligue*, Gilbert Schrenck highlights that L'Estoile lacked objectivity both as an observer and as a collector. He points out that even though the propagandistic pamphlets often attacked the princesses of the court during the Wars of Religion, L'Estoile's *Belles figures* contain very few women, with the exception of Catherine-Marie de Lorraine, Duchesse de Montpensier, and her mother.[11]

For L'Estoile Catherine-Marie de Lorraine (1552–1596), sister of the assassinated Guise brothers, was the person who embodied the monstrosity of the League. Married to Louis de Bourbon, Duc de Montpensier, and subsequently widowed at the age of thirty, she returned, childless, to her clan. Frederic Baumgartner's blunt assessment of L'Estoile's feelings toward her says it best: "L'Estoile utterly despised Guise's sister, Catherine, Duchess of Montpensier, for her zeal for the League and her success in stirring up the Parisians against the king."[12] As we shall see, rather than attributing her power to a keen awareness and intelligent knowledge of the most effective strategies to attain her objective—the demise of the king—L'Estoile instead stoops to a misogynistically-driven strategy: ascribing her success to louche behavior, where her body is put in the spotlight as part of L'Estoile's own discursive defamation campaign. Supported by his selectivity bias in what he collects, foregrounds, and comments upon, L'Estoile aims to corroborate his hate-filled portrait of Catherine-Marie de Lorraine.

After the assassination of the Guise brothers in 1588, Catholic fury against the king exploded. As I have shown elsewhere, this reaction was fueled by the female Guise triumvirate and the support the three widows gained through their highly organized campaign against him.[13] The double assassination led not only to Henri III's excommunication by the Pope, but also resulted in sermons from the pulpits

11. Pierre de L'Estoile, *Les belles figures et drolleries de la Ligue*, ed. Gilbert Schrenck (Geneva: Droz, 2016), XXVI, fn 119. For illustrative materials relating to Catherine-Marie de Lorraine, see 18, 41, 90, 185, 296, 356, 357.

12. Frederic Baumgartner, *Dictionary of Literary Biography*, 260.

13. For the ferociously effective polemical verbal and visual campaign waged on the home front against Henri III by Anne d'Este and Catherine-Marie de Lorraine, see Dora E. Polachek, "Le mécénat meurtrier: l'iconoclasme et les limites de l'acceptable: Anne d'Este, Catherine–Marie de Lorraine et l'anéantissement d'Henri III," trans. Sylvie Déléris, in *Patronnes et mécènes en France à la Renaissance*, ed. Kathleen Wilson-Chevalier (Saint-Etienne: Université de Saint-Etienne, 2007), 433–54. See also the groundbreaking work of Eliane Viennot concerning historians' erasing the important role of women in the sixteenth century, "Des 'femmes d'Etat' au XVIe siècle: les princesses de la Ligue et l'écriture de l'histoire," in *Femmes et pouvoirs sous l'Ancien Régime*, ed. Danielle Haase-Dubosc and Eliane Viennot (Paris: Rivages, 1991), 77–97.

of at least eight churches, denouncing the king, along with mounds of pamphlets, broadsides, and street corner harangues against him.[14] Catherine-Marie de Lorraine was without a doubt a driving force behind the humiliating Day of the Barricades of May 12, 1588, as a result of which the king was forced to flee Paris.[15] Seven months later, with the December 23 and 24 assassination of her brothers, the Duchesse de Montpensier was a ubiquitous presence in the visual, written, and oral rhetorical polemics that ensued. Along with her widowed mother and now widowed sister-in-law Catherine de Cleves, she had her hopes set on a specific goal, which culminated eight months later in the assassination of Henri III at the hands of Jacques Clément, marked by bonfires of celebration throughout Paris once the news was disseminated.[16]

L'Estoile regularly accuses the Duchesse de Montpensier of gaining what she wants through grotesque sexual wiles, bordering on sacrilege. As we see in his description below, in one case she purportedly allows herself to be manhandled and groped, dressed in a provocatively thin and revealing garment. This is made all the more outrageous because she hypocritically joins religious processionals organized by her henchmen where she and her clan can exploit the naïve, zealous masses who unsuspectingly become victims of a scene of sexual debauchery. According to L'Estoile, she encourages such debauchery in order to excite the crowd and thus incite rebellion against the King after the double assassination.

L'Estoile reports this scene in a passage that includes the epithet "The Holy Widow of Paris" [La Sainte Veuve de Paris], a play on "the Holy League" [La Sainte Ligue], which she metonymically embodies. At the same time, he mocks her saintly behavior:

> The Holy Widow [. . .] covered only with a sheer low-cut garment, allowed herself to be led, held under her arms, across the church of Saint

14. For the push to have the pope excommunicate the king, including letters from the Guise women, see Richard Cooper, "The Aftermath of the Blois Assassinations of 1588: Documents in the Vatican," *French History* 3/4 (1989): 404–26.

15. For a description of the king's humiliation, see Stuart Carroll, *Martyrs and Murderers: The Guise Family and the Making of Europe* (Oxford: Oxford University Press, 2009), 274–79.

16. See Denis Crouzet, *Les guerriers de Dieu. La violence au temps des troubles de religion (vers 1524–vers 1610)*, 2 volumes (Seyssel: Éditions Champ Vallon, 1990); for the apocalyptic justifications for regicide and their relation to the League, see volume 2, Chapter 19, "La Ligue et le régicide: la trame d'une expérience mystique," 464–539.

Jean, letting herself be sweet-talked and touched, to the great scandal of many good devout people who in good faith were part of processions, led by a devout and religious zeal, mocked by those who had organized them [i.e., the processions], having been instituted for the sole purpose of keeping the people always on the side of the League, and to cover with a veil of religion the infamous perdition, high treason and revolt of those gathered against their king, their natural prince and sovereign lord. (*Registre-journal* VI, 146)

Other sexual allusions abound through the inclusion of ephemera found by L'Estoile. For example, in a satirical piece entitled *The Manifestos of the Ladies of the Court*, the entry for the Duchesse de Montpensier reduces her to her body as she makes the following confession: "My body never was disposed to anything but lubricity and madness, and my mind only to diabolical machinations and perturbations" (*Registre-journal* V, 347). In another piece included by L'Estoile, *Sacrificium Deo Spiritus contribulatus*, the Duchesse de Montpensier's sacrifice is described in the following way: "she thought she had made a great sacrifice to God, by lending out her front in order to advance the affairs of the League" (*Registre-journal* V, 347).

L'Estoile's numerous examples leave no doubt as to where he positions himself when it comes to Catherine-Marie de Lorraine. At no time does he even allude to the possibility of her having been motivated by anything that could garner the reader's admiration, let alone sympathy. Reduced to an objectified, diabolical, oversexed monster, she is depicted as a force of chaos who uses her body to destabilize a legitimate ruler and thus to destroy an entire kingdom along with him.

L'Estoile's vitriolic rhetoric persists even when he describes her death in May 1596:

Monday the sixth, at one hour past midnight, Madame de Montpensier died, in her house on the rue des Bourdonnais, in Paris, from a great outflowing of blood which poured out from all parts of her body: which was a death fitting her life; as was the great thunder and storm which took place that night which corresponded to the tempestuous humors of her evil spirit, muddled and tempestuous, by which, according to even the League, she was the cause of the death of her two brothers, for having boasted aloud of giving the late king the crown of Saint Gregory. When she was dead, she was put on her processional bed, where for a long time many good people had wished to see her;

and there was a gentleman who, after having kissed her, dead, said aloud that he had wanted for a long time to give her that kiss.[17]

In a fashion similar to his description of the assassination of the Guise brothers, L'Estoile's reportorial style begins objectively, giving the who, what, when, where, and how of the event, but the "why" interjects the kind of editorializing we have already seen, with an appeal to higher forces at work. This time, instead of directly invoking God, L'Estoile suggests that the stormy weather replicates on a grand scale the turbulent personality of Madame de Montpensier. Without any substantiation for his claim, he attributes the Guise brothers' death to her because of the threats she made to the king.[18] This opinion thus exonerates the king of any long-standing animosity regarding the Duke's political aspirations. If anyone is to blame for her brothers' death, it is surely she; the rhetorical question L'Estoile seems to be asking is, would those of the League echo this opinion ("according to even the League") if it were not true?

L'Estoile then proceeds to destroy any solemnity that a member of the nobility's processional deathbed normally evokes, by claiming that numerous "good people" (gens de bien) had waited to see this happen—that is, to see her stretched out, dead—for a long time. L'Estoile's final discursive move is to sexualize the morbid scene through the words of a gentleman expressing his satisfaction after having kissed (après avoir baisé) the dead Duchess.

It is easy to discern reasons for L'Estoile's outlook. Because his sympathy lies with the king, he was offended by Catherine-Marie de Lorraine's unwavering determination to destroy the king through a propaganda campaign that was designed to, and succeeded in, winning over the hearts and minds of the population. Nevertheless, the virulence of his own misogynistic defamatory campaign is striking. Such polemical strategies are not unusual in propaganda campaigns. Nevertheless, the danger of this kind of evaluation is evident if one is not aware that there is another viewpoint, as Brantôme's makes perfectly clear.

17. *Journal de L'Estoile pour le regne de Henri IV, 1589–1560*, ed. Louis-Raymond Lefèvre (Paris: Gallimard, 1948), 481.

18. As for the crown of Saint Gregory, L'Estoile is probably alluding to the golden scissors that Madame de Montpensier always wore at her waist, and the taunts she made, threatening to tonsure the king with them, and force him to retreat to a monastery; see *Registre-journal* VI, 12–13.

One may prefer Brantôme's sympathy-inducing portrayal of the Duchesse de Montpensier, but, as we shall see, it is equally biased in the other direction, and for the same reasons as L'Estoile's account is: social allegiance and political alignment. Our earlier sketch of Brantôme was designed to prevent any possible surprise as to what we can expect when Brantôme turns his pen to Catherine-Marie de Lorraine, who is not only the daughter of the man alongside whom he fought and whose wife he extols, but is also the sister of the Duc de Guise whose death he mourns as an incommensurate loss. For him, she is "Madame de Montpensier, sister of the late Monsieur de Guise, who was a great woman of state, and who contributed her good share of resources, of inventions of her fine mind, and of the work of her body, to build the said League" (Brantôme 703).

This description underscores that Catherine-Marie de Lorraine provided concrete resources, creative ingenuity, and physical strength to the construction of the ultra-Catholic League. Brantôme legitimizes her by underlining that she is a woman with intellectual capacities that rightfully make her a woman of state, in the most positive meaning of such an epithet. Her physical strength ("travail de son corps") coupled with her mental inventiveness ("inventions de son gentil esprit") create something of substance that is respected by Brantôme: the League.

It is worth noting that Brantôme uses broad strokes in his portrayal of Catherine-Marie de Lorraine. His adulatory terms underline the important role she played in creating the League, but he does not explain in detail what the League's purpose was. Hence, one is left with the only conclusion possible: that she is worthy of our admiration. Brantôme provides more detail when he turns to the specifics of her actions once she becomes aware of the murder of her brothers, but unlike L'Estoile, who vilifies these kinds of actions, Brantôme justifies them:

> [She] goes out of her hotel with the children of Monsieur her late brother, holding them by the hand, leads them through the city, makes her deploration before the people, animating it with tears, cries of pity, and words commanding all to take up arms and rise up in fury, and to do all manner of violence to the house and picture of the King [. . .] and to deny him any fidelity, but on the contrary to swear total rebellion, which soon after resulted in his murder. [. . .] Certainly the heart of a sister who loses such brothers could not stomach such poison without avenging this murder. (Brantôme 703)

To be sure, Brantôme also emphasizes Catherine-Marie de Lorraine's body, but never reduces it to just that. What she does with her body distinguishes her from other women. Nowhere does he allude to the sexual deployment of her fame for lascivious pleasures or hypocritical ends. Her actions here are not depicted as the machinations invented by the League, but rather as an affect-inspired response to the news of the killings. As Brantôme tells it, once she hears the news of her brothers' assassinations and the ensuing arrests of her mother and sister-in-law, instead of grieving in her house, she displays a powerful loyalty to her clan through what she physically undertakes. What we would today call her "emotional intelligence" enables her to heighten the sympathy and outrage already present among the Paris population, and thus she purposefully displays her dead brother's orphans to rouse the crowd to a fever pitch so that they engage in violent, iconoclastic acts. As was the case in his conclusion concerning Anne d'Este's virulent diatribe against the king, Brantôme's depiction attributes the Duchesse de Montpensier's exhortations to a strictly human and comprehensible motive: how could a loyal sister tolerate such a murderous king who has robbed her of her two brothers? Grief and a justifiable desire to avenge the death of her brothers drive her to enlist the mob to carry out her wishes. Brantôme continues underlining her physical strength and her far-from-crazy journey from that point on. Once she has roused the crowd to action, she then rides swiftly out of the city to rally powerful princes to her cause and to ensure their support.

THE GUISE ASSASSINATIONS AND BEYOND

If we compare these two chroniclers' narration of the same events, what are we to conclude, except that it is naïve to expect an unbiased account of the events that transpired during the French Wars of Religion? However, as these analyses have shown, if we know more about where the chroniclers are positioned, both socially and politically, we can arrive at a better understanding of what drives Brantôme to describe the Guises with such glowing admiration and L'Estoile with such utter derision. Then, as now, it is impossible to deny that professional and political affinities, coupled with a writer's narrative goals, generate biases.

As we have seen here, narratives depend on a narrator's loyalties, whether through social network affinities or political or religious alignments. Were the Guise women "right" in staging their grief in public? Was Catherine-Marie de Lorraine "justified" in enlisting the help of an entire population in avenging the deaths of her brothers? Can one ever defend a call to kill the leader of a nation? Reading Brantôme's account of the Guise assassinations would lead us to one set of answers, while L'Estoile's would elicit precisely the opposite response.

Brantôme's account of the Guises during the period after the 1588 double assassination differs radically from Pierre de L'Estoile's. Which one do we believe? If, as Hayden White posits, historians shape the fragments of the past into a whole, we also engage in a similar process as we digest each chronicler's version of "the facts." As readers, we, too, are interpreters, and what we label as "truth" is filtered through our own set of values. The research of social scientists demonstrates that what we label as true or false is strongly correlated with where our sympathies lie in relation to the event. How we affiiliate socially or politically elicits an emotional response that infiltrates other facets of our world view. As a result, our response to a historical episode—what political scientists have termed "partisan affect"—can reveal much, not only about the event itself but about ourselves and our own beliefs.[19] In short, many lessons remain to be learned from unsettling events that took place more than 400 years ago.[20]

19. See Shanto Iyengar and Sean J. Westwood, "Fear and Loathing Across Party Lines: New Evidence on Group Polarization," *American Journal of Political Science* 59/3 (July 2015): 690-707; DOI: 10.1111/ajps.12152

20. Portions of this research were first presented at the Sixteenth Century Society Conference in San Juan, Puerto Rico in October 2013. I thank the participants for their questions and comments, as well as more recently, Howard Brown, Gila Stadler and the editors of this volume for their invaluable suggestions for shaping this article into its present form.

SHIRA WEIDENBAUM

From Monologue to Dialogue: The Uses and Misuses of Genre in *Le pacifique*

Scholars of early modern dialogue have often seen the genre's popularity as evidence of a Renaissance spirit of openness, and the use
of dialogue as a sign of humanist movement away from rigid medieval dialectic in favor of a form permitting shared inquiry, critique
of authority, and appreciation of differing perspectives.[1] Nonetheless,
even the Platonic and Ciceronian models of this capacious genre exhibit a high degree of control over an argument, while simultaneously providing the appearance of free debate. The historical realities
of the second half of the sixteenth century in France, with bloody
civil wars and failed truces, also remind us of the cultural challenges
to open-minded discussions. Yet dialogue retains some mystique as
a multivocal form, an educational and intellectual model that profits
from the inclusion of different voices. The dialogic form, especially
in works of religious propaganda, thus contains a core tension between the value of depicting multiple perspectives and the fact of its
single authorship. A case study of *Le pacifique*, a Protestant dialogue
published in 1590 and staged between an Evangelical and a Catholic,
serves to illuminate a genre that contains both dialogic and monologic elements.[2] This work, which has received no previous scholarly

---

1. Eva Kushner raises these perennial issues and acknowledges the perspective
that the dialogue's popularity might have signaled "the possibilities of openness to
truly divergent thinking, thus one sign among others of fragmentation of authority" (7,
my translation), declaring finally, "the Renaissance was truly the age of dialogue" (16,
my translation). Kushner, *Le dialogue à la Renaissance: Histoire et poétique* (Geneva:
Droz, 2004).
    2. Théophile Friderick, *Le pacifique* (N.p.: n.p., 1590). The text is available on
Gallica. All translations are my own.

YFS 134, *The Construction of a National Vernacular Literature in the Renaissance:
Essays in Honor of Edwin M. Duval,* ed. DeVos and Hayes, © 2018 by Yale University.

attention, *appears* to embrace a dialogocentric spirit, yet remains closed to alternative viewpoints. The very purpose of the dialogue— to argue for Christian unity—requires the paradox of a resolutely univocal message communicated through the fiction of multiple voices. The high political stakes at the moment of the dialogue's publication accentuate the importance of communicating a single message persuasively, but the same historical context likewise transforms the imagined peaceful exchange between members of opposing religions into a message itself. Through the following description and analysis of *Le pacifique*, I will argue that the work illustrates both the appeal of the dialogue as a means for depicting religious unity and the ways in which the genre silences other voices.

Le pacifique, written by the presumably pseudonymous Théophile Friderick,[3] stages a conversation between two French travelers, identified as the Evangelical and the Catholic. In many works of religious propaganda, the interlocutors form an adversarial relationship that emphasizes the disagreements between Catholics and Protestants; instead, *Le pacifique* follows an educational model and creates a more amicable relationship between interlocutors, despite their religious difference. The Evangelical is the primary speaker, acting as a teacher to the Catholic willing student. The Evangelical explains how Protestantism and Catholicism are but one Christian religion, and the Catholic appears by the end of their conversation to have fully understood this lesson. Although the Evangelical seems to present a theological argument about the unity of Christian beliefs, the content is overwhelmingly historical, with long passages about the Great Western Schism (1378–1417) and discussions grounded in syllogism rather than scripture. From the title page[4] to the closing prayer, the dialogue stresses that Christians should no longer fight each other, so that they can come together to protect themselves from threats such as the Ottoman Turks. While the core of the dialogue contains obvious Protestant propaganda, the work also transmits a political plea for Gallican unity to support the Protestant Henri IV, who is fighting

3. I have found no other works by Théophile Friderick, nor any other evidence of his existence. The Bibliothèque Nationale de France identifies Friderick as a pseudonym, and the meaning of the name—a lover of God in a peaceable kingdom—is suspiciously relevant to the work's message and recalls such pseudonyms as Eusèbe Philadelphe of the *Réveille-matin*.

4. The title is followed by a full paragraph summarizing the argument of the dialogue.

the Guise family and the Catholic League for control of Paris and the nation.

It is the political urgency of the moment that inspires Friderick to compose *Le pacifique*, in the hope of convincing others "more graced by God" to build something "more solid and more suitably arranged" (4). In the dedicatory epistle, Friderick reduces his authorial role by claiming only "the effort of having collected, distributed, and ordered" ideas that he has read elsewhere (4). This modesty exceeds the humility typical of a dedicatory epistle, and his claim only to have gathered and reorganized other works is borne out in my research. A close examination reveals that over a third of the text consists of an almost verbatim reproduction of passages written by the Protestant jurist Innocent Gentillet (1535-1588) in *Discours sur les moyens de bien gouverner et maintenir en bonne paix un royaume ou autre principauté—contre Machiavel*, commonly known (and hereafter referred to) as the *Anti-Machiavel*, first published in Geneva in 1576. Not only does the existence of this source text support Friderick's repudiation of his authorship, but, more interestingly, comparisons of Friderick's and Gentillet's respective works also illuminate relevant differences between dialogue and monologic genres. With its structure of responses to Machiavellian maxims, the *Anti-Machiavel* is dialogic, or at least dialectical, in spirit, but only in the sense that we might consider much of language dialogic, that is, aiming at an audience and incorporating the words of others in a Bakhtinian dialogism. *Le pacifique*, on the other hand, translates the subject matter into a theatrical dialogue, a conversation reported in direct discourse between interlocutors who, though fictitious and unnamed beyond their religious labels, nonetheless embody characters with whom a reader may identify. It is this aspect of the dialogue, the representation of characters, and not just ideas, that proves vital for the persuasive potential of the dialogue.

Friderick's slim dialogue—under seventy pages in-octavo—between members of different religions fits into a considerable corpus of sixteenth-century dialogues with religious and political aims, as well as into a context of actual conferences between theologians, such as the Colloquy of Poissy (1561).[5] Dialogues provided a convenient way

5. For information about the Colloquy of Poissy, where Théodore de Bèze and other Reformed ministers convened with Catholic archbishops and members of the royal family, see Donald Nugent, *Ecumenism in the Age of the Reformation: The*

for writers of both the Reformation and Counter-Reformation to contrast theological positions, as they worked to differentiate among different forms of Christianity and to distinguish correct beliefs from heresy.[6] While some of these dialogues focused on the doctrinal issues dividing Catholics and Protestants and thus included detailed discussions of scriptural and patristic sources, other dialogues, such as *Le réveille-matin* (1574) and *Le maheustre et le manant* (1593), commented instead on political events, from the St. Bartholomew's Day Massacre to the League's struggle for control of the throne after Henri III's assassination. While religion and politics can never be completely disentangled during this period of French history, most works of propaganda nonetheless have a distinct orientation toward either political or religious issues. In contrast, *Le pacifique* clearly aims at both political and religious goals, which are in fact at odds. *Le pacifique* explicitly wishes to convince Frenchmen to transcend their religious differences in order to unite, but beneath this political goal lies the same intention as religious propaganda: to convince readers of *the* correct form of Christianity. I argue that the harmonious conversation forms part of the political strategy to model unity, and that certain textual strategies communicate Protestant views in ways that avoid conflict. The analysis of these strategies suggests how the author of *Le pacifique* might have hoped to navigate successfully between his two competing goals, but this exploration will also reveal the improbability of success, if success is defined as persuading Catholics to accept Protestant doctrine. Despite the ways in which the dialogue seems designed to encourage readers to identify with the Catholic, and might therefore imply a Catholic readership, the likelihood of an intended Protestant audience becomes progressively clearer.

In order to recognize and understand the persuasive strategies at work in *Le pacifique*, I employ two avenues of analysis. One, as men-

---

Colloquy of Poissy (Cambridge: Harvard University Press, 1974). See also Isabelle Hentz-Dubail's dissertation, *De la logique à la civilité: disputes et conférences des guerres de religion (1560–1610)* (Université Grenoble III, 1999).

6. Peter Ascoli explains the attraction of literary dialogue for pamphleteers as "a useful form of propaganda because it could appeal to the dramatic and draw its readers into the debate. It was also an effective way of presenting both sides of an issue, while giving one side a clear advantage over the other" (6). Ascoli, "A Radical Pamphlet of Late Sixteenth-Century France: Le dialogue d'entre le Maheustre et le Manant," *Sixteenth Century Journal* 5/2 (October 1974): 3–22.

tioned above, is to compare *Le pacifique* to the *Anti-Machiavel* and probe the meaning of small variations between the two. The other analytical tool consists in uncovering the underlying organization of the dialogue, an endeavor that may initially seem futile. Unlike a volume of verse, a play divided in scenes and acts, or a novel with chapters, literary dialogues contain little internal architecture. Conversations wander, interlocutors ramble or monopolize the floor, and the formlessness frustrates a Duvalian search for a logical design, much less a significant center. An appreciation of the symmetries of *Le pacifique*, however, helps us to understand the importance of one of the dialogic elements, the frame story.

Like many dialogues, *Le pacifique* involves no extra-dialogic material but rather begins immediately with the direct discourse of the interlocutors. But unlike many dialogues in which the interlocutors offer only perfunctory greetings before entering abruptly into a contested question, the Evangelical starts with a pious soliloquy to thank God for his successful journey thus far. He notices another traveler who appears to be an "homme de qualité" (a gentleman), turns back, and greets him: "Monsieur, may God grant you a good day, and keep you from evil" (7). The Catholic returns the blessing, "May Jesus Christ son of God and the Virgin Mary, give all happiness and contentment to you, Sir, my friend" (7). These invocations are formulaic but meaningful, as the Catholic explains that the Evangelical's greeting "in the name of God and his son Jesus Christ" (9) immediately reassured him and gave him hope of a good travel partner. The pious language signals to contemporary readers the Christian faith of the author and, by extension, vouches for the acceptability of the dialogue's content. The blessings also indicate the Catholic's accommodation of his conversation partner. While the Evangelical mentions only God in his original greeting, the Catholic includes Christ and the Virgin Mary in his. When the Catholic cites the Evangelical's greeting, he includes Christ, but omits the Virgin Mary, thereby adapting both his own words and the Evangelical's for a more ecumenical public and foreshadowing the dialogue's irenic conclusion.

The interlocutors continue to express their good will and confidence in one another, their common feelings of distress about the violence in France, and the Catholic conveys his genuine interest in understanding the Evangelical's claim about Christian unity. They delicately share their religious affiliation, accompanied by assurances that they are not "massacreurs & bruyans" (murderous and blustering)

(11, 12) and that they abhor all the violence that has been committed in the name of religion. Phrases such as "open my heart" (10) and "I will not be coy to say" (10, 12) imply both the honesty of the interlocutors and their readiness to trust one another. The Catholic's curiosity and his requests for further explanation justify the Evangelical's increasingly long speeches without losing the sense of a noncoercive conversation. Even if the Evangelical dominates the dialogue by sheer word count, the Catholic's regular interventions never allow the reader to forget his presence. This depiction of voluntary participation is indispensable if later sections of agreement and persuasion are to appear convincing. The Catholic's interventions, as well as the slow progression toward the difficult and controversial topics at the center of *Le pacifique*, mimic the unhurried pace of a naturally flowing conversation, an essential element for portraying a realistic scene of persuasion.[7] This preamble makes sense as part of a realistic story, where interlocutors who are strangers to one another must lay a groundwork of trust and amity before discussing controversial topics. At the same time, the interlocutors exhibit kind and respectful treatment toward strangers, and the introduction becomes itself a lesson to readers about Christian behavior.

In parallel to the extensive opening, the conclusion to the dialogue highlights the Catholic's metaphorical journey and the evolution of the interlocutors' relationship. The Evangelical has dominated the dialogue with his explanations whereas the Catholic has participated through questions, requests for information, brief reactions, and short answers about his own faith. The conversational imbalance is reversed in the final pages of the work, when the Catholic concludes with a statement of agreement, a summary of the main points, and a prayer to which the Evangelical responds solely, "May it be so" (74). The Catholic does not express his persuasion as a change of faith. Instead, he has a realization about Protestant beliefs:

7. This analysis owes much to the work of Jean-Claude Carron, "The Persuasive Seduction: Dialogue in Sixteenth-Century France" in *Contending Kingdoms*, ed. Marie-Rose Logan and Peter L. Rudnytsky (Detroit: Wayne State University Press, 1991), 90–108. Carron emphasizes the mimetic aspect of dialogue and lucidly explains the mechanics of persuasion in a dialogue as "a seductive scene in which systematic argumentation plays no role in bringing a dialogue to its end" (103). Instead "the represented submission of the addressee, the true 'action' of the dialogue" happens within a fiction of an open conversation that is "controlled by a single 'voice'" (102). Carron suggests that the interactions between interlocutors may be just as, if not more, convincing to readers as the substance put forth in their arguments.

And however, considering your reasons and speech, which I have heard with great pleasure and for which I am grateful to you, I must tell you that *never have I believed otherwise* the points that you have touched upon, except as you have said: and as for me, I would never have thought that you others would have been in such agreement with Catholics, as I hear from your words that you are. (71, my emphasis)

This declaration demonstrates an understanding about the compatibility of Protestant beliefs with Catholicism, but it also underscores the stability of the Catholic's perception of his own faith. The Catholic reinforces the persuasiveness of the Evangelical's speech while still maintaining his own Catholic identity. Having stated his belief that Protestants and Catholics share a core Christian faith, the Catholic interlocutor turns his attention to the current state of affairs, deploring the recent bloodshed in France and beyond, the indifference of the Pope to this suffering, and the Ottoman threat that requires Christian unity. This troubling political situation moves him to pray to God "after so much misery and calamity to bend the hearts of Princes and Christian peoples to peace" (72) and to advocate a specific agenda of refusing obedience to the Pope, ensuring freedom of conscience, and holding a universally recognized council; these are the same points found on the title page and throughout the Evangelical's argument. The staging of the dialogue, from start to finish, represents the patient and civil interactions necessary for members of different religions to converse and to find sufficient religious concord to support a unified political will for peace.

In addition to the narrative framing, the symmetry of the dialogue includes a central section that addresses specific doctrinal issues, buffered on both sides by historical information about the Great Western Schism, the period following the Avignon Papacy from 1378 to 1417. The Evangelical raises this subject in response to the Catholic's initial objection to the claim of religious unity. The Catholic does not use doctrinal disagreements to question the Evangelical's assertion that Catholicism and Protestantism are one religion, but rather he argues that the current war and bloodshed are proof that religious differences exist. The Catholic cannot believe that Christians would fight against each other if they actually held the same faith. This objection allows the Evangelical to offer a refutation based on a counter-example: the Great Western Schism is evidence that Christians have fought one another in the past. Toward the end of the dialogue, the Catholic leads the Evangelical back to the topic of the Schism; he explains that he has found all the arguments convincing, but obedience to the Pope remains an important difference between them. The Evangelical uses the Schism to prove that Catholics have in the past survived without a Pope and he repeats the historical information from earlier in the dialogue with similar detail. The Schism therefore provides an analogy for the current strife that conveniently displaces responsibility for the conflict onto an absent third party (the Pope), suggesting that the civil war is the result of greedy and power-hungry individuals who care little for Christendom or for France, and using the example of a French king, Charles VI, who refused obedience to Rome.

Le pacifique borrows the content about the Great Western Schism primarily from a single passage of the *Anti-Machiavel*, but instead of presenting the information as a long intervention by the Evangelical, Friderick inserts original material in the form of interjections spoken by the Catholic. In addition to maintaining the fiction of a dialogue, the Catholic's interventions emphasize certain lessons and display appropriate emotional reactions upon learning this information. After hearing of conflicts between Clementine and Urbanist factions, the Catholic comments, "There is surely a deplorable blindness of Christians, eating one another while the Turk and his empire grow daily. But how was it possible, I ask you, to appease such great uprisings?" (19). When the Evangelical explains how the king and his advisors wanted the popes to come to a Council to resolve the problems, the Catholic responds, "There is, in my opinion, a good means wisely put forward by the King and his Counsel, the gentlest and most proper manner to put an end to Christendom's misery" (63). In reaction to the popes' refusal to listen, the Catholic asks, "But can the King endure patiently such obstinacy, without admonishing and soliciting them further, to get them to their objective, or did he not look for another means to force them to reason?" (63–64). These interventions underscore the attitude of praise or blame that readers should adopt, such as appreciation for the king's wisdom.

The inclusion of historical content and the dialogic additions serve multiple purposes when considered as strategies to balance the competing political and religious goals. Discussion of the Schism maintains the focus on political rather than theological causes of conflict. As an active interlocutor, the Catholic shows genuine curiosity and peaceful interaction; he thus acts as a character with whom readers, both Catholic and Protestant, may identify. Like the narrative frame, the symmetrical sections about the Great Western Schism provide a buffer, delaying treatment of the thorniest issues. The digression, explicitly identified as such by the interlocutors, reinforces the fiction of a conversation that can wander and take its time, but also provides more space for the Catholic and Protestant to build trust before they arrive—almost a third of the way through the text—at the contentious doctrinal issues.

If Catholics were reading *Le pacifique*, the insulation of the doctrinal material would allow them to advance further in the text before encountering objectionable ideas. This central section, however, makes it clear that Catholics are not the real audience for this work. A Catholic is unlikely to read, let alone be convinced by, the undeniably Protestant discussion of doctrine. *Le pacifique* differs from other religious propaganda in a subtle but significant way. Since propaganda aims to convince its audience of a single correct belief, it proves, by extension, that other beliefs are wrong. The author of *Le pacifique* must portray Evangelical beliefs in a way that does not show them to be different from the faith of a Catholic. The very purpose of this propaganda then changes; instead of persuading readers to accept certain *beliefs* (which they presumably already hold), this dialogue shows Protestants their similarity to Catholic *believers*. In order to argue for Protestantism without arguing against Catholics, *Le pacifique* must avoid suggesting any Protestant superiority to Catholicism. In fact, *Le pacifique* must argue for Protestant faith in a way that does not admit the existence of two different religions. The dialogic transposition of an argument against transubstantiation from the *Anti-Machiavel* illustrates how the use of dialogue shifts the focus from beliefs to believers.

The *Anti-Machiavel* contains a section that I label proto-dialogic, because it presents an imagined conversation, reported in indirect discourse. In this section, Gentillet becomes a narrator, rather than an orator, recounting a scene where he overheard a Protestant argue that the two religions were but one. Within this reported speech the Protestant demonstrates common beliefs through hypothetical interrogations in which he imagines a Catholic's response to certain questions:

> In the first place, if you ask a good Catholic, if when he receives the
> holy sacrament at Easter, he believes he is crushing and breaking be-

tween his teeth the actual flesh and bones of our Lord Jesus Christ, he will answer you that he does not believe this and that he detests and abhors this discourse of crushing and breaking in one's teeth the flesh and bones of our Savior. If you ask him, if he does not believe that in receiving the Holy Sacrament he receives spiritually the body and blood of our Lord Jesus Christ, he will respond that yes, he believes it so. If you ask him again, if in receiving the sacrament of the host he believes that he receives and drinks by the same means the sacrament of the blood [. . .] he will say that he does not believe that at all.[8]

This proto-dialogic material is easily adapted in the direct discourse of *Le pacifique* with some significant additions, highlighted below:

Evangelical: In the first place, Sir, I ask you, when you receive the holy Sacrament of the Altar at Easter, do you believe that you crush and break between your teeth the actual flesh and bones of our Lord Jesus Christ?

Catholic: I do not believe that. I even find these words a horrifying abomination, to crush and break in one's teeth the flesh and bones of our Lord Jesus Christ.

Evangelical: *That is however what the Sophists want Christians to believe, on pain of being taken for heretics.* But I beg you, tell me, don't you believe that in receiving the holy Sacrament, you receive spiritually and by faith the body and the blood of our lord Jesus Christ?

Catholic: Yes, I believe it so.

Evangelical: *And so do we believe it as well.* But in receiving the sacrament of the host, do you believe that you receive and drink by the same means the sacrament of blood [. . .] ? (35–36)

Equating transubstantiation with cannibalism, as both texts do here, repeats the misrepresentations of the Eucharist found in the most virulent Protestant propaganda.[9] The inclusion of such extreme material is a sign that *Le pacifique* is directed at a Protestant audience. Not only would a Catholic audience find this suggestion of cannibalism outrageous, but the Catholic would also have no difficulty in refut-

8. Innocent Gentillet, *Anti-Machiavel*, ed. C. Edward Rathé (Geneva: Droz, 1968), 172 (my translation).
9. Frank Lestringant identifies a "true cannibal hermeneutic" of the Catholic Mass in the critiques of Marcourt, Calvin, Bèze, and Viret. *Une sainte horreur ou le voyage en Eucharistie XVIe—XVIIIe siècle* (Paris: PUF, 1996), 64 (my translation).

ing this representation of his beliefs.[10] Protestants, however, might have encountered propaganda accusing Catholics of theophagy. This argument against transubstantiation is therefore included not to convince Catholics to believe differently but to convince Protestants that Catholics are good Christians and not cannibals.

The original material that the Evangelical inserts into his questioning emphasizes the unity of Christian beliefs, both by asserting his agreement with the Catholic and by providing an external source for the heretical beliefs. Not only are the Sophists (the Evangelical's blanket term for theologians of the Sorbonne and others who insist on obscure reasoning) responsible for the misunderstanding about the Eucharist, the Evangelical argues, but they are also to blame for the discord and the threats against supposed heretics. Friderick's additions remind us that there are at least three levels of persuasion occurring simultaneously in the dialogue. *Le pacifique* shares one of its aims with the *Anti-Machiavel*, that of persuading a reader that Catholic and Protestant beliefs are the same, by imagining how a Catholic would respond to certain questions. But the Evangelical must also appear to convince the Catholic of their shared beliefs in order to create a scene of persuasion, which is itself necessary to convince Protestant readers to accept a vision of peaceful and reasonable Catholics.

The transposition of the third-person hypothetical discourse of the *Anti-Machiavel* to the direct first- and second-person speech changes relatively little in terms of the content, but the Catholic's expressions of belief appear more plausible in *Le pacifique* because of the distance created between the author and his characters. As Jean-Claude Carron acknowledges, dialogue "remains fundamentally a performance of persuasion rather than a true instrument of persuasion. The reader is not convinced by the arguments of the exchange but through the representation of someone being convinced."[11] Certainly, in both the *Anti-Machiavel* and *Le pacifique*, the perspective of the Catholic is imagined, and is therefore no more than a Protestant fiction, but the dialogic form enhances the verisimilitude of the Catholic's utterances and buttresses the admittedly questionable fiction that Catholics agree with Protestants on this contentious issue. Whether the shift to direct discourse indeed has such an effect on readers is unknowable,

10. It is the Catholic, in an interesting transposition from Gentillet, who likens this depiction of the Mass to a meal for Polyphemus (38).

11. Carron, "The Persuasive Seduction," 102.

but we can surmise that Friderick imagined that his reader would be more inclined to accept the depiction of Catholicism as truthful if offered through the performance of a dialogue.

This scene of persuasion depends not on the Evangelical's persuasiveness, let alone upon the actual theological content, but on the Catholic's expressions of understanding and agreement, as the passage quoted above and the concluding prayer demonstrate. The Catholic's agreement cannot come too easily, however, and it cannot come across as conversion or capitulation. The wording of the Catholic's agreement often avoids direct statements in favor of provisional or highly periphrastic support. For example, "Up to now I would not be able to find any heresy, not even an error in what you believe" (31). Rather than expressing approval of the Evangelical's statements, he uses negatives: "Never would it happen that I would want to condemn that" (53) or "I would be careful not to deny that" (57). These restrained expressions may compensate for the Catholic's heterodox agreement, as he manages to concur with the Evangelical, while simultaneously avoiding the impression that he is misrepresenting Catholicism or changing his mind.

Le pacifique illustrates how a dialogue can, by deliberate misrepresentation, silence other voices; it thereby serves as a counter-example to claims that Renaissance dialogue embodies a spirit of openness and toleration. The genre is, however, useful in this case precisely because it *seems* to advocate for openness and toleration, which is the ultimate goal. This analysis of *Le pacifique* thus indicates some risks and paradoxes of interfaith dialogue, which are still present today in efforts to find unity rather than to understand and accept diversity. By its structure the dialogue embodies the value of hearing multiple voices and is therefore the optimal form to represent a resolution to religious conflict, given that the first step to peaceful coexistence requires coming together and listening. It is hard to reconcile the form with its functioning, however, when difference is erased in a way that may in fact be intolerant and coercive, forcing perspectives upon an interlocutor who does not or cannot defend himself. Above all, this textual paradox highlights an extra-textual tension between a devotion to one's faith and a desire for national unity and peace, so critical in 1590 during the crisis of Henri IV's succession. The tension in *Le pacifique* between the form and the functioning of the form thereby mirrors the difficulty of resolving a political crisis that is entwined with deeply held religious beliefs.

This study of *Le pacifique* demonstrates both the importance of the dialogue as the medium for a political message of toleration and the failure of the religious rhetoric to achieve real toleration. The dialogue presents a distinctly Protestant version of Christianity, with arguments for Christian unity cloaking its polemical elements. Likewise, the staging of a dialogue conceals the inherently univocal nature of a work that offers a scene of co-existence only by creating a likeable but unlikely Catholic character. Since the dialogue follows an educational model, we might assume that the reader, learning along with the Catholic, will identify with the Catholic interlocutor. But, as I have argued, the dialogue must be intended for a Protestant audience, which leads to a further paradox. *Le pacifique* enacts a scene of persuasion in which a Protestant reader identifies with the interlocutor who is not of their faith and accepts the lesson that Protestant and Catholic religions are still a single Christian religion. In this way, the work enables Protestant readers to feel both comforted in their own beliefs and unified with Catholics. The portrayal of a reasonable and open-minded Catholic, however fictional, may have helped Protestants to see Catholics as partners in the interest of French unity and may have constituted the real lesson of *Le pacifique.*

V. Ethical Legacy of Humanism

DAVID QUINT

Of an Allusion in Montaigne

The beginnings and endings of Montaigne's individual essays bear special attention, as Edwin Duval has taught us.[1] The endings at times
have the effect of the "sting in the tail" produced by the final twist
of an epigram, a reversal of the meaning or logic of what has preceded
it, a saving of the worst or most malicious sense for last.[2] Montaigne
produces one such ending, but he stealthily disguises it, at the close
of "De la cruauté" (2.11), a key chapter in the *Essais'* radical project
to substitute a modern, vernacular ethics (and Montaigne's own example) for classical moral philosophy:[3] "And Plutarch had scruples,

1. Edwin M. Duval, "Le début des *Essais* et la fin d'un livre," *RHLF* 88/6 (1988):
896–907; "Lessons of the New World: Design and Meaning in Montaigne's 'Des Can-
nibales' [I:31] and 'Des coches' [III:6]," in *Montaigne: Essays in Reading*, ed. Gérard
Defaux, *Yale French Studies* 64 (1983): 95–112; "Rhetorical Composition and 'Open
Form' in Montaigne's Early *Essais*," *BHR* 43 (1981): 269–87; "Montaigne's Conver-
sions: Compositional Strategies in the *Essais*," *French Forum* 7 (1982): 5–22.
2. "Les esguillons dequy Martial esguise la queuë des siens" ("The stings with
which Martial sharpens the ends of his [epigrams]"). French citations come from *Les
Essais de Michel de Montaigne*, ed. Pierre Villey (Paris: Presses Universitaires de
France, 1965), 412. All translations from Montaigne come from *The Complete Essays
of Montaigne*, ed. Donald M. Frame (Stanford: Stanford University Press, 1958.) 2:10,
Essais 412, *Essays* 299.
3. On the radical nature of Montaigne's position, see the important article by
Philip Hallie, "The Ethics of Montaigne's 'De la cruauté,'" in *Oh un amy!: Essays on
Montaigne in Honor of Donald M. Frame*, ed. Raymond La Charité, French Forum
Monographs 5 (Lexington, KY: French Forum, 1977), 156–71, Judith Shklar, *Ordinary
Vices* (Cambridge, MA: Harvard University Press, 1984), 7–44, and the brief remarks
of Géralde Nakam, in *Les Essais de Montaigne: Miroir et proces de leur temps* (Paris:
Nizet, 1984), 438–39. Timothy Hampton traces the movement from ancient to modern
example in *Writing from History: The Rhetoric of Exemplarity in Renaissance Litera-
ture* (Ithaca: Cornell University Press, 1990), 159–71. See also David Lewis Schaefer,

YFS 134, *The Construction of a National Vernacular Literature in the Renaissance:
Essays in Honor of Edwin M. Duval*, ed. DeVos and Hayes, © 2018 by Yale University.

he says, about selling and sending to the slaughterhouse, for a slight profit, an ox that had served him long."[4] As is often the case in the *Essais*, we appear to have followed the train of thought of the essayist quite far from where he started. "De la cruauté" initially seems to be about the distinction between true virtue, defined in Stoic terms as a heroic struggle against vicious inclinations, and a simple goodness that comes with souls who are *"bien nées,"* a deliberately ambiguous phrase that can mean both well-born from a good, noble family, and being blessed with a good disposition by nature. Some particularly virtuous exemplars, Cato the Younger and Socrates, have turned their mastery over vice into second nature and into a kind of Epicurean pleasure. Cato even takes pleasure in contemplating the supreme test of his virtue, his ripping out of his entrails in suicide—"I know not what rejoicing of his soul, and an emotion of extraordinary pleasure." Socrates finds similar pleasure—"I know not what new contentment"—in drinking his hemlock.[5] Montaigne judges this quieter death to be even more beautiful than Cato's.

Montaigne then confesses that he does not himself possess virtue at all as he has defined it. He depends instead on his good fortune: "It had me born of a race famous for integrity, and of a very good father." He also depends on the "instinct and impression that I brought away from my nurse" and "the chance of my birth."[6] He is one of those souls who are "bien-nées," in both of its senses. As we finally come to the subject announced in the title, he cites his hatred of cruelty as an example of his native and naive innocence. He cannot watch a chicken's throat being cut or hear the crying of a hare pursued by his hunting dogs. It is physical cruelty that is at stake.[7] After several celebrated pages that denounce torture, executions that go beyond simple killing,[8] and the atrocities of the French Wars of Religion tak-

---

The Political Philosophy of Montaigne (Ithaca: Cornell University Press, 1990), 227–36, 245–50; David Quint, *Montaigne and the Quality of Mercy* (Princeton: Princeton University Press, 1998), 42–74.

4. *Essays* 318, *Essais* 435.

5. 2:11, *Essays* 310, *Essais* 424

6. 2:11, *Essays* 311, 312, 313, *Essais* 427-29

7. Shklar, *Ordinary Vices*.

8. "As for me, even in justice, all that goes beyond plain death seems to me pure cruelty," (*Essays* 314, *Essais* 431). The papal censor of the 1580 edition of the *Essais* objected to this pronouncement, which Montaigne repeats verbatim in 2:27, "Couardise mere de la cruauté" (*Essais* 700). Montaigne retained both passages in subsequent editions. See Nakam, 327 and note.

ing place around him, Montaigne returns to the theme of cruelty to animals—to creatures united to human beings because of their embodied, physical nature. The essay takes a final, positive turn as it asserts the "general duty of humanity" owed not only to animals but to all living things: "We owe justice to men, and mercy and kindness to other creatures that may be capable of receiving it. There is some relationship between them and us and some mutual obligation."[9] Justice is one thing, and it is directed to humans as rational beings; mercy—for that is the primary meaning of Montaigne's "grace" in the French text—and kindness are owed to animals as physical beings. This is all the more true for domesticated animals with whom humans have a kind of contractual relationship: horses, dogs, beasts of burden. The essay concludes with classical examples of men honoring animals who have done them service, feeding them at public expense, and building them funeral monuments. And so we come to the final sentence: Plutarch had scruples, he tells us, about selling and slaughtering, for the small profit it would bring, an ox that had long served him.

Well, did Plutarch sell the ox and take the money, or not? The essay leaves us in a kind of suspense about this philosopher, and raises again the question of philosophical virtue versus the simple good nature of the essayist that we may have felt by now we have left behind. But the anecdote, when we read it in its original context, is not really about Plutarch at all, but a different ancient. It and most of the material in the two paragraphs that precede it (including the descriptions of the honors done and monuments built to animals) come from Plutarch's *Life of Marcus Cato the Elder*, Cato the Censor. Plutarch is, in fact, appalled by Cato's treatment, not of his old used-up animals, *but of his old slaves*, whom he would sell off, even when they were of no use to anyone, adding dishonesty to avarice. Here is Amyot's version, from which one can get an idea of just how much Montaigne has lifted:

> Nonetheless, thus to sell slaves or drive them away from the house, after they have grown old in your service, no more nor less than if they were mute beasts, when one has drawn out of them the service of all their life: that seems to me to proceed from an overly harsh and rigidly austere nature, and from one who thinks that there is between one

9. 2:11, *Essays* 318, *Essais* 435.

man and another no larger society that mutually obliges them than
the profit or utility they can derive from each other. Nonetheless we
see that goodness extends further than justice, because nature teaches
us to use equity and justice only toward human beings, and mercy
and benignity sometimes even to brute animals: that which proceeds
from the fountain of loving-kindness and humanity that should never
dry up in a man. [. . .] And as for me, I would never have the heart to
sell an ox who had for a long time worked my land, because he could
no longer work on account of age, and still less a slave in expelling
him, as if from his homeland from the place where he had long been
nourished and from the manner of life to which he had been accus-
tomed—all for the little money which I might obtain in selling him,
when he would be as of little use to those who would buy him, as to
he who would sell him.[10]

So, to be clear, Plutarch would *not* sell off his old ox. But Cato inhu-
manely did to his human slaves what should not be done to house-
hold beasts, and defrauded those who bought them as well. In this
ethically luminous passage that Montaigne repeats, Plutarch distinguishes between mere justice and equity on the one hand and, on the
other, a goodness that we may even extend to animals, though in doing so, he might suggest that we are kinder and more obligated to animals than to our human kindred. He also ambiguously positions the
slave as both human and beast. We treat other rational beings with
reason—and in "De la colere" (2.31) Montaigne will depict, and raise
his eyebrows at, a Plutarch who claims to be a dispassionate judge
as he orders the flogging of one of his own misbehaving slaves.[11] But
insofar as the slave is a bodily creature, he has a claim to mercy that
goes beyond equity. For Montaigne, if not for Plutarch and certainly
not for the elder Cato, *this is the overriding moral claim, the claim
based on shared animal embodiedness, that all human beings, free
and slave, have on one another.* It is a claim that the *Essais* repeatedly attempt to balance with justice but that finally outweighs it.

Cato the Elder's violation of this claim is not only shocking in
itself: the buried allusion at the essay's end, once unpacked, also implicates his great-grandson Cato the Younger who is depicted at the

10. Plutarch, *Les vies des hommes illustres grecs et romains*, trans. Jacques Amyot
(Paris: Michel de Vascosan, 1559), 236. My translation.

11. 2:32, Essays, 541-42; *Essais* 716-17; see Quint, "Letting Oneself Go: 'De la
colere' and Montaigne's Ethical Reflections," *Philosophy and Literature* 24 (2000):
126-37.

beginning. The Elder Cato disdained philosophy, but his inhumanity seems to have been handed down and entered into the stoic philosophy of his descendant. Cato the Younger takes so little account of the body that he can seem to Montaigne to enjoy—"esjouissance [. . .] plaisir extraordinaire"—watching himself rip out his own intestines, too similar for comfort to some of Montaigne's contemporaries whom the essay goes on to describe: licensed by civil war, they dismember and torture solely for the sadistic pleasure—"de jouïr du plaisant spectacle"—of watching other human beings suffer and die in anguish (2:11; 432). The Catos, too, might boast descent from a famous, well-born family, but Montaigne balks at the cruel virtue they profess: he prefers his own family's (and, by implication the human family's) inherent good-nature, what it truly means to be "bien-né." The modern essayist who hates cruelty offers himself as a substitute exemplar for the heroes of antiquity. And Montaigne senses, here as in "De la colere," how classical ethics is deeply compromised by the institution of slavery that was at its social foundations. Reason's supposed control over the body—the perfected virtue of the younger Cato and Socrates celebrated at the essay's opening—conforms to a practice of brutal mastery over the bodies of others.

Montaigne takes up these issues again in the essay that follows "De la cruauté," the "Apologie de Raimond Sebond" (2.12), where he recounts the story of the slave Androdus (more familiarly, Androcles) and the lion, told by Aulus Gellius (Noctes atticae 5.14).[12] Having run away from his master, a Roman lord of consular rank who flogged him every day, Androdus is befriended by the lion from whose paw he has removed a splinter; after three years of companionship, sharing the meat the lion brings back to his lair, Androdus leaves, is recaptured and immediately sentenced to death by beasts in the arena. There he meets his lion, who fawns on him, beating his tale on the ground like a dog in front of his master. "battre de la queuë à la mode des chiens qui flattent leur maistre." The two, slave and beast, embrace, to the delight and pleasure of the audience: "it was a singular pleasure to see

---

12. In light of the end of my essay, it is worth noting that medieval versions of Gellius's tale circulated, attributed to Aesop. One was incorporated as "The lion and the shepherd" into Heinrich Steinhöwel's collection of Aesop's Fables (Ulm, 1476). It would subsequently appear in other editions and translations of Aesop based on Steinhöwel, including a French translation (Lyon, 1480). Hieronymus Osius translated the story as "The lion host to man" in his versification of the Fables (Wittenberg, 1564).

the caresses and greetings that they lavished upon each other."[13] At the cries of joy of the public, the Emperor hears Androdus's story, pardons him, frees him, and gives him the lion, whom Androdus leads through Rome on a leash as a kind of moneymaking attraction.

Montaigne translates word for word the anecdote recounted by Aulus Gellius, but he makes one significant addition in the story: Androdus explains why he came into the wilds and found himself in the lion's lair: "When my master was proconsul in Africa, I was constrained, *by the cruelty and rigor with which he treated me*—he had me beaten daily—to steal away from him and take flight."[14] The cruelty of the slaveholder, a high Roman noble of consular rank, links the story to the preceding essay in Montaigne's book. Such physical cruelty stands in contrast to the mutual affection between owner and pet. Montaigne plays on the different uses of "battre"—flogging and tail-wagging—and the two inflections of "maistre." (These, too, are Montaigne's own elegant embellishments of the Latin original.) Human cruelty is witnessed in treating other humans like beasts, so many bodies to be beaten or, in the last instance, to be fed to wild beasts in uneven combat. We see its opposite in the kind treatment of animals, animals from whose virtues we have something to learn, the "Apologie" continuously argues, not least our presumption in thinking ourselves superior to them. All of the passages I have cited so far come from the 1580 A] text. In two 1595 C]-text additions, first to "De la cruauté," Montaigne confesses his weakness (that is really his moral strength) of being unable to refuse the "feste" that his dog offers him even in inconvenient moments (2:11, *Essais* 435), and he famously states in the "Apologie": "When I play with my cat, who knows if I am not a pastime to her more than she is to me?"[15] The lion of the anecdote is evidently a big cat that plays like a dog.

But Montaigne had already made an addition to the 1588 B] text of "De la cruauté" that tells another side of the story and that influences how we read both essays.

> At Rome, after they had become accustomed ("apprivoisé') to the spectacle of the slaughter of animals, they proceeded to that of men and of gladiators. Nature herself, I fear, attaches to man some instinct for inhumanity. No one takes his sport in seeing animals play with

13. 2:12, *Essays* 351, *Essais* 477.
14. 2:12, *Essays* 351 (emphasis added), *Essais* 477.
15. 2:12, *Essays* 318, 331, *Essais* 435, 452.

and caress one another, and no one fails to take it in seeing them tear apart and dismember one another.[16]

Montaigne repeats his argument that cruelty to animals is continuous, even causally continuous with cruelty to other human beings, in this case to the gladiators, who were slaves like Androdus, and sent to kill each other. But he now qualifies his argument to the point of contradicting his assertions of an inherent good human nature. The story of the arena audience taking delight in the caresses between Androdus and lion appears to be a singular exception: nobody likes to see animals play and caress, but everybody enjoys seeing them dismember each other. The pleasure that Cato took in watching his spectacular suicide may not only be philosophical cruelty toward the body, but an expression of a deeper human nature. In our own twenty-first century empire, cute cat pictures on the internet pale before nature documentaries that provide the thrill of being in on the kill: scenes of tooth and claw. They inure us to social Darwinism, if not to outright slavery.[17]

The pessimistic force of the passage, Montaigne's fear about what may be a naturally inherent *inhumanity*, is perhaps softened by the force of "apprivoisé."[18] The Roman people had to be trained to enjoy the murders of animals, and the verb has a special ironic charge, since "apprivoiser" for the most part is used to describe training animals themselves to be less ferocious, to tame them. The Romans were domesticated to cruelty, and thus brought down to the level of wild beasts. So inhumanity may be a question of education or of custom. Near the beginning of "De la coutume" (1:23), Montaigne, in fact, rehearses the same chain of ideas and examples, as he complains how parental indulgence ingrains vices in the very young:

> I find that our greatest vices take shape from our tenderest childhood, and that our most important training is in the hands of nurses. It is a pastime for mothers to see a child wring the neck of a chicken, amuse itself by hurting a dog or a cat; and there are fathers stupid enough to take it as a good omen of a martial soul when they see a son unjustly

16. 2:11, *Essays* 316, *Essais* 433.

17. I owe this observation to Margaret Doody, who remarked on it in conversation many years ago.

18. Montaigne, notably, cannot be "apprivoisé" to the many atrocities of the French civil wars in the 1580 A] passage one page earlier (2:11, *Essays* 315, *Essais* 432) to which the use of the word in this 1588 B] addition is meant to correspond.

striking a peasant or a lackey who is not defending himself, and as a
charming prank when they see him trick his playmate by a bit of malicious dishonesty and deceit. Nevertheless, these are the true seeds
and roots of cruelty, tyranny, and treason; they sprout there, and after-
ward shoot up lustily, and flourish mightily in the hands of habit. And
it is a very dangerous educational policy to excuse our children for
these ugly inclinations. In the first place, it is nature speaking, whose
voice is all the purer and stronger because it is more tenuous.[19]

However much Montaigne may claim in "De la cruauté" to have received good instincts and hatred of cruelty from his nurse, he recognizes that other children may receive opposite instincts from nature:
Montaigne cannot bear to watch a chicken die; they would happily
wring its neck. He loves to play with dog and cat; they take pleasure
in injuring theirs. The mistreatment of slaves in classical antiquity
finds its updated equivalent in the contemporary child's striking a
socially dependent peasant or servant: what one does to animals, one
will do to other people. But Montaigne also suggests that such cruel
and sadistic tendencies can be checked, before they become custom
or second nature, while the child's own nature is still weak, and while
one can educate the child and teach it the "natural deformity" (1:23;
110) of vice. In "De l'experience," he further informs us of his father's plan to raise him in his earliest years among peasant villagers,
to learn his commonality with them, with the effect that "I am prone
to devote myself to the little people, whether because there is more
vainglory in it, or through natural compassion, which has infinite
power over me."[20] The essayist is alert to the ironies: that there is
something self-aggrandizing ("la gloire") in this patronage of depen-
dents, that such "natural" compassion has been engineered in him by
his father's educational design. Like cruelty, this compassion can be
unnatural and natural at the same time.

The *Essais* have similar educational designs on the reader. The
possible contradictions they articulate do not end in aporia, but in
moral judgment.[21] Montaigne appeals to our best instincts even as he
acknowledges the simultaneous pull of our worst ones. Reviving the
terms of "De la cruauté," he offers himself in "De l'experience" as a
moral example of easy-going goodness and compassion, a model we

19. 1:23, *Essays* 78, *Essais* 110.
20. 3:13, *Essays* 844, *Essais* 1100.
21. Duval, "Le début"; "Lessons of the New World."

can find it in ourselves to imitate as opposed to that of the *inimitable* Catos: "that inimitable straining for virtue that astounds us in both Catos, that disposition, severe to the point of being troublesome."[22] He does so, in this last of the *Essais* by describing his self-knowledge, which is a knowledge better than what any doctor, physical or spiritual, could achieve, of his own body and his habits.[23] He catalogues the latter in exhaustive—and, to some of his exasperated contemporary readers, superfluous—detail, and discusses the kidney stone disease of which he is slowly dying. The essay reminds us that we, too, have bodies and habits, and that we are mortal; in these respects, we already imitate Michel de Montaigne. It also reminds us that such shared embodiedness carries a moral obligation: it concludes with the warning that attempts to deny our bodies and to escape the human ("eschapper à l'homme") do not turn us into angels but rather into beasts, and *not* the beasts with whom we share domestication, but savage ones.

This was the case of Alexander the Great, who fancied himself a god. His lieutenant Philotas congratulated Alexander on godhood but pitied subjects who would have to live beneath a ruler not content to be a man ("la mesure d'un homme"). It was a self-fulfilling prophecy: the tyrannical Alexander cited these very words to condemn Philotas to prolonged torture and execution.[24] This anecdote, at the end of the book's final essay, retrospectively explains another at the end of its first essay, where Montaigne is puzzled by Alexander's horrifying treatment of his captive Betis and of the vanquished defenders and inhabitants of Thebes (1.1; 9–10). Now he understands the cause of Alexander's cruelty: the conqueror's disavowal of his human condition, his fear of living itself. These stories of Alexander frame the *Essais* as admonitions.[25] The last words of the opening essay describe the Thebans' fate and the results of inhumanity: "thirty thousand slaves."

"De l'experience" has just offered, a few sentences earlier, an earthier version of Philotas's speaking truth to power, here in the mouth of a slave himself: "Aesop, that great man, saw his master pissing as he walked. 'What next?' he said. 'Shall we have to shit as

---

22. 3:13, *Essays* 851, *Essais* 1109. The passage notes that even these stoics had to submit to human nature, and indulge in Venus and Bacchus.

23. Jean Starobinski, *Montaigne in Motion*, trans. Arthur Goldhammer (Chicago: The University of Chicago Press, 1985), 138–84.

24. Quintus Curtius, *History of Alexander*, VI.ix.18.

25. Schaefer, 232.

we run?'"[26] The drop in diction and decorum is meant to bring up short both the reader as well as the master within the anecdote, stopping them to make them think. It is one of several instances on this final page where the entire *Essais* seem to reach their epigrammatic conclusion; perhaps this is the most memorable one. Aesop teaches his master that they both have bodies that have needs and it is a mistake—a ridiculous, but also an ethically distorting one—to try to deny these needs. The slave who has been reduced to an animal body demands, in turn, that we give the body its due. The *Essais* teach us to extend that care to all human beings, bodies each and every one.

26. 3:13, *Essays* 856, *Essais* 1115.

Contributors

MARY BYRD KELLY is a lecturer in the Department of French, Francophone, and Italian Studies at the University of Kansas. She has translated articles and books by Tzvetan Todorov, Alain Finkielkraut, Pascal Bruckner, Christian Delage, and others.

RICHARD COOPER is Emeritus Professor of French at Brasenose College, Oxford. He works on Renaissance authors such as Rabelais, Marguerite de Navarre, the Pléiade, and Montaigne, as well as on court festivals, and relations between France and Italy. Recent publications include an edition of Marguerite de Navarre's poetry, *Chrétiens et mondains, poèmes épars* (2007), an edition of the 1549 romance *Histoire et ancienne chronique de Gérard d'Euphrate, duc de Bourgogne* (2012), and a monograph, on *Roman Antiquities in Renaissance France* (2013).

FRANÇOIS CORNILLAT is Distinguished Professor of French at Rutgers University–New Brunswick and a specialist of 15th- and 16th-century French poetry. His publications in this field include *"Or ne mens." Couleurs de l'Éloge et du Blâme chez les "Grands Rhétoriqueurs"* (1994) and *Sujet caduc, noble sujet. La poésie de la Renaissance et le choix de ses "arguments"* (2009). He is currently working, in collaboration with the historian Laurent Vissière, on a critical edition of Jean Bouchet's *Panégyrique du chevalier sans reproche*, to be published by Éditions Classiques Garnier.

JESSICA DEVOS is a Lector of French at Yale University. In addition to her passion for teaching (and learning) languages, she never tires of exploring the complexities of Renaissance France and Italy. Her current research focuses on women writers, female voices, and gender as a lyric construct.

YFS 134, *The Construction of a National Vernacular Literature in the Renaissance: Essays in Honor of Edwin M. Duval*, ed. DeVos and Hayes, © 2018 by Yale University.

BROOKE D. DI LAURO obtained her Ph.D. from Yale University in 2006 and is an Associate Professor of French at the University of Mary Washington. She is interested in the interconnections between literature and the visual arts and has published two articles on the relationship between the poems and emblems of Scève's *Délie*. Most recently she has contributed to two collected volumes, *Memory and Community in Sixteenth-Century France* (2016) and *Polemic and Literature Surrounding the French Wars of Religion* (forthcoming).

BRUCE HAYES is an associate professor and chair of the Department of French, Francophone, and Italian Studies at the University of Kansas. His research focuses primarily on polemical humor in Renaissance France. His first book was *Rabelais's Radical Farce* (2010) and he is currently preparing for publication a second monograph, *Castigating Comedy: Polemical Humor and the French Wars of Religion* (forthcoming).

MIREILLE HUCHON is Emerita professor at the Université Paris-Sorbonne, an honorary member of the Institut universitaire de France, vice-president of the Société d'histoire littéraire de la France, and a specialist of 16th-century literature and language. Her numerous publications include *Rabelais grammairien* (1981), the edited volume *Œuvres complètes de Rabelais* (1994), a biography of the author, *Rabelais* (2011), *Histoire de la langue française* (2002), and *Louise Labé, une créature de papier* (2006).

RICHARD E. KEATLEY's research focuses on the relationship between technological and sociological changes and the construction of identity in the late sixteenth century. His forthcoming book titled *Textual Spaces: French Renaissance Writings of the Italian Voyage*, examines the use of symbolic space in the travel diaries, poems, and narratives of French Renaissance travelers to Italy.

DORA POLACHEK is Visiting Associate Professor of French in Binghamton University's Department of Romance Languages and Literatures, where she is also its Director of Undergraduate Studies. She has published extensively on Marguerite de Navarre, Montaigne, Brantôme, and women's roles in the French Wars of Religion. Her interests include issues related to gender, sexuality, and power in comic texts. She is currently working on a monograph on Brantôme and the "woman question."

DAVID QUINT is Sterling Professor of English and Professor of Comparative Literature at Yale University, where he has been privileged to have Edwin Duval as a friend and scholarly model. A specialist of the European Renaissance, he has published widely on diverse literary genres. He is the author of *Epic and Empire* (1993), *Montaigne and the Quality of Mercy* (1998), *Cervantes' Novel of Modern Times* (2003), *Inside Paradise Lost* (2014), and *Virgil's Double Cross* (2018).

FRANÇOIS RIGOLOT is Meredith Howland Pyne professor of French Literature Emeritus at Princeton University. He has written books on individual Renaissance authors, such as *Les langues de Rabelais* (1972), *Louise Labé lyonnaise, ou, La Renaissance au féminin* (1997), and *Les métamorphoses de Montaigne* (1988), as well as several general studies of the Renaissance.

EDWARD TILSON is a researcher with the Graduate School of Trent University and a director of Canada's Humanities Digital Degrees Project. Based on readings of 16th-century texts, Montaigne's *Essais* in particular, his work examines connections between understandings of modernity on the one hand, and constructions of the Renaissance and of humanism on the other.

SHIRA WEIDENBAUM is a Tutor in French and Humanities at Quest University Canada in British Columbia. She completed her dissertation on religious propaganda and the dialogic genre under Edwin Duval in 2009. Her article on the *Discours familier* by Pierre Regis appeared in *Les états du dialogue à l'âge de l'humanisme* (2015). She has a forthcoming article on the *Dialogues rustiques* of Jean de Moncy in *Topographies of Tolerance and Intolerance: Responses to Religious Pluralism in Reformation Europe*, edited by Victoria Christman and Beth Plummer.

CATHY YANDELL is the W. I. and Hulda F. Daniell Professor of French Literature, Language, and Culture at Carleton College. The author of *Carpe Corpus: Time and Gender in Early Modern France* (2000) and co-editor of *Vieillir à la Renaissance* (2009) and *Memory and Community in Sixteenth-Century France* (2015), she has published articles on dialogue, gender, the body, sexuality, and visual culture. Her current project examines the Renaissance body and corporeal knowledge from Rabelais to Descartes.

Yale French Studies is the oldest English-language journal in the United States devoted to French and Francophone literature and culture. Each volume is conceived and organized by a guest editor or editors around a particular theme or author. Interdisciplinary approaches are particularly welcome, as are contributions from scholars and writers from around the world. Recent volumes have been devoted to a wide variety of subjects, among them: Levinas; Perec; Paulhan; Haiti; Belgium; Crime Fiction; Surrealism; Material Culture in Medieval and Renaissance France; and French Education.

Yale French Studies is published twice yearly by Yale University Press (yalebooks.com) and may be accessed on JSTOR (jstor.org).

For information on how to submit a proposal for a volume of *Yale French Studies*, visit yale.edu/french and click "Yale French Studies."